W9-BIS-449

FROM MOTHERHOOD TO CITIZENSHIP

. . . . . . . . . . . . . . . . . . . . . .

# From Motherhood to Citizenship

## Women's Rights and International Organizations

*Nitza Berkovitch*

The Johns Hopkins University Press

*Baltimore and London*

© 1999 The Johns Hopkins University Press
All rights reserved. Published 1999
Printed in the United States of America on acid-free paper

8   6   4   2   9   7   5   3   1

The Johns Hopkins University Press
2715 North Charles Street
Baltimore, Maryland 21218-4363
www.press.jhu.edu

Library of Congress Cataloging-in-Publication Data will be
found at the end of this book.
A catalog record for this book is available from the British Library.

ISBN 0-8018-6028-8

# CONTENTS

. . . . . . . . .

# LIST OF TABLES AND GRAPHS

. . . . . . . .

## TABLES

## GRAPHS

PREFACE AND ACKNOWLEDGMENTS

. . . . . . . . .

Although I started to work on this project while in graduate school at Stanford, its roots can be traced back to the country where I was born and raised—Israel. Israel is characterized by many contradictions and myths, notable among them the myth of sexual equality. While women have to deal with various instances of inequality and oppression in their daily lives, the myth of equality shapes the local discourse on gender relations, prevents large-scale feminist mobilization, and inhibits the recognition of women's rights within the Israeli public agenda. The struggles of Jewish women at the beginning of the century to participate equally in the Zionist project of settlement in Palestine and to gain the right to vote was unknown to many. Moreover, this period, considered to be the formative period of the Israeli state and society, was portrayed as the "golden age" as far as equality was concerned. During the 1970s the first cracks started to appear in this glorified image of Israeli society. Jewish feminist activists, mainly of North American origin, formed the embryonic women's movement. Many of us in Israel then did not realize that it was part of a much larger-scale phenomenon, that known as the second wave of feminism. It took almost a decade for the new ways of thinking to trickle into academia, and in the 1980s the first harvest of feminist scholarship in the social sciences started to be published.

It was exactly at this time when these new ideas were beginning to circulate that I attended school and completed my bachelor's and master's degrees at Tel Aviv University. I vividly remember the deep impressions that the pathbreaking works of Dafna Izareli and Deborah Bernstein left on me when I was first exposed to them while still under the spell of "gender equality." But my true introduction to the world of feminist knowledge and research, my model of feminist academic practice was Hanna Herzog, and she remains an important model. To her I owe my first gratitude.

The 1980s was also the period during which a new kind of sociology emerged. I was lucky to be a student of Yonatan Shapira and Gershon Shafir; their sociological thinking challenged much of the mainstream sociological analysis of Israeli society. Many of the friendship ties that were forged during that stimulating period at Tel Aviv University and afterward still serve as sources of support, advice, and assistance whenever I need them. I can name only a few here: Uri

Ben-Eliezer, Adriana Kemp, Danny Levy, Motti Regev, Ilan Talmud, and Yuval Yonai. I was also fortunate to meet and befriend Yehuda Shenhav, who has provided continual encouragement and intellectual stimulation throughout the years.

Being exposed to parts of American society and culture while attending graduate school at Stanford, I was struck by the similarities as well as the clear differences between the social and gender systems of Israel and the United States. The sociological imprints gained at Tel Aviv University sensitized my perception of difference and power plays everywhere, while the sociology I was first exposed to at Stanford focused my attention on the "bigger picture," in which national differences play a smaller part than is usually assumed. This bird's-eye view is the one I chose to employ when I began to investigate the ways in which the evolving world polity—the world political and cultural system— shapes the history of "women's issues" and "women's rights."

Most Israelis (including social scientists) hold firmly to the belief that Israeli society is a unique case that refuses to conform to many sociological theories. Much to my surprise, when I started to work on this project, I discovered that many of the events that shaped ways of thinking and acting on gender issues in Israel were not unique to Israel. For example, the report published in 1976 by the Commission on the Status of Women (appointed by the late prime minister Yitzhak Rabin) and which unmasked the pervasive inequality that exists in all walks of life is singled out by many as the first important catalyst in shaping feminist consciousness and organizing in Israel. Being loyal to local tradition, many tried to explain the emergence of the embryonic women's movement by looking at political and social factors. I was amazed to find out, however, that such commissions were appointed around the world, and their resulting reports had a similar impact in many countries.

Macro-institutional sociology that weaves together global-level factors with the processes of meaning construction enabled me to account for this phenomenon as well as other events regarding the history of women's status which became the focus of this book. Undoubtedly, John Meyer has had the greatest impact on my work in this respect. In his thought-provoking way he taught me to ask the "big questions" and encouraged me to embark on this project, which at the time seemed unattainable. I consider it a privilege to have been his student. Francisco Ramirez inspired me to challenge conventional sociological thinking. He was also the first to show me how gender issues can be conceptualized within a global frame of analysis, an approach that I have found to be most fruitful.

There were several groups of which I have been fortunate to be a part. The lively discussions that were held during the meetings of the Institutional Comparative Seminar at Stanford (a seminar that became a notable institution in and of itself) helped me to shape and clarify my ideas. I especially benefited from the spirited and learned conversations I had with Marc Ventresca. I found the greatest pleasure in participating in what we named the "San Franciscan Chicana Jewish group," which included Debbie Barrett, Gili Drori, Laura Gomez, and Manuella Romero. Our meetings consisted of the winning combination of serious discussions, great food, and lots of laughter. I cherish the memories of our lengthy debates on sociology and life, which typically lasted through the night.

I owe special thanks to two people—Debbie Barrett and Karen Bradley. Both have been great friends and valued colleagues. Debbie made my stay in the United States so much more enjoyable and interesting than it would have been otherwise. I admire the strength and persistence she showed through some very hard times when I could not be close by. Karen inspired my work, showed me how cooperative projects can be both beneficial and enjoyable, and supported me all the way.

Upon my arrival in Israel I found in the Behavioral Sciences Department at Ben-Gurion University, where I currently teach, a unique and welcoming academic community. The Sociology program there, headed by Steve Sharot and Ran Chermesh, has assisted and encouraged me in many ways. Lev Grinberg, Sara Hellman, Andre Levi, Fran Markovitz, Uri Ram, and Niza Yanai have provided me with social support, intellectual stimulation, and many opportunities for the exchange of ideas. Their friendship has supported me during the long periods of making this book come into existence. I most appreciate the fact that in their work they prove that a deep political commitment to ideals of justice and equality results in original and challenging sociological thinking. I find such commitment to be too rare in the Israeli sociological scene. I also want to thank the School of Humanities and Social Sciences for their generous financial support.

At the Johns Hopkins University Press, Henry Tom provided me with much needed guidance and offered help all along the way. Elizabeth Gratch did a wonderful and thorough job of editing the manuscript.

This book was completed at a time when the political climate in Israel was very bleak. Gaps have been widening among all the social groups that constitute the collage called Israeli society. Heartless "free-market" spirit and policies, coupled with chauvinistic nationalism, prevail. Both trends affect women's situation in many ways. News from around the world does not present a rosier picture. Women's situation has worsened in Russia, as a result of the transition to a market economy; in Algeria and Afghanistan, with the rise of Islamic fundamentalism; and in Serbia and Croatia, due to the rise of more frenzied nationalism, to mention only a few examples. At the same time, research and news reports document women's various modes of struggle. In many parts of the world women are organizing to resist and transform current social and political institutions and processes. The twentieth century began with many high hopes and is ending with much disillusionment. For women the new millennium will begin with cautious expectations but with a firm conviction not to forsake hard-won victories. I hope that the great women of history will serve us all as examples in their continuous struggle to transform the world into a better place for both women and men.

# FROM MOTHERHOOD TO CITIZENSHIP

. . . . . . . . . . . . . . . . . . . . .

. . . . . . . . .

# CHAPTER ONE

# *Introduction*

## Women's Rights and Global Discourse

In 1929 a little celebration took place in a courtroom where a member of the London Judicial Committee read a court decision in full to the representatives of various women's organizations and their supporters crowding the chamber. Telegrams came from across the Atlantic, and newspaper editorials congratulated women on the progress they had made. The reason for the celebration was the following decision: "The word 'person' may include members of both sexes, and to those who ask why the word should include females, the obvious answer is, why not?" (qtd. in Sachs and Wilson 1986, 40).

This decision ended a series of cases brought before the British courts beginning in 1867. They came to be known as the "person cases." These cases were a response to a series of new laws that had granted to any "person" who possessed certain qualifications the rights to hold public office, enter professions, and vote. When women decided to "test" these new laws, however, they found that they bore the burden of proof in the courtroom for demonstrating their inclusion in the category of persons. Until the 1929 case they failed in that mission.

Today in most countries what had been a topic of endless debate has become a taken-for-granted notion. Very few countries still have internal discussions over whether or not women are persons. In the few in which the topic has not yet been resolved, there is growing pressure, both internally and externally, for a resolution. Nearly all countries have established legal rules aimed at granting rights to women in some areas of public life, in their constitutions or in statutes (see Morgan 1984). In politics women have been granted suffrage in 96 percent of the countries in the world (Ramirez, Soysal, and Shanahan 1997). In the wage economy, the focus of this book, women have gained the right to be rewarded equally with men in about 130 countries.

Through these legislative and organizational activities the contemporary nation-state now constitutes women as a social category of citizens: a category that is comparable to that of men at least in one important respect, its entitlement to participate in public institutions. This construction has implications that extend far beyond the realm of ideology and formal rights. Women have gained access to various institutions in the public sphere which in the nineteenth century were defined as exclusively male domains in most nation-states. The overall process started at the beginning of this century, gained momentum after World War II, and has accelerated since 1975. Women's participation in higher education has increased dramatically in recent decades, and at a faster rate than that of men, in most nation-states, regardless of their levels of development and modernization (Bradley and Ramirez 1996; Ramirez and Weiss 1979). Similar trends have been observed in women's share in secondary education (Benavot 1989), in the paid labor force (Joekes 1987; Standing 1989), and in upper-echelon occupations (Adler and Izraeli 1988).

All this is not to say that women have indeed gained full equality everywhere, or anywhere, or that nation-states are identical in their capacity or intention to implement women's rights. An abundance of evidence shows that "constitutional equal rights coexist with institutionalized male privilege" (Parpart and Staudt 1989, 6). Various degrees of gender segregation continue to characterize all educational, political, and employment systems (see, e.g., Charles 1992). Decoupling policy and implementation, legislation and action, allows nation-states to adopt "progressive" programs and structures and at the same time to continue oppressive practices (Meyer, Boli, Thomas, and Ramirez 1997). Research continues to accumulate and to document real gaps between men and women in every conceivable domain. Moreover, it has been shown that "unisex policies" (Wilson 1992) and gender-neutral legislation have differential impact on men and women and might, in some cases, worsen women's situation. Feminist scholars have exposed the underlying assumptions about men and women which frame the seemingly universal discourse of rights and citizenship.

Thus, the story of the process of proliferation of rights and women's entrance into various public institutions is not a story of "progress." But nor is it a story of everlasting, never-changing gender oppression. Considering the overall pervasiveness of the hierarchical character of gender relations, it is clear that official rights cannot abolish patriarchy. But, at the same time, official rights, state policy, and state action do participate in helping to shape the meaning of gender. Official rights, bestowed by the state, almost everywhere constitute women as legitimate actors in the public sphere, as a group to be legitimately mobilized and empowered to mobilize others. In doing that, it opens new avenues for social action and instigates new social dynamics that were neither possible nor conceivable before. Women as a group now can make legitimate claims on the state and can demand action on their own behalf.

Note that the notions of "inequality" and "discrimination" are meaningful only when the unequal and discriminated-against individuals are conceptualized as having a similar ontological status to those with whom are compared. And, in the case of a de jure equality, it makes it possible and legitimate to measure a group's distance from de facto equality, constructing inequality as a problem that requires intervention. Using standardized measures, the status of women is compared to that of men, and the gap that is found (and it always is) is defined as discrimination considered to be a social problem and treated as an injustice to be rectified and corrected through state action and state policy.

In this book I use the history of one type of state policy, that of the regulation of women's employment, as an instance of this process. Since the mid-nineteenth century, in almost all European countries (and not only European), the state produced a wide variety of measures that were relevant to women's patterns of employment. These laws mark the beginning of the history of the modern state's acknowledgment and regulation of women's participation in the public sphere. It was the first time that the state was mobilized to regulate women's participation patterns in public activities. In other domains, such as politics or education, either women's participation was not regulated by state law, or it was banned altogether. It is important to note that these early gender-specific laws did not prohibit women's employment. Rather, they created a gender-differentiated workforce in which each gender was subject to a different regime. Thus, women were permitted into paid employment but only when constituted as a different type of worker.

Yet, more than any other activity in the public sphere, women's engagement in paid work also means diminishing their dependence upon men. This kind of activity constitutes the greatest deviation from the traditional role of women. The prevailing image is that paid employment might jeopardize the wife's commitment to her domestic and maternal responsibilities, which are thought to be her primary ones. The evidence for this assertion is the fact that until recently women in many countries needed their husbands' authorization to enter a labor contract. Alternatively, the burden of proof was on them to show that their jobs did not have negative effects on the family (Berkovitch 1994). Thus, the appearance in the second half of the twentieth century of the notions of the "right to employment," to "equal pay," and "equal opportunities," undermines women's inferior position both at home and in the labor market. It transforms (though not abolishes) one of the central pillars of the gender system—that of the economic dependence of women upon men.

Early labor laws, however, did not intend to grant women equality. Gender equality in employment was not a concept that states endorsed. The route to (nominal) equality in paid economy—that is, in the "public"—had to follow an alternative path: one that went through the "domestic" sphere. Early labor laws incorporated women through their social and functional capacities. Women's participation in the economy was to be affected by their maternal roles, and their association with the domestic sphere shaped their patterns of and entitlement to participation in the public sphere. Then, in the latter part of the twentieth century, national policies were adopted which granted women expanded and equal political rights. Only during the second half of the century did national policies "liberalize" women in the sense that they were incorporated as citizens into the public sphere as individuals and not as women.

This process is not unique to the economic domain but is a characteristic of other public institutions as well. Women were granted educational and political rights at an increasing rate. But more intriguing is the fact that the process was not confined to a specific group of countries but, rather, became part of women's history in many countries around the world and at about the same period. Thus, a series of questions emerge: how should we account for the fact that, for example, during one decade alone (1960–70), more than forty countries from all regions and continents granted women equal economic rights (and the rest followed suit)? What drove most countries, from the mid-1970s on, to revise their laws and regulations restricting women's employment to certain occupations and certain times of the day? What motivated almost all countries to establish one form or another of state agency designated for the sole purpose of promoting women's status? Considering the immense variation in their economic, political, and social structures, their ideologies, and the regimes of the countries involved, these processes pose a puzzle that cannot be sorted out unless one considers the global context in which nation-states are embedded.

Most studies that explore women's position use case studies and look at factors such as the political constellation, the level of modernization, women's degree of organizing, and the existence of democratic principles and practices. Whereas this type of study is highly useful for understanding the particular situation in each individual country, the focus on individual countries tends to mask the similarities among them. Studies that compare policies in similar areas of different countries highlight the country-level differences even further (e.g., Adams and Winston 1980; Jenson 1988). For example, Ruggie (1984), in her study of women's employment policies in England and Sweden, asserts that both countries were attempting to achieve some measure of equality for women. The fact that they chose a different path, claims Ruggie, reflects differences in state-society relations which are historically contingent within a national context. I take one step backward, however, and ask: why is it that in such different societies (and one can think of a much larger variety of societies) women were granted the same kinds of rights, at approximately the same period of time?

In addition, when studying each phenomenon related to women's rights separately, researchers tend to use explanations that are unique to the phenomenon under investigation. For example, it has been suggested that the expansion of the service sector and the decline in fertility account for the increase in the share of females in the labor force. Or that factors such as level of development, religion, and/or the overall expansion of higher education explain the growth in women's share in higher education. But when we think about the prevalence of all the various trends, we need to consider the possibility that they are different manifestations of the same process and, as such, need to be conceptualized within the same theoretical framework.

## *World Polity, the State, and Women's Rights*

The increasing isomorphism described here is not unique to state's action regarding women. Evidence has accumulated that different countries, especially in the last five decades, tend to develop similar structures, programs, and policies that concern a wide variety of issues and domains: similar educational systems (Ramirez and Boli 1987), welfare policies (Strang and Chang 1993; Thomas and Lauderdale 1987), science policy-making organizations (Finnemore 1993), anti-natalist population control policies (Barrett 1995), record-keeping and data collection systems (McNeely 1995; Ventresca 1995). Looking at individual nation-states and their internal characteristics, be they political, economic, cultural, or social, would not help us account for the transnational character of these processes. We need to look elsewhere. The vast array of similarities point to the fact that external factors—that is, the global context—is a major determinant of state's structure and actions in general and concerning women's issues in particular. One cannot ignore the fact that "the constitution of women's position in society and economy, and of women's position in the home . . . owes much to changes and trends that are international and transnational . . . At the cost of some exaggeration, it is possible to . . . assert that 'the personal is international' " (Halliday 1988, 421–22).

How should one conceptualize the international and the nation-state to account for the process under investigation—the worldwide distinct patterns of incorporation of women into the public sphere?

Following institutional theory,[1] conceptualizing nation-states as subunits of a world polity—a cultural-political system—enables us to understand why units that are so different in so many respects share a common view of what is and what should be done about such things as the "women's question." The main proposition is that "many features of the contemporary nation-state derive from worldwide models constructed and propagated through global cultural and associational processes" (Meyer, Boli, Thomas, and Ramirez 1997, 144). From this perspective the world is seen as an increasingly integrated (though not conflict-free) social system organized around institutionalized cultural rules that affect nation-states as system subunits. These subunits share, to various degrees, common conceptions about what they are, what kinds of activities they ought to be engaged in, and what kinds of social entities their own members are. In this perspective social actors (e.g., states, citizens) do not exist a priori but are constituted and reconstituted by a wider cultural context (Meyer 1987; Thomas, Meyer, Ramirez, and Boli 1987).[2]

The logic of the institutional perspective can be used to understand social action at various levels, be they the individual, organizational, or nation-state level. It emphasizes the way in which institutions and shared systems of rules and meanings structure action and make order possible (Dimaggio and Powell 1991). These ways of operating come to be defined as taken for granted or as taking on a rule-like status in social thought and action. Cognitive elements are highlighted in such a way that even norms and values come to be thought of as taking on the status of facts, scripts, and rules (Meyer and Rowan 1977). In other words, institutions are "cultural rules giving collective meanings and value to particular entities and activities, integrating them into a larger scheme. . . . Institutionalization is the process by which a given set of units and a pattern of activities come to be normatively and cognitively held in place, and

1. Thinking of the world system in terms of world culture and world polity is a tradition that emerged within sociology (e.g., Meyer and Hannan 1979; Wuthnow 1987; Zucker 1983). The theoretical foundations can be found in Berger and Luckman 1967. Geertz (1973) and Douglas (1986) used similar lines of theorization in their analyses of culture and institutions. For general analytical and historical reviews, see Dimaggio and Powell 1991; Finnemore 1996; Scott 1987 and 1991.

2. This approach differs markedly from international relations perspectives including neorealism, neoliberalism, and international regimes and from world systems theory in sociology. See reviews and comparisons in Grieco 1990; Krasner 1983; Meyer 1987. The main criticisms are that these theories reify social actors, ignore the highly institutionalized nature of global society, and do not pay adequate attention to culture.

practically taken for granted as lawful (whether as a matter of law, custom or knowledge)" (Meyer et al. 1994, 9).

Thus, it is clear that, contrary to most sociological accounts, both the existence of actors and their patterns of activity are seen as socially constructed by the wider cultural rules. They do not exist a priori as essential entities with a given set of interests and preferences that guide their behavior but, rather, as constructed and embedded. Following this logic of explanations, Friedland and Alford see "each level of analysis [individual, organization, state] as equally an abstraction and a reification . . . none is more 'real' than the other . . . we conceive of these levels of analysis as 'nested'" (1991, 242).

Along these lines the global level—world polity defined as a broad cultural order—is constitutive of the state's characteristics and action. In contrast with most theoretical formulations, the processes that operate on the global level are not being reduced to the interests of individual nation-states, and they should not be seen as mere instances of interstate exchange (Bergesen 1990; Robertson 1992).

Substantively, world culture originates from the modern Western tradition that emphasizes instrumental and purposive action and constitutes both society and the individual as a means to collective ends such as progress, justice, and equality. In this process of rationalization these entities, which are defined as means, are given an ontological status. Thus, with the increasing levels of rationalization comes a wider and more sharpened conception of the individual and the state (Meyer, Boli, and Thomas 1994).

This process gained a general character over time and now operates worldwide. The emerging global infrastructure in the form of international organizations of various kinds is coupled with an increasing flow of resources and information and by increasing rationalization. It encompasses more and more nation-states with tighter links connecting them. This kind of world culture is a historical phenomenon that is unique to the modern period, culminating in the aftermath of World War II.

This is not to say, however, that in previous times there were no linkages among parts of the world or that this is the first period in which Western ideas have penetrated other parts of the world. What is unique about the contemporary system is its highly rationalized, interconnected structure, in which its standardized subunits follow similar models of organizing. They all take the same political form—the nation-state—and are thus all defined as having an equal (ontological) status. Previously, international organizations and international agreements regulated mainly economic and political relations among the states. Nowadays, world models set the rules for nation-states about how to organize internally—that is, how to define and manage relations with its inhabitants. The proper model that is actively promoted is that of citizenship: members of nation-states are to be defined as citizens, as individuals with a standardized and elaborate set of rights and responsibilities.

In contrast with conventionally held wisdom, state's jurisdiction, global authority, and individual rights do not contradict one another and are not in zero-sum relations. The expansion of world culture (i.e., more and more domains falling under one body's growing rationalization and being defined as means to attain collective goods) leads both to the expansion of the nation-state (authority and organization) *and* to the "expansion" of the modern individual as embodied in the status of citizenship—which is to say that more rights, more responsibilities, and more aspects of the individual's lives have become rationalized and incorporated into the polity. Boli (1987), for example, shows that citizens' rights and states' jurisdiction are mutually enhancing. Similarly, Meyer and others note: "The modern state may have less autonomy than earlier but it clearly has more to do than earlier as well, and most states are capable of doing more now than they ever have been before" (1997, 157).

Part of the process of expanding states' jurisdiction is that an increasing number of issues are being defined as "social problems" and as such fall under the scrutiny of the state. One such new problem is gender inequality. With the expansion of global and state's polity, more and more aspects of men's and women's lives and activities are subject to quantification. International standards are being formulated so that cross-national comparisons can be made. The gaps that are found call for action. Countries are being rank-ordered according to the magnitude of these gaps. Social scientific theories of various persuasions formulate all sorts of possible relations between gender inequality and modernization/development: that the low level of modernization is the cause for women's lower status; that women's restricted access to public institutions (high levels of inequality) is a major factor explaining the backwardness of certain societies; that equality in and of itself is an indicator of a country's level of development. And highly rationalized prescriptions are being issued which specify the programs, policies, and structures that nation-states should adopt to correct all manifestations of inequality.

Again, this is not to say that inequality is a new state of affairs. It is to say that world processes drove many nation-states to define this situation as a state's concern that requires special legislation, public policy, and a designated state agency. A situation that for many long centuries was defined as either "natural" or ordained by God came to be defined as acts of social wrongdoing which should be rectified through appropriate social engineering implemented by the nation-state.

Conceptualizing global society as a highly institutionalized but stateless structure leads one to acknowledge the significance of a set of nonstates—global social structures and associations (Meyer, Boli, Thomas, and Ramirez 1997). These world-level entities assume various structures and are composed of individuals, groups, state's representatives, or any combination of the three. In the last several decades there have been several thousand such associations and several hundred bodies of a more official character which operate in every conceivable domain (Boli and Thomas 1997). As noted by Inis: "In quantitative terms, the growth of international institutions in the past half-century has been nothing but phenomenal" (1988, 112). Their structure and mode of operation vary considerably (Smith et al. 1997). They produce a multitude of organizational networks, projects, plans of action, treaties, and a variety of activities that extend to all parts of the globe, which especially in the post–World War II era have started to play a major role as carriers of world culture and creators of a global agenda. The multiplicity of organizational activities, resources, and texts together constitute what can be termed a global discourse. Within this global discourse world models of general principles and prescribed ways of organizing are being formulated and advocated and, as such, shape states' actions and structures in a variety of areas. Science (Finnemore 1993), welfare (Strang and Chang 1993), data collection (Ventresca 1995), and population policy (Barrett and Frank 1999) are only a few examples.

This book focuses on activities carried out by a wide range of global actors who emerged and organized around women's issues and follows the transformation in the global discourse that they produced. It begins in 1875, with the launching of the first international crusade that concerned women—that to abolish the state regulation of prostitution—and which was accompanied by the international suffrage movement and the campaign for labor legislation. It then moves through the interwar era, in which women's affairs were handled extensively by two official world bodies, the International Labour Organization and the League of Nations. It ends in 1985, with the third-world conference on women, which marked the end of the United Nations Decade for Women. The UN Decade signaled a new era in women's global organizing. During these 110 years the meaning of womanhood, women's issues, and women's proper role and place has changed fundamentally, together with the extent, form, and agenda of global discourse itself.

The new ideological constructs of citizenship, rights, and equality which emerged in the global arena mainly after World War II started to shape much of world activities regarding women. And, with the increasing involvement of the United Nations in women's rights in the 1970s, it became much more so. The change in content was accompanied by an expanding jurisdiction and intensification of activities of world bodies. The result was that world models regarding the proper type of citizenship and rights gained more authority than before and fashioned much of national activities.

More specifically, the increasing extent of world activities that "liberalized" women led to increased adoption rates of liberal national policies. Policies that aimed at standardizing individuals (in terms of making them comparable) proliferated and replaced gender-differentiated ones. This is not to say that all countries are exposed in the same degree to world pressures, yet one of the factors that influences nation-states to adopt certain kinds of models of citizenship is their exposure to these world pressures. Note also that those that "resist" and follow models that deny women "personhood" and citizenship are marked as deviant cases and "backward societies."

Indeed, the worldwide definition of the appropriate model of statehood includes as one of its building blocks the universal notion of modern citizenship, women included. In order to understand the process of the extension of citizen rights to women, however, we need to consider the ways in which the process has been shaped by the institution of gender.

## Rights, Citizenship, and Gender

Modern nation-states are predicated on citizenship as the principle that organizes the relations between the state and its members. T. H. Marshall's earlier formulation defined citizenship as "a status bestowed on those who are full members of a community" (1965, 92). Later, the notion was expanded to include a set of practices that constitute individuals as competent members of a community (Turner 1986). In all its variations the concept of citizenship implies participation in public institutions and a notion of personhood in the legal and bureaucratic sense. It means that members of a community are and should be autonomous individuals capable of owning their personhood.[3]

Marshall's original list of three categories of rights—civil, political, and social—was elaborated to include also economic, cultural, regional, global, and environmental rights (see, e.g., Steenbergen 1994). Alongside the proliferation of types of rights, more and more groups of people were found to be entitled to

3. See recent collections of Steenbergen 1994; and Vogel and Moran 1991; also vol. 26 of *Theory and Society* (1997).

rights and citizenship. Indeed, one of the phenomena with which scholars have dealt is the extension of rights over the last three centuries to different groups of people. Within mainstream social scientific scholarship the process of the extension of rights to women has not received much attention. It was assumed that it could be subsumed under the general process of extending rights to all social classes. Only with the emergence of new feminist critique, was it "discovered" that, for example, the historical process that Marshall described does not fit women's history. In many European countries women were granted social rights much earlier than political rights. Civil rights, the first type to be granted to men, were denied to married women well into the twentieth century. Thus, we first have to acknowledge that there is no single unified history of citizenship (Vogel 1991).

The general process of extension of citizenship was assumed to be either a bottom-up process—that is, a response to demands for the right to participate in the polity and the economy—or as a co-optation strategy on behalf of the ruling class (Bendix 1974; Mann 1987). Neither of these explanations can account for the fact that women have become citizens in places where there was no organized women's movement to demand it. Also, it is hard to imagine situations in which women challenged the existing regime to the degree that they needed to be co-opted. In the few studies in which there is an explicit reference to women the explanation is local and cannot be applied to the transnational nature of the phenomenon. For example, Turner claims that "it is reasonably argued that the growth of citizenship rights for women was a consequence of wartime conditions and female employment in heavy industry rather than an enlighted altruism on the part of political parties" (1986, 95). This might be true for the United States and a few European countries, but it cannot account for the vast majority of cases.

Institutionalist arguments, as suggested by Boli (1987), Meyer (1987), and Ramirez (1981), see the process of the extension of citizenship status to women as part of a general process of incorporating previously peripheral groups. Ramirez and Weiss (1979), for example, shows how the general expansion of state jurisdiction increases the extension of citizenship to women via their participation in areas outside of familial domains. The overall process of extending rights is seen as resulting from world models that specify the appropriate ways in which societies should organize *and* define their inhabitants. This kind of explanation can account for the worldwide proliferation of rights to previously excluded groups, women among them. Indeed, within this framework one can conceptualize women as one such marginalized group, that is, as being excluded to various (diminishing) degrees from different institutions. In most countries women were granted the political status of citizenship, the franchise, much later than any group of men. In England, the United States, and Canada, for example, women got the right to vote only after World War I, and in France and in Italy they were enfranchised only after World War II. Still, worldwide, their participation in active political bodies remains blocked, and they are excluded from top positions in most institutions.

But this perspective implies that there is a generic status of citizenship that, once "invented," can be applied, as is, to all "newcomers." It does accept the assumption that citizenship is indeed generic, disembodied, and gender neutral. The recently emerging feminist critique that explores the way the concept of citizenship has been developed in Western political thought reveals that this is not the case. It is a male model; that is, it is based on the construction of what "male" is and is predicated on the very exclusion of women. Therefore, its extension to women can result only in a partial and incomplete notion of citizenship. This understanding encouraged scholarship that focuses on highlighting the different histories, meanings, and relevance that citizenship and rights, as conceptualized by liberal thinkers and practiced by nation-states, have for men and women (Arnaud and Kingdom 1990; Lloyed 1984; Okin 1989; Pateman 1989; Walby 1994).

The notion of citizenship is based on the liberal ideas of individualism and equality developed in the West in the seventeenth century, which marked a radical departure from traditional ideas of society as made up of natural hierarchies and inequalities. The basic idea is that all individuals are born free and equal. This modern individual has been seen as the bearer of formal rights granted and protected by the state (Dietz 1992; Marshall 1991). This abstract individual seemingly had no gender, but, in fact, it possessed all the qualities that women were assumed not to have (Okin 1979). In her analysis of classical texts Pateman shows how men alone were assumed to "possess the capacities required for citizenship, in particular they are able to use their reason to sublimate their passions, develop a sense of justice and so uphold the universal, civil law. Women . . . cannot transcend their bodily nature and sexual passions; women cannot develop such a political morality" (1989, 4).

Whereas the category of "individual" represented the disembodied male person, the "female persons become held to be virtually saturated with their sex which then invades their rational and spiritual faculties" (Reily 1988, 8). It was not only reason but also autonomy, economic independence, and the right to bear arms that were tightly coupled with the notion of citizenship. These were exactly the properties that women were denied systematically throughout most periods of history and maybe even more so in the nineteenth century, when the modern nation-state arose and the claim for universal citizenship was first voiced.

Equally important is the fact that citizenship applies to the rights, entitlement, and patterns of participation in public institutions. The exclusive focus on participation in public domain tells only one part of the story. The missing part is hidden in the private/domestic sphere, a domain that did not get much attention in most theories and debates that concerned citizenship. Thus, understanding the ways in which the public-private split is being constructed and interwoven within the concept of rights and that of gender is crucial.[4] As Carol Pateman puts it: "the dichotomy between the public and the private is central to almost two centuries of feminist writing and political struggle: it is ultimately what the feminist movement is about" (1989, 118). But this dichotomy keeps changing. Following Nicholson (1986), I argue that the public-private gendered dichotomy needs to be investigated within a historical perspective since its territoriality, meaning, and consequently its implication for women's citizenship change over time. For the present purposes it is important to explore the history of the public-private split *alongside* the history of citizenship.

To put it very briefly, the concept of modern citizenship emerged with the differentiation of the political and the family, both being created out of the older institution of kinship. Seventeenth-century political theories reflected this emergence of the family and state by separating its theory into the familial and the political. The sphere of the family differentiated from the economic in the nineteenth century, with industrialization, when the production of goods ceased to be governed by familial principles and, instead, became organized through the principle of the market. Since that time the private realm has increasingly come to be defined as that which concerns personal and domestic relations alone (Nicholson 1986). The public is designated for all those activities and institutions such as the market, politics, and education.

The public and the private are valued differently, governed by a different logic of action, and gendered. The two domains are gendered in the sense that women, women's activities, and women's characteristics are relegated to and associated with the domestic realm. The public, on the other hand, is men's arena. The domestic was constructed as governed by mutual responsibilities, altruism, trust, and caring (and patriarchal authority as well) and, as such, as an inappropriate site for applying the principle of rights (Okin 1989). The public is

---

4. There is abundant literature on the ways in which the construction of the public/private is implicated within gender relations (see, e.g., Nicholson 1984; Okin 1989; Rosaldo 1974 and 1980; Thornton 1991).

governed by competition and self-interest, but at the same time it is also regulated by principles of justice. Modern political ideas developed from this very
differentiation, conceiving of the public sphere as the domain in which to apply
their radical theories of equality and rights. The private, the women's sphere,
was left untouched by these ideas.

But domestic relations are characterized by hierarchy and subordination as
well. Thus, the exclusion of the domestic from justice theories, and its definition as private, legitimates the de facto authority relations, constitutes the
source of the "power of the patriarch" (Okin 1989, 129), and delegates power to
the head of the family, the modal citizen. The result is that, "by the beginning of
the 20th century, marriage alone (if we exempt the case of parental power over
children) had retained some of the peculiar attributes of feudal bondage.
Women, as wives still lacked some of the basic attributes of autonomous legal
agency" (Vogel 1994, 79).

This development is relevant for understanding both women's and men's
citizenship. Men's citizenship was predicated on women's exclusion and on the
domestic patriarchal power they were given. This was exactly the reason why
women's citizenship was problematic from the beginning. When women were
allowed access, their participation in the public domain, their ability to exercise
their public rights, and their ability to own their personhood were determined
to a large degree by their association with the domestic arena. Their patterns of
incorporation were shaped by their assigned domestic characteristics. Note that
the public is populated with "individuals," "citizens," and "workers," and not
with "men" and "women." Early modes of citizenship incorporated women as
women, thus leading to an incomplete and partial inclusion. The patriarchal
base of gender relation intersects with the process of the extension of citizenship in a way that creates a distinct pattern of incorporation of women which
cannot be explained unless one takes patriarchy seriously.

The purpose of this book is to investigate the worldwide transition from
social models in which women were defined as "property," as "minors," or only
in relation to their reproductive capacities, to those models in which they are
defined as persons and as such, entitled to participate in public institutions.
Here I follow Riley in looking at the category of woman as a historical and
cultural construct and tracing the process that she calls "the woman-to-human
transition" (1988, 18). The constitution of woman as a "legal, bureaucratic and
social scientific 'person'" (Wilson 1992) was entwined with diminishing their
association with the domestic sphere. This new model followed the decline of
women as a functional and gendered group, earmarked for incorporation into
society through family roles such as that of "mother." Women are not inherently

domestic, nor are they essentially similar to men. Both gender categories are historical and social constructs; they are cultural products and normative myths that eventually come to be taken-for-granted notions prevailing in the contemporary modern world. These myths are grounded in material reality, embodied in political arrangements, and enacted through a variety of social practices.

## Overview of the Book

This book explores three interrelated processes: (1) the consolidation of a world polity made up of international bodies and the increasing interconnectedness between them; (2) the general increase in attention given to women's issues; and (3) changing notions of womanhood and women's rights. These three processes run through and weave together the chapters of the book, which are organized chronologically. Each chapter will deal with the transformation in the contents and practices of international and national discourses, along with the changing relations between the two.

The focus of chapter 2 is a discussion of three international campaigns, the first to deal with women and women's issues, which were carried out during the second half of the nineteenth century, until World War I: the movement for women's political rights; the crusade against states' regulation of prostitutes and against international trafficking in women; and the campaign for international legislation of protective labor laws. These three movements were part of and contributed to the emerging world organizational agenda that had expanded to include social and humanitarian questions for the first time. In the context of the progressive vision of society carried out by transnational social reformers, these campaigns promoted the notion of protection: women had to be guarded and saved from various evils and hazards that lurked around them. Women's distinctive character and capacities were highlighted and underscored whenever their participation in the public sphere was considered. Thus, the suffrage campaign constituted women as gendered political citizens, and the campaign for state's regulation of women's employment constituted them as gendered economic citizens. The campaign and action for women's international and national protective labor laws receives special attention and will be followed in chapters 2 through 4.

The interwar era is the focus of chapter 3. During that period global linkages gained more coherence with the establishment of two major supranational organizations, the League of Nations and the International Labour Organization. The crusades against international trafficking in women and for protective legislation for women were taken up by the league and the ILO, respectively. Under their tutelage these activities expanded, bureaucratized, and came to incorporate larger parts of the world than ever before; that is, there was an increasing interconnectedness between these intergovernmental organizations and their constituent nation-states. Via their elaborate network of activities, the new global political authorities extended and institutionalized the prewar conceptions of women: as precariously located in the public domain and as associated primarily with the domestic sphere. Efforts to transform this dominant discourse turned out to be futile. During that period various women's movements lobbied the league and the ILO to take action on behalf of "women's equality" but to no avail. Ideological constructs such as equality and women's rights were not a legitimate concern for world bodies, but women's protection was.

The case of the women's peace movement that was active during World War I and after exemplifies a more complex case. It shows how the movement's ideology and practice was shaped and constrained by the spirit of the period and, at the same time, empowered by it. On the one hand, the rhetoric that accompanied the claim that women should have a say in international politics reinforced once again the gendered nature of women. But, at the same time, it reclaimed many of its constitutive symbols, inverted their meanings, and made them into powerful resources in their campaign for the promotion of women as agents of social improvement.

The post–World War II major transformation of the world polity, global discourse, and states' action regarding women are the topics of chapters 4 and 5. In chapter 4 I show how the establishment of a new supranational body with a broad mandate, the expansion of the nation-state system, and the emergence of human rights as an international concern have changed dramatically the way women have been discussed globally. For the first time women's rights as individuals and citizens were articulated and promoted by major global actors. The creation of the United Nations Commission on the Status of Women, the first body of its kind, presents one such institutional manifestation. The transformation of international employment policy provides another instance of this process. In earlier periods the goal of social progress was translated into policies that aimed at setting international standards for the better protection of women and children. During the period under investigation it came to be expressed in guidelines for nation-states to ensure that women's incorporation into the economy would measure up to that of men. Protective legislation was stigmatized as having negative effects on women's opportunities and has declined. Maternity protection, on the other hand, was seen as an essential antidiscriminatory device and, as such, has expanded even further. The replacement of the notion of "working mothers" with that of "workers with family responsibilities" contributed in yet another way to the diminishing association of women with the domestic sphere.

Nation-states complied with these guidelines. As a result, equality-in-employment policy, revised protective legislation, and expanded maternity provisions became an integral component of labor codes of most countries. Statistical analysis show that indeed the process is not internally generated but is, rather, externally driven. The changes in states' legislation can be accounted for by considering world-level events and states' linkages to world polity rather than the economic and political characteristics of the individual states.

The effects of the fusion of the global discourse of development with that of women's rights are discussed in chapter 5. When the economic logic of national development began to dominate global action regarding women, "women" were transformed into "underutilized human resources," and discrimination was defined as an "economic waste." As such, rapid and comprehensive action was seen as needed in order to "incorporate women into the process of development." The UN Decade for Women, marked by three world conferences (in 1975, 1980, and 1985), was a major turning point in the process. A full-blown, multilevel (international, regional, national) campaign was launched promoting rights in the name of development. This campaign embedded women's issues in a rapidly growing and highly rationalized bureaucratic infrastructure and intensified global action regarding women's issues to an unprecedented degree. The growing coherence of the world polity intensified also the extent to which nation-states were mobilized in the global campaign. The increasing attention to women was expressed in the formation of state organizations for "the promotion of women." Nowadays, almost all countries have at least one official body that is designated for women's issues. The overwhelming majority of these bodies were established in the 1970s with the specific purpose of promoting women's equality. A very specific set of guidelines, articulated by major global organizations, was responsible for this worldwide coordinated states' action.

Thus, the history of women's rights is implicated in the history of world polity, and the story needs to be told as such. This book follows the two narratives and points at the ways in which the history of the one was shaped by the history of the other.

# CHAPTER TWO

# "Improving the Lot of Womanhood"

## The Emerging World Social Agenda

In the second half of the nineteenth century international linkages on issues other than security, technical cooperation, and standardization of trade and transportation were first established (Taylor 1969). Global bodies were created, and international documents were drafted to deal with social and humanitarian issues. Also at this time a wide variety of social reform movements flourished in Europe and the United States. Some of them, such as the socialist, the temperance, and the suffrage movements, sought and found alliances in other countries and formed transnational movements. Other groups—such as those promoting public health and hygiene and those fighting to stop international trafficking in women, children, and narcotics—managed to mobilize governmental support and secure intergovernmental cooperation as well. The following statement, said in one of the international congresses held at the turn of the century, expresses the spirit of the epoch: "We have been baptised in that spirit of the twentieth century which the world calls internationalism" (IWSA 1909, 63).

The feeling was that none of the era's problems could be solved within national boundaries. Those that were engaged in improving employment conditions thought that only by standardizing labor laws would they be able to protect their respective countries from losing in the international economic competition, and those who sought to stop international trafficking in women and children realized that, without international cooperation, their whole effort would be in vain. But it was more than an instrumental logic that drove this effort; it also was a vision of an interdependent world in which all would share a similar fate. This idea was promoted explicitly by the socialist and the suffrage movements: "our task will not be fulfilled until the women of the whole world have been rescued from those discriminations and injustices which in every land are visited upon them by law and custom" (IWSA 1909, 63). The drive to cooperate beyond national boundaries was motivated by a desire not only to improve one's own society but also to create an *international* moral community.

One of the conditions that enabled the emergence of this universalism was the prolonged peace in Europe which was interrupted only by relatively short wars, lasting from 1815 to 1914. Whether it was the political (Kedouri 1984) or economic (Polani 1944) organization of Europe which enabled this prolonged state of peace, nevertheless, it was conducive to universal movements. The way the matters of Europe were handled assumed, and expressed, the consciousness of a common civilization, common political attitudes, and a common language of international politics (Kedouri 1984).

To be sure, this spirit of universalism was very much the result also of a colonial-style internationalism (Boulding 1988). This was the heyday of European colonialism in which most of Africa and large parts of Asia were under the direct control of European nations. Latin America was no longer under colonial rule and was incorporated into the international capitalist economy, developing its own inter-American institutions but maintaining only a marginal position within the emerging international system based in Europe (Cammack, Pool, and Tardoff 1989). Under these conditions the notion of the "world" was ambiguous. On the one hand, for most of the transnational reformers at that time the boundaries of the "civilized world" (a term widely used) were marked by race and included mainly the West—that is, Europe, North America, and the white British colonies. On the other hand, some of these movements set themselves the target of reforming also, and sometimes mainly, the "noncivilized world." This missionary zeal stemmed from a notion that similar standards of behavior should be set and similar state regulation should be imposed in all parts of the world. Such was the case, for example, with the abolitionist movement, which made the point that state regulation of prostitution should be abolished in Europe as well as in its colonies. But others, like the World Christian Temperance Movement, were motivated more by the need to protect the West from the dangers (e.g., opium) of the Orient. Only after World War I did the notion of the world expand, and in the post–World War II era it came to include literally all geographical parts of the world. It was then that the emerging conception of the world as an arena for social and cultural action (in addition, of course, to the older arenas of political and economic action) materialized.

International women's movements played an important role in this process. These movements were led mainly by educated elite women from Europe and

North America who could afford traveling the world and attending world fairs and international congresses. They themselves initiated and held international conferences and created international bodies. Interwoven with their specific agendas, which reflected their background, was a notion of universalism, characteristic of its time, as was said in 1888: "the position of women anywhere affects their position everywhere. Much is said of universal brotherhood, but for weal and for woe, more subtle and more binding is universal sisterhood" (qtd. in Sewall, 1914, 8). And they were set to give tangible shape to this universal sisterhood.

The focus of this chapter is on the creation of a new world agenda that expanded the subject matter of international relations to include nonpolitical questions. In this new world agenda women and women's issue became prominent. Within the vision of a better society women's lot had to be improved. Their inferior position and situation constituted a wrongdoing that required action on behalf of individuals and states.

The form and content of this new global agenda should also be seen as a reaction and response to changes in gender relations which took place around that time. With industrialization and women moving into the paid labor market, middle-class women's rising educational aspirations, and women's expanding role in society through social and philanthropic work, previous notions of women's proper place were being challenged. The very action that was designed to "improve women's situation" also enacted and recreated women's distinct nature as gendered persons. This constituting of women as gendered persons figured into the ways in which they were incorporated into the public sphere (as economic and political citizens). Women's citizenship was constituted as problematic and nonstandard—that is, incomparable to men's political participation and economic activity.

Three main international campaigns formed the early stage of global discourse on women: the international suffrage campaign; the crusade against international trafficking in women; and the campaign for international legislation of women's labor laws. Usually, these three issues are treated separately, within different theoretical frameworks and different historical narratives. Indeed, each relates to a different domain—rights and politics, "vice" and morality, and labor and the economy—yet each represents a different response to what has become known as the "woman's problem." Via these responses, similar notions of womanhood and its relations to the public or domestic spheres were conveyed and enacted in global discourse. In addition, while struggling with similar obstacles, each led to the creation of new international bodies and to the expansion of international cooperation.

The first campaign to raise much international sentiment was women's suffrage. The women's suffrage movements did not lobby heads of states to form international cooperation. The whole arena was in the hands of women activists who fostered linkages and created organizations with members from various countries to promote their cause. For most of these groups suffrage was only one item on a larger agenda of social reform. They operated within the existing paradigm of "separate spheres" and women's domestic nature but used it to promote their cause in a way that eventually modified the paradigm. Their very activity helped to erode it and presented revised models of action for women in the public sphere.

The second campaign, the crusade against prostitution, began as a struggle to abolish the state regulation of prostitution and ended up as an effort to end international trafficking in women. It was one of the first large international campaigns for "moral" and "health" issues to attract a substantial number of individuals, organizations (national and international), and heads of state. As opposed to the first campaign, the various groups involved aimed at fostering official world action and indeed succeeding in bringing about one of the first multilateral agreements of its kind. In the first stage of the campaign the emphasis was on the injustices done to women, to be corrected by, among other means, giving women the right to vote. In the second stage women's vulnerability was the image most widely used. Women involved in prostitution were portrayed not as dangerous seducers who lead astray good family men but rather as innocent, helpless girls who were "ruined," exploited, and transported without their consent. Indeed, this was the winning image that mobilized a whole international movement, which in turn set the path for the League of Nations, which picked up the issue after World War I.

In contrast with the two previous campaigns, the one for international labor legislation was led mainly by state officials and was directed early on at forming official international cooperation. This campaign demonstrated both the drive and caution manifested in countries' actions regarding cooperation on social matters. It was not the case that states were requested to cooperate on novel matters; in fact, the reverse held true. During this period quite a few countries had already instituted legal measures to regulate women's employment. By the turn of the century it was already a widespread practice for states to impose labor measures that restricted women's (and children's) employment. What was new, however, was the idea of homogenizing these measures in a coordinated and institutionalized form, to be embodied in an official document. The very idea of creating international legislation was an alien one. For several decades official representatives met and discussed whether it should or could be done. What facilitated this cooperation and actually made it possible was the widely shared agreement that women workers, as a group, required states' special protection. This was the only matter on which all agreed to cooperate.

Gender-specific labor legislation was a clear manifestation of the ambivalent attitude toward women's role in the public sphere. Women's nature and the harsh realities of the industrialized world were thought to contradict each other. This contradiction was dealt with by an extra protection granted by the states resulting in a set of restrictions not imposed on adult males. Thus, while protective legislation did acknowledge women's presence in the labor market, it did so in a way that highlighted their peculiar position. The struggles that were involved in the attempt to internationalize labor laws made clear that the very jurisdiction of the emerging world polity was highly contested and that its appropriate roles were still being negotiated. In constrast to the post–World War II era, it did not create new models of citizenship and states' behavior. Thus, in the period under discussion it was national labor legislation that preceded and set the path for international action. Even attempts to homogenize existing laws were challenged. In later periods, with the expansion of world organizations' jurisdiction, the order was reversed: then authoritative world organizations provided guidelines to be followed by nation-states.

These three international campaigns—the first to concern women's issues—constituted a significant part of the new world social agenda. All three were part of a general reform movement that was motivated by a progressive vision of society in which women occupied a special role. In order to enable women to fulfill their specialized functions, a global effort was required.

## "United Womanhood" for the "Betterment of the World": The International Campaign for Women's Suffrage

There were many suffrage organizations active around the world during the nineteenth century (Dubois 1991). By the turn of the century the first attempts were made to foster cross-national linkages and to create international associations on the issue. Several international organizations incorporated it into their agendas, but only in 1904 was the first international organization to focus exclusively on women's suffrage created—the International Woman Suffrage Alliance (currently under the name the International Alliance of Women). Once created it had much effect on women's international organizing in general and on the internationalization of the idea of suffrage in particular. The majority of international women's organizations that were founded before World War I (twenty-two altogether), however, were social reform movements that aimed at getting women to work together mainly for a vague ideal of "bettering the world." Access to politics (in addition to education and the professions) was considered as one such means that women could use to attain their goals.

Thus, though suffrage was a central theme on the world scene, it was promoted mainly as part of a wider social reform and not as a goal in and of itself. It was not justice but an argument for "expediency" which provided the rationale for the demand for women's political rights. The justice argument said that women ought to have political equality because of the natural equality of all human beings; denying women equal rights violated the principle of justice. Expediency theory, on the other hand, used a utilitarian approach: suffrage was needed as a means of attaining higher goals such as enhancing the good of society as a whole (Kraditor 1981). Note, for example, the words of Josephine Butler, leader of the Abolitionist Society: "Give women the vote and see what will be the result . . . think what we could do in the cause of morality, think of the pain and trouble and martyrdom that we might be saved in the future, if we had that little piece of justice" (qtd. in George and Johnson 1909, 153–54).

Interwoven in the expediency theory was the assumption that women's distinctive characteristics and unique contribution to the public arena stem from their domestic functions and maternal roles. Women's domesticity is what nurtures the very qualities needed in the public sphere. Thus, while operating within the paradigm of the "domestic woman" and "public man," this argument undermines the hierarchy it implies. Women used the notion "separate spheres" while turning it into a powerful symbolic resource in their struggle for equal rights and for the transformation of society. Subverting the existing notion of gender roles was also achieved in terms of citizenship. Citizenship had historically been connected with soldiering and the right to carry arms. Within the feminist-pacifist discourse the two were disentangled and their meanings reversed. Thus, in a keynote speech given in 1911 the speaker praised women's inability and unwillingness to fight as a rather positive attribute for citizens. Not only did a lack of soldiering abilities make a woman a better citizen, it would also enable her to bring peace and end all wars: "Another argument against women is that they cannot be soldiers . . . And what is more, when they get the ballot, they will use it to make war impossible" (Kaplan 1988).[1]

But this ideology also had its limitations. The story of the International Council of Women (ICW), founded in 1888, and its ambivalent attitudes toward suffrage as a sole goal presents a good example. It shows how, through the

---

1. To be sure, not all feminists were pacifists. Yet the pacifist "nature" of women was part, though a contested part, of the feminist discourse of the time. See also chap. 3.

process of trying to internationalize, suffrage—originally the main motivation behind this organizing—gained secondary importance as other issues surfaced; soon it disappeared completely from the council's agenda and only later reappeared as part of a much larger program.

In 1882 two of the leaders of the National American Woman Suffrage Association (NAWSA), the largest American organization for women's suffrage, Elizabeth Cady Stanton and Susan B. Anthony, during a trip to Europe decided that the time had arrived to unite forces and to organize an international society for political rights for women. They raised the issue in a suffrage meeting in Liverpool, where it was decided to form a committee to work toward forming an International Woman Suffrage Alliance. That committee never met, but its members kept sending letters to the two women urging them to initiate action. In the 1887 NAWSA meeting the idea of an International Woman Suffrage Congress had been put on the agenda. The controversy that arose around the matter reflected the polarization of opinions regarding the appropriate relations between women's rights and a wider social agenda. The older, pioneer suffragists advocated the idea that the congress should be limited to the advocacy of equal political rights, whereas the younger generation preferred a broader agenda that would not emphasize suffrage over other demands (Sewall 1914). The final resolution that announced the decision to hold an international congress of women in Washington, D.C., shows that the latter prevailed: "convening an International Council of Women to which all associations of women in the trades, professions and moral reforms, *as well as* those advocating the political emancipation of women, shall be invited" (Sewall 1914, 7; emph. added).

The congress was scheduled for 1888. That year was chosen because of its symbolic meaning as the fortieth anniversary of the convention held at Seneca Falls, New York, which marked the beginning of the women's movement in the United States. Representatives of organizations from Canada, Denmark England, Finland, France, India, Norway, and Scotland attended the congress. It was then that the idea of a permanent international body that would function as an umbrella organization for all women's associations, clubs, and organizations had been endorsed, and the International Council of Women was officially created. At that point the demand for suffrage had disappeared; the preamble to the constitution reads: "We, women of all nations, sincerely believing that the best good of humanity will be advanced by greater unity of thought, sympathy and purpose, and that an organised movement of women will best conserve the highest good of the family and of the state, do thereby band ourselves in a confederation of workers to further the application of the Golden Rule to society, custom and law" (Sewall 1914, 19).

The "golden rule," then, replaced suffrage. The idea that women are entitled to the same rights as men had no expression in the newly formed organization. Only in 1904, when the International Woman Suffrage Alliance was founded, the International Council of Women finally passed a suffrage resolution, and a standing committee on women's suffrage was formed (ICW 1966).

The International Council of Women is typical of its period. It shows how women entered the public sphere and got involved in organizational and political activities, both at the national and international levels, while appropriating the social and moral reform motive. In doing so, they incorporated the "women's cause" into the emerging global vision of social reform, thus helping to expand world polity, both its agenda and organizational infrastructure. One of the leaders of the International Council of Women, for example, advocated at the World's Congress of Representative Women held in Chicago in 1893 (in conjunction with the World Columbian Exposition): "[the idea of a] . . . throwing the influence of a united womanhood in favor of better conditions for humanity, better educational opportunities for all children, and in favor of that equality between man and women, which shall give to man the high privilege of living, not with his social and political inferiors, but with his social and political equals and which shall lend its influence toward world peace and human welfare" (qtd. in Spencer 1930, 13–14).

Alongside the prevailing notion of universalism and "united womanhood," the perception that the existing differences among the countries constitute a real hindrance was still held by some. The founders of the International Council of Women tackled this problem in their effort to look for a suitable woman to become the president of the new organization. One such candidate was Millicent Fawcett, a prominent figure in England. She, however, rejected the offer repeatedly. A draft document compiled in 1914 by Sewall, one of the leaders of the organization, listed the reasons she gave for her refusal. This draft includes also marks made by an anonymous editor (maybe Sewell herself). Note the lines, here set in italics, which were edited out: "She felt that she had already enough work at home and that in Great Britain conditions are not ripe for federating the existing organizations of women, *and finally to the disappointment of Mrs. Sewall, Mrs. Fawcett declared that to her mind it was 'quite impossible that English and American women should have anything in common, the conditions of their lives and the purposes of their respective societies being so different'*" (Sewall, 1914, 37). This story was not mentioned in the different historiographies of the movement. Maybe because it contradicted the spirit of "sisterhood" on which this movement was based and which it was supposed to embody and foster.

The International Council of Women was not only the product of its times;

it also helped shape them. It started early on to rationalize and standardize its activities on the national and international levels. This type of activity later became widespread. In 1889 the Canadian section recommended the establishment of a Bureau of Information in which "statistics regarding the women of the country shall be collected and kept to date . . . to give accurate information regarding the position, employment, education, pursuits, etc., of the women of the country" (cited in ICW 1966, 22). Together with the establishment of an Information Bureau in most of the national councils, a reporting procedure was established. Each national council had to present a formal report on the work it had accomplished since the last meeting, to be discussed in the meetings of the international body. In 1913 it had national councils in twenty-three countries, including Argentina, Persia, and Turkey.

The same two leaders who had founded ICW, Stanton and Anthony, did not abandon the idea of forming a federation of national suffrage associations. For that purpose they convened a meeting in Washington, D.C., in 1902 with representatives from Australia, Canada, Chile, England, Germany, Norway, Russia, Sweden, Turkey, and the United States. The opening speaker was fully aware of the historical importance of the event: "But ladies, it is an epoch in the history of the world that your coming marks. For the first time within the written history of mankind have the women of the nations left their homes and assembled in council to declare the position of women as women before the world, bringing to national and international view the injustice and the folly of the barriers which ignorance has created and tradition fostered" (NAWSA 1902, 21). A provisional committee was formed which arranged a second congress at Berlin in 1904, and it was there that the International Woman Suffrage Alliance was officially formed (IWSA 1913).

The forming of the IWSA had a big effect on further international organizing. Its leaders toured Asia and Latin America to promote the cause of suffrage and to help form national associations. Indeed, national sections of suffrage organizations were formed and affiliated themselves with the international organizations, as did previously existing ones, so that by 1914 it had members in twenty-four countries.[2]

The IWSA, more than any other organization of the period, emphasized the "justice argument" in order to promote suffrage. It adopted the enlightenment rhetoric of natural rights—a rhetoric that historically had been associated with men's rights—and used it in its demand for rights for women, the same

2. Not all existing suffrage societies, however, were admitted as full members. For example, the Women's Social and Political Union, from England, was considered too militant, and as such its members were admitted as fraternal delegates only (Schreiber and Mathieson 1955).

strategy that had been used first by bourgeois and then working-class men when they demanded political rights. A typical statement is the first article of the declaration of principles presented in Berlin in 1904: "men and women are both equally free and independent members of the human race; equally endowed with intelligence and ability, and equally entitled to the free exercise of their individual rights and liberty" (qtd. in Whittick 1979, 32).

Led by American activists and influenced by American rhetoric, they invoked powerful American myths from the fight for independence, such as the claim "no taxes without representation" or the "consent of the governed." These statements were, for example, echoed in their declaration: "That governments which impose taxes and laws upon their women citizens without giving them the right of consent or dissent, which is granted to men citizens, exercise a tyranny inconsistent with just government" (qtd. in Whittick 1979, 32).

Using the natural rights claim, however, was not their exclusive rhetoric. Being shaped by the dominant discourse of their times, they also pointed to the ways in which women's suffrage would benefit the whole society. Depriving women of rights constituted injustice not to women alone but to society at large. Indeed, much of the current problem was the result of this perverted situation. Thus, for example, the activists claimed that "the existing economic disturbances throughout the world" had intensified as a result of women's lack of rights. In a special report that they published on women's political rights in different countries, additional "evidence" was provided. It was argued that Australia and New Zealand, two countries that had granted suffrage, were "the healthiest countries in the world." The general mortality rate and that of infant mortality were lower there than for any European country, all being the result of women's suffrage (IWSA 1913).

The IWSA and its national sections became the leading force in the international campaign for political rights for women and were the trigger for further organizing. But they did not monopolize the campaign. Other groups—the temperance movement (which was much larger) and socialist women (who were much more organized)—were part of it as well. Each group operated within a different organizational and ideological context, and each held its own version of international work and feminism in general and of suffrage in particular.

The World's Woman's Christian Temperance Union (WWCTU)[3] was the

---

3. The singular possessive form (*woman's*) used in the title was chosen deliberately: "The women of the World's WCTU are as one woman, one heart, one soul, on one purpose intent, the protection of the homes of the world, by the annihilation of the traffic in intoxication drink, opium, and other narcotics" (qtd. in Staunton 1956, 17).

first and largest single constituency supporting the ballot for women (Giele Zollinger 1995). Many of the women activists within the suffrage movement were mobilized from within the ranks of the WWCTU; a good many of them had experience in the antislavery movement. In many of the colonies, especially the white British colonies, suffrage organizations were formed only after the temperance movement had taken hold (Tyrrell 1991). Though appealing to a different constituency (the upper-middle class rather than the poor), applying different methods (political activities rather than charity and community work), and diverging on some issues, (Giele Zollinger 1995), the two movements maintained cooperative working relations.

As a typical transnational reform movement of the late nineteenth century, the temperance movement was a sort of international Puritanism inspired by religious and moral concerns. It had been active in the United States well before women took the lead; in the 1850s women had been refused permission to speak at a number of temperance conventions run by men. As a result, they decided to form their own organization. By the 1870s an effective women's temperance movement was under way, leading to the founding of the Woman's Christian Temperance Union in 1874. Temperance associations and national unions were soon organized in other countries as well, and in 1883 the World's Woman's Christian Temperance Union was initiated (though its first convention was not held until 1891).

Internationalism was an integral and necessary part of the mission and activities of the WWCTU. Its symbol was a flower-formed world encircled by a white ribbon. The white ribbon symbolized the pledge to total abstinence. The group's goal was, indeed, to "tie" their white ribbon around the whole world. This drive to act globally was motivated by both instrumental logic and moral missionary zeal. It became clear that fighting against alcohol use and other vices could not be handled within the confines of any single country. According to the group's own accounts, this realization came about when in the early 1880s, during a visit to San Francisco, Frances Willard, the leader of the American Union, was horrified by the "opium dens side by side with the houses of shame" she saw there (Stanley 1983, 11). It was then that she decided to take vigorous action: "We must be no longer hedged about by the artificial boundaries of States and Nations, we must utter, as women, what good and great men long ago declared as their watchword—'The whole world is my parish'" (qtd. in Staunton 1956, 8).

Four women members were commissioned to travel the globe, spreading the idea of organized action against the use of alcohol and other substances and setting the foundation for a coordinated network of national organizations.

They visited, among other places, China, India, "Little Asia" (Turkey), and the Pacific islands. Willard tried to get states' officials to join in a campaign to set a standard of purity and total abstinence. In order to impress state officials and to raise public support, she initiated a petition ("the polyglot") addressed to all heads of states asking them to cooperate in the matter. It was the first petition of its kind, and it has been claimed that it contained one and a half million signatures. The initiators were very well aware of the fact that it would not bring immediate state action and that it was mainly an act of symbolic politics: "the object is rather to focus public sentiment" (qtd. in Staunton 1956, 25). This project did serve as the crystallizing force for the founding of the international body. By the turn of the century the WWCTU was the largest international women's movement.[4] By the time of the first international convention, in 1891, eighty-six unions in twenty-six countries were in operation (Stanley 1983).

Some argue that WWCTU's internationalism should be seen as part of a much larger outreach of American power and culture. This assertion might be true. For the present purpose, however, what is relevant is the actual internationalizing of the women's cause, a process in which the WWCTU played a central role, and, in its course, a highly politicized women's consciousness and activity spread to different parts of the world.[5]

The WWCTU worked in the contexts of both international feminism and the missionary endeavor. They combined notions of religiosity and domesticity, feminist commitment with an emphasis on gender antagonism. The latter characterized this group much more than any other women's movement operating at the time (Epstein 1981). What contributed to its gender antagonism was the special role that the domestic sphere, "home," and maternalism played in their discourse. Their main mission was protecting families (i.e., women and children) from the "rum curse" (i.e., drunk men). Men, the providers, waste money needed for the household on alcohol; drunk men neglect their families and become abusive husbands and fathers. In more general terms drinking, the product of masculine culture, was the major cause of moral degeneration and the ruin of homes and families. One of the most effective methods in the war against "the rum" (in addition to rehabilitation) was the imposition of legal restrictions, and for that the women's vote was needed. Therefore, political equality and the good of the family were conceived as one

---

4. Later they were superseded by another missionary movement, the World Young Women's Christian Association.

5. For more on the complexities involved in the movement's cultural imperialism, which characterizes any missionary work, see Tyrrell 1991.

and the same goal, and the struggle for women's suffrage was carried on in the name of "protection of the home and community." "Prohibition, Woman's liberation and labor's uplift" were the "blessed trinity of the movement" (Stanley 1983, 23).

Like other social feminists and social reformers of the nineteenth century, temperance women saw women's disenfranchisement as one main wrongdoing that needed to be corrected in order to remedy other injustices. But, unlike them, they did not focus on women's position in the public sphere. The main injustice done to women, as they saw it, was not their discrimination in the public domain but, rather, the evil they suffered at home by their own (drunken) men. Where there is no prohibition and men drink, the home becomes the central arena of women's oppression. Thus, coupled with gender antagonism was an emphasis on maternalism.

Their demand for rights and states' action was justified by a maternalistic logic. It was a woman's duty *as a mother* to demand suffrage: "It is the right, and ought to be the purpose of every woman of this country to demand every ounce of power which will enable her to do for her children the very best and noblest service. The distiller is armed with the ballot . . . the drunkard—the male drunkard—is armed with the ballot. The home maker, the child rearer, is powerless against such a foe without the ballot which determines political conditions in this country, and it is the crime of our day" (qtd. in Gordon 1924, 170).

Thus were women's role in and association with the domestic sphere presented as the main reason, cause, and justification for their struggle for public rights. Maternalism and domesticity provided women with powerful rhetoric that allowed them to act effectively in the public sphere and to demand the right to enter politics as well as other areas of social and civic life.

In contrast with the temperance women, the women's circles within the socialist movement had much more problematic relations with the suffrage organizations. Still, they played a significant and distinct role in the fight for women's rights, contributing their own version to the international discourse about women.

To be sure, many of the prominent women figures in the socialist movement were not sympathetic to the feminist cause. They adopted the socialist stance that women's oppression was inherent to the capitalist system and that both would disappear with the coming socialist revolution—socialism was the answer to all types of oppressions, women's included. This indifference to feminism was clear in the socialist activist Rosa Luxemburg's hostility to any attempt to deal with issues concerning women (Mullaney 1990). Still, beginning in the

1890s, an open and assertive feminist[6] movement began to develop within international socialism. As part of the first internationally organized political movement, feminist socialists had access to the arena provided by the organizational infrastructure of the First and Second Internationals (Boxer and Quataert 1978). This enabled them to reach and recruit masses of working-class women, a fact that contributed to their power base within the party. The largest groups were in Austria, Germany, and the United States, but there was also activity in Argentina, Australia, France, Italy, the Netherlands, Russia, Scandinavia, and South Africa (Dubois 1991).

Adhering to socialist thought, they saw the woman's question as part of a larger problem of class society and rejected the bourgeois feminists' focus on achieving sexual equality within the existing capitalist system. They saw class and not gender as a base for solidarity and cooperation, arguing that the feminist agenda reflected the interests of middle-class women only. Thus, for example, they could not accept the feminists' demand to extend the vote to women "on the same terms as men." In many European countries the right to vote was restricted to property owners, and, thus, this demand was meant to benefit the propertied classes only (Tax 1980). Similarly, the emphasis on married women's right to property seemed irrelevant to women from the working class. Another dividing issue was protective labor legislation for women, favored by the socialist feminists but of little concern to and even opposed by many middle-class suffragists. In general, the socialists objected to the emphasis put on political rights. This point was made very clear in a speech delivered by Clara Zetkin at the founding conference of the Second International in 1889. This speech became one of the key texts of the socialist women's movement (Sowerwine 1987): "We expect our full emancipation neither from women's admission to what are known as free trades, nor from equal education with men—although the demand for both of these rights is natural and just—nor from the granting of political rights . . . Electoral rights without economic freedom are neither more nor less than an exchange without currency" (qtd. in Bell and Offen, 1983, 90).

The feminist socialists had an uneasy relationship with their fellow socialist men as well. In general, though socialism prides itself on having an ideological commitment to women's emancipation, the issue was considered secondary at best, if not subversive and antirevolutionary. All feminist efforts were suspected

---

6. Note that the use of the term *feminist* for these women is problematic. The socialist women reserved the term for the suffrage movements, from which they tried to disassociate themselves.

of bourgeois tendencies. On that ground the Working Women Association, for example, was expelled from the First International (1864–67), whose members were hostile also to wage labor for women and unenthusiastic about allowing women into politics. The Second International had a more positive attitude about the women's cause, but it adopted the official policy, backed by resolutions adopted by the women's circles, which forbade any cooperation with bourgeois groups (Dubois 1991; Meyer 1977).

It was exactly this nexus of international feminism and international socialism which shaped the ways in which the socialist feminists have operated. They promoted the women's cause, speaking broadly of the woman's question, emphasizing the economic base of their exploitation, and pointing at the patriarchal bourgeois family as a site of women's oppression. But the woman's question was promoted also as a part of a strategy for recruitment of women, being a large portion of the working class, to the Socialist Party (Gluck 1983). Accordingly, suffrage was supposed to play a role not only in women's emancipation but also in class struggle. The socialist version of expediency theory was that women's suffrage was needed so that women would participate alongside working-class men in the political struggle. Thus, suffrage and class struggle went hand in hand, but the former was a means for the latter: "For the proletariat there is an increasing necessity to revolutionize the minds and to place its adult members into the battleground well armed, without regard to sex difference. The fight for universal female suffrage is the most suitable means to use this situation in the interest of the proletarian struggle for liberation" (qtd. in Meyer 1977, 94).

Women's domesticity and gendered nature did not occupy a central role in the socialist feminism of the period, nor were these themes coherently conceptualized. In contrast to the suffragists, the home was a site not so much for women to nurture their nature and the traits needed in the public sphere but, rather, a site of oppression. Just like the temperance women, they saw current wife-husband relations as particularly oppressive. The feminist socialist did not wish to restore the traditional "good" family, however, but to abolish it altogether.

At any rate the main focus was on liberating women through their gaining economic independence within a just social system. For that purpose, just like the temperance women, the feminist socialists created a separate organization, but, unlike them, they remained within the framework of the men's organization, the International. The German socialist women's organization, organized and led by Zetkin, was the leading force in the international organizing of the socialist feminists. (The German Socialist Party was also dominant within the

Second International.) One of its sources of power was its semiautonomous structure within the party. Two main reasons motivated its formation. First, women were not allowed to join political parties in Germany until 1908. Second, Zetkin recognized women's need for free space to be able to exercise their skills fully and to have an impact on the general movement. Therefore, she initiated the idea of a separate organizational structure for women, both within the German party and at the international level. This structure was carried on throughout the International, when each national party created its own women's section (Honeycutt 1981; Sowerwine 1987).[7]

The First International Conference of Socialist Women, attended by members from fifteen countries, was held in conjunction with the 1907 International Socialist Congress (Evans 1977). The question of "women and the vote" dominated the meeting. The focus of the debate was whether to forgo suffrage for women and to focus, instead, on universal men's suffrage, as suggested by the delegates from Austria, Belgium, and Sweden. Finally, the conference adopted the position of full commitment to suffrage for all men and women; the vote was 47 to 11 (Farnsworth 1980). It was the first time that the socialist women declared their commitment to the suffrage cause. Once that was determined, the women delegates decided to mobilize the whole International for the cause. After much debate the Second International adopted Zetkin's resolution: "wherever a struggle is to be waged for the right to vote, it must be conducted only according to Socialist principles, *i.e.*, with the demand for universal suffrage for both men and women" (qtd. in Sowerwine 1987, 416). This event was considered a major achievement for the whole international women's movement and a turning point for the International. Recognizing the significance of autonomous organizing, an independent women's secretariat with Zetkin at its head—the Socialist Women's International (SWI)—was set up. It lasted for almost a half-century, until 1955, when it ceased to exist as an independent body.

The suffrage movement played an active part in the international campaign against prostitution. The campaign was part of the vision of a better world that had no moral vice which could be brought about when women got the vote. The emphasis on suffrage changed with the transformation of the campaign. There were actually two distinct stages in this campaign; each involved a different level of international organizing, and each employed a different notion of womanhood and gender images.

---

7. Note, however, that it was still an auxiliary to the all-male party. Honeycutt (1979) argues that this structure was both a source of strength for the feminist socialists among working-class women and also a limitation as a women's emancipatory movement.

## The "Whole Civilized World" Fights the "Hideous Social Evil"

Prostitution and trafficking in women, also called "white slavery,"[8] was one of the hotly debated social issues in Europe and in the United States from the second half of the 1800s until World War I. It was a major preoccupation for governments, the medical establishment, state administrations, and social reformers in the different Western countries, all sharing the view that the fight against this "vice" could not be confined to national boundaries. "Transnational moral entrepreneurs"—that is, international associations of individuals—led the campaign to fight this social vice (Nadelman 1990). They held international conferences and managed to convene two major international diplomatic meetings that resulted in international agreements signed by a large number of countries. It turned out to be one of the first major international social reform movements, and it was the first international movement that focused on women; in some countries it was led by women.

One of the widespread concerns of the time was public health, especially venereal disease. One of the means to control the spread of the disease, as advocated by the medical establishment, was to put prostitutes under medical and police control (Bristow 1982). By the mid-nineteenth century European states had complied and adopted the system of state regulation of prostitution in their countries and territories. The regulation policy was based on the assumption that prostitution was necessary since it fulfilled an important function for the family and society. Therefore, it should not be outlawed altogether but, rather, should be tightly controlled by the state (Winick and Kinsie 1971). The type of control that was adopted emulated the old "French model" that dated back to 1802. According to the French system, a special police unit—a Bureau of Morals—was appointed. Prostitutes had to register with the bureau and to practice their profession in designated "tolerated" houses. They were subject to compulsory medical examinations and compulsory treatment, if necessary. In the case of refusal or not appearing they were imprisoned (George and Johnson 1909).

When similar measures were adopted in Britain in 1864 and 1866 in the form of the Contagious Diseases Act, a widespread protest emerged and led to the formation of numerous committees and associations. The emerging resistance called for the abolition (hence, the name abolitionists) of any state control of

8. Note that not all prostitutes were whites, nor was trade in women limited to the "white world." Appealing to existing racism, usage of the term *white* was expected to be more evocative and more disturbing.

prostitution and of prostitutes. Some of them, like the National Ladies Association, began corresponding with similar associations abroad with the aim of establishing some form of cooperation across national borders (Fawcett and Turner 1927).

An International Medical Congress that was held in 1873 alarmed the various national abolitionist organizations, signaling that a coordinated action was needed. The congress had reaffirmed the opinion that state regulation was the only method for dealing with the diseases accompanying prostitution. It demanded an international and administrative law in order to widen the scope and increase the severity of regulation (Fawcett and Turner 1927). The abolitionists became aware that an international front was needed: "a large and powerful organization on the continent was seeking to increase the efficacy of the measures employed, and for that purpose it was appealing confidently to England to take the lead in organizing among all the governments of Europe an international system which would bring the whole world within its scope . . . they are supported by the International League of the Doctors, International Medical Congresses . . . etc." (British, Continental, and General Federation 1876, 2).

If the medical establishment were ready to bring the "whole world within its scope," so were the abolitionists. Josephine Butler, the main figure in the British national campaign, was commissioned to mobilize public opinion in Europe against this system, to "produce the necessary revolutions in the minds of people, the people of the whole civilised world" (qtd. in Fawcett and Turner 1927, 119). Upon her return to Britain, in 1875, the first International Association for Moral Reform (later to be called the International Abolitionist Federation) was founded: "This was one of the earliest unofficial international societies of legal and social reform" (Fawcett and Turner 1927, 112). Its mission was to work toward abolishing the regulation of prostitution. The abolitionists won a victory in England, and in 1886 the Contagious Diseases Act was repealed. Encouraged by this gain, a big meeting was held, attended by delegates from Europe and America, to "consolidate the attack on regulation throughout the world" (117).

At that time there were already committees to fight regulation in other European countries as well. The International Abolitionist Federation became the leader and the vivid spirit in the campaign, providing means of communication and making connections among the various national committees and associations (Pivar 1973). The main difficulty in working internationally, however, was the perception that there were immense differences among the various countries. The leaders listed some possible differences: "The differences of language, of national and social traditions, of the state of public opinion and of the laws—and above all, the differences in the status of women" (qtd. in Fawcett and Turner 1927, 119). Cross-national variation was mentioned frequently by both advocates and proponents of international cooperation at the turn of the century as a hindrance for such cooperation. In the post–World War II period, even though differences were acknowledged, they were not perceived as barriers to formulating international standards for state conduct. On the contrary, the main mission was to eliminate these differences by getting as many states as possible to pass similar regulations and legislation regarding the status of women.

Some of the associations, such as the British one, saw prostitution within a larger social context and advocated a wider agenda of reforming the morality of society at large and women's position in particular. Butler, for example, was active in Britain in promoting the suffrage cause. In order for international activity to become possible, however, this wide agenda had to be narrowed down and a focus on putting pressure on governments to repeal all the relevant state laws and regulations had to be established.

Moreover, this well-defined goal should be applied universally, that is, to European as well as non-European countries and colonies. No compromise would be accepted. The relativist position that such regulation could not be tolerated in Europe but was found appropriate for the colonies, for the latter presented a totally different reality than the former, was rejected altogether: "The abolitionist arguments concerning the futility of regulation were found to be as apt to Indian as to European conditions, for they were inspired by principles which are permanent and of universal application, and as much they were unaffected by difference of climatic or social conditions" (Fawcett and Turner 1927, 131). This universalistic approach led the reformers to work in Australia, Ceylon, Gibraltar, Hong Kong, Malta, Singapore, and South Africa in addition to their previous work in the European countries.

Two main arguments were advocated during the campaign. Whereas some were looking for "scientific evidence" for the ineffectiveness and even the harmfulness of the system of state regulation (Bristow 1982; Fawcett and Turner 1927), Butler and others were prepared "to take a stand against regulation *even if it could have proven effective from the administrative and medical standpoint, because it was an attack upon human liberty*" (qtd. in Fawcett and Turner 1927, 58). The system of state regulation, in and of itself, was condemned for being oppressive and arbitrary; it constituted a violation of the most basic principles of justice. Butler invoked the Magna Carta and the writ of habeas corpus to show that under the regulation policy women were deprived of what was guaranteed by these documents—that is, safeguarding and personal security. Using these texts was very powerful symbolically. The two texts were central to

Western political thought and claimed to have universal applicability. Butler's act had two subversive implications. First, she extended the ideas of the two texts to apply them to groups of individuals beyond their original intention—that is, women in general and, more important at this point, prostitutes in particular. Second, she pointed to the contradiction between current state regulation and the principles embodied in these two texts, thus challenging the legitimacy of the former and reinforcing the latter.

The notion of the double injustice done "because it is unjust to punish the sex who are the victims of a vice, and leave unpunished the sex who are the main cause both of the vice and its dreaded consequences" led to a deep feeling of gender antagonism expressed in very evocative language (qtd. in George and Johnson 1909, 71). All women were the victims of the system, and it was men who were responsible. Men were the cause of prostitution, and men were the ones to initiate and implement the system that punished prostitutes and caused all women shame. In addition, it was emphasized that the harm done was not only to the prostitutes but was, in fact, an assault on all women. Thus, the fact that women led the campaign gained major importance and was frequently mentioned. "Women revolt" it was called in contemporary essays: "Thank God that women had risen up for the emancipation of their sex from the tyranny of vice, and that a woman had been appointed to touch their hearts with the sharp arrow of conviction" (British, Continental, and General Federation 1876, 18) and to "claim a practical repentance from the Parliament which had flung this insult in their face" (qtd. in George and Johnson 1909, 67).

Alongside the rhetoric of women united rising to fight against injustice done to their own kind, the imagery of slavery gained currency as well: "the slave now speaks. The enslaved women have found a voice in one of themselves." This image, based on metaphors of the powerless victim—"The cry of women, crushed under the yoke of legalized vice . . . is simply a cry of pain, a cry for justice"—prevailed in the following phase of the campaign (qtd. in George and Johnson 1909, 113).

The imagery of white slavery became dominant during the second phase of the campaign when the notion of recruitment to prostitution by force or fraud was introduced (Bristow 1977; 1982). Whereas the first image of women revolt declined and disappeared completely by the eve of World War I, the latter lasted well into the 1930s and 1940s and was expanded and institutionalized with the work of the League of Nations. Egalitarian talk, such as "if the same standard of morality were required of men which they require of us women, many things would be turned upside down," characterized the abolitionist crusade (qtd. in

British, Continental, and General Federation 1876, 19). It was replaced by an image of helpless innocent young women being "ruined," transported, and sold by traffickers to brothels in other countries, where they had nobody to turn to. This was the result of the change in emphasis from the antiregulation campaign led by Butler to the anti–white slave trade—the fight against trade in women for the purpose of prostitution—led by William Coote. The latter image was much more enthusiastically adopted and crystallized much energy on both the national and international levels. Butler herself commented that Coote's project aroused "immense zeal and interest" which was "in much contrast to the little interest taken in our direct Federation work, which is much more difficult to arouse" (qtd. in Bristow 1977, 176).

It seems that the switch to the images articulated in the antitrafficking movement was a reaction, a kind of a backlash, to the first signs that the old gender order was beginning to change. Bristow argues that "in an age of female emancipation it was comforting for men to subscribe to the white-slave myth, with its connotation of female helplessness, because it symbolized the simpler days before women demanded personal and political rights" (1977, 189). This interpretation finds support in the following quote by the head of the Scotland Yard's special new White-Slavery Bureau: "is it not reasonable to suppose that with the modern desire for independence and liberty of action which has become so characteristic of women, it is not only the man who is to blame for some of the deplorable consequences which follow in the search for a free and uncontrollable life?" (qtd. in Bristow 1977, 190).

The popularity of the white slave campaign was skyrocketing. It was no longer confined to the narrow circles of activist women but became widespread throughout society. Bristow (1977) describes a series of mass publicity about how white slave traffickers lurked everywhere, waiting to lure unsuspecting females into bondage. It was the topic of films, newspapers, story series, and books that were popular at that time. A landmark in this mass hysteria was a demonstration of tens of thousands marching behind Salvation Army bands in Hyde Park for the "protection of virgins" (see also Connelly 1980).

The anti–white slavery campaign shifted the focus from the relations between the state and its citizens (in that case, the citizen being the female prostitutes) to fighting international trade that was based on cooperation among individuals (pimps, traffickers, etc.) across national boundaries. It was clear that an international network was needed. Social reformers and activists in various countries were mobilized, and new kinds of international organizations emerged. The first was the International Federation of Friends of Young Women, which was created in 1877 by a group of thirty-two women from seven countries. Its official purpose was quite similar to most of the international and national organizations that mushroomed in the same period: "to establish an international protection by centralizing and coordinating the efforts being made to form a network of protection around every young woman who has to leave her home to search elsewhere for her living, and, so far as possible, every young woman who is isolated or lives in a bad environment whatever her nationality, religion or occupation" (qtd. in White 1951, 183).

During the 1880s and 1890s more organizations were created for the sole purpose of coordinating efforts to combat the social vice, including the Jewish Association for the Protection of Girls, Women and Children and the International Catholic Society for Girls. Already established organizations, either suffragist or religious ones, were mobilized as well, devoting organizational energy and resources. They included the Salvation Army, the St. Joan's International Alliance, the Jewish Council of Women, the Woman's Christian Temperance Union, the International Woman Suffrage Alliance, and the International Council of Women.

The World's Purity Federation, founded in 1900, represented the spirit of the purity crusade of that time. It combined religious conviction and moral justification with preaching on hygiene matters. The motto of the *Light*, the organization's official publication, declared its members conviction that "the white slave traffic and public vice can and must be annihilated." Promoting "higher standards of morals, and the safe and sane instruction of our young in sex hygiene" (1912 [March], 1) was their way of achieving the "annihilation of public vice" and "eradicating traffic in women."

William Coote, a well-known evangelical social reformer, was the leading figure in this crusade. In 1898, feeling that he had been "called by God" to "join the crusade," he launched his campaign. In the same year the medical establishment, for the first time, changed its position and started to voice opinions against state regulation. In an international conference in Brussels it abandoned its favored regulation policy and called on states to take better measures to protect young girls in order to "prevent their being drafted into the service of organized vice" (George and Johnson 1909, 199–200).

The battle was to be fought on two fronts: to prevent "falling" and procurement and to foster international cooperation. For the former Coote organized an ambitious force of paid and unpaid port and station watchers called the International Guild of Service for Women. Whereas the previous travelers' aids societies aimed at helping the innocent, the International Guild also sought to intercept prostitutes and send them back home (Bristow 1977).

On the other front, in an effort to join forces with organizations in other countries Coote decided to convene an international congress in London (Bristow 1982). A questionnaire was circulated among interested countries in order to gather relevant information. This soon became typical preparatory work before such international conferences. The requested information covered several domains: the existing legal and administrative arrangements regarding suppressing trafficking, the availability of statistics regarding the wide spread of the phenomenon, and the extent to which "preventive" work (or "moral uplifting") was already being done (The White Slave Trade 1899). Of utmost importance was the question on the desirability of international cooperation and its preferred form. It was not clear how state officials would react, since nothing like this had ever been done before—bringing about cooperation among governments on moral and social issues in general and those that pertain to women in particular.

The congress took place in London in 1899 under the name the International Congress for the Suppression of Traffic in Women and Children, and it was attended by delegates from Austria, Belgium, Denmark, France, Germany, the Netherlands, Norway, Russia, Sweden, Switzerland, the United Kingdom, and the United States. The preface to the transactions of the congress presents the group's typical depiction of white slavery and of the misery of its women victims, for whose rescue they were gathered: "In all such houses, the position of women is that of servitude. Their isolation, their friendlessness, the contempt with which they are usually regarded by respectable society, keep them under the control of the keepers of the house . . . young girls are being decoyed, or persuaded away to foreign parts . . . the poorer parts of Europe are visited by traveling agents, who have their local purveyors, and conduct their victims to the East and West, whereby they are lost in the bad houses" (The White Slave Trade 1899, 9).

The resolutions that were adopted in the congress called for immediate action. First, it was declared that each national committee should put pressure on its respective government to modify legislation to be in accordance with the aims of the movement. It was agreed unanimously to institute an international committee that would act during periods between congresses. Thus, a basis was laid for ongoing activity for the purpose of advocacy and raising public concern. In addition, international coordination was sought on two levels: an official level, by an agreement among governments, and an unofficial level, by agreement among charitable societies in the different countries.

The fact that the issue of abolition of state regulation was not mentioned only helped matters. By avoiding this issue, the national committees established during and after the 1899 congress managed to obtain the financial support of governments and the patronage of royal families and leading politicians across the continent (Bristow 1977). But securing international cooperation was not without difficulties.

The 1899 congress resulted in the establishment of the International Bureau for the Suppression of the Traffic in Women and Children. The significance of the international bureau was that it took steps to involve state officials and governments in the crusade in order to reach an official international agreement. After much effort and deliberation a diplomatic conference was convened in 1902, resulting in a minimalist agreement—the 1904 International Agreement for the Suppression of White Slavery. This convention did not require any controversial national legislation. It called on the thirteen states that signed it to coordinate their activities, and it provided for the setting up of "central authorities" to collect and communicate information about white slavery, to have ports and stations watched for procurers, to supervise employment agencies who sent women abroad, and to instruct officials to collect information leading to the detection of the traffic. Six years later, in 1910, another agreement was reached. This one, however, bound its signatories to take punitive steps against the people involved—to punish any person who helped a girl under twenty to enter a career as a prostitute or who procured an adult by force or fraud (International Bureau 1949).

Similar treaties that dealt with issues of controlling the infiltration of "unwanted elements" were already in existence during that period. For example, Russia and Sweden had signed a treaty in 1861 on repatriation of vagrants; Belgium and the Netherlands agreed in 1886 on expulsion of foreign prostitutes to their home countries (The White Slave Trade 1899).Yet the 1904 and 1910 treaties were the first multilateral treaties to regulate these issues internationally. They signify one of the first attempts to create an international social agenda. In this social agenda women—their rescue, protection, and rehabilitation—were the first item.

Alongside and sometimes in conjunction with this web of organizations and activities was a Jewish network that devoted itself to fighting Jewish trafficking. Jewish involvement in the organized traffic in women was rather conspicuous and thoroughly covered by newspapers. Because it was widely used in the anti-Semitic propaganda at that time (and later, in the 1930s, by the Nazis), Jewish communities all over the world initiated a widespread action. A network of committees was formed that drew in some of the major Jewish philanthropists. The Jewish Association for the Protection of Girls and Women was established in 1896. Local branches were formed all over Europe, South Africa, Egypt, India, and Argentina. Their activities included guarding travelers, lobbying for legal changes, gathering intelligence and sharing it with the police, stopping and prosecuting traffickers, rescuing girls, and reforming prostitutes (Bristow 1982).

Though many of the Jewish reformers worked together in interdenominational associations and organizations, the effort of the Jewish organizations was focused on "Jewish victims" and had to be carried by "Jewish workers" from a "specifically Jewish basis" (Jewish Association 1910, 3–4). Actually, they followed the same methods practiced by others; promoting the ethnic base of their activity allowed them to form quick contacts with other Jewish communities that were spread throughout the world and to secure the cooperation of community leaders. In the name of the harm done to the Jewish community as a whole, they were able to raise substantial funds and manpower. In any case, the Jewish activity constituted a significant part of overall international activity during that period and afterward.

In general, the international crusade over matters of prostitution was one of the largest global social reform movements in the second half of the nineteenth century and lasted well into the first half of the twentieth century. The need to correct the ways prostitutes were treated by the states where they lived and, later, the need to mobilize states to stop international trade in women for the purpose of prostitution were put forward forcefully and successfully by various social reformers. In both cases the harm that was done and needed to be remedied had a potential effect on all women. The two crusades, however, portrayed this harm, and consequently women, in two different ways. The rhetoric of discrimination, a double moral standard, and deprivation of human liberty which characterized the first phase of the crusade did not survive long. It was replaced by the image of the helpless, innocent young woman who could only be rescued through a massive effort of organizational activities at all levels, international, national, and community. Instead of discourse about women united rising to fight against injustices done to their own kind, we hear talk about "virgins and whores." The justice and rights discourse that defined prostitutes as autonomous human beings whose rights were being violated was replaced by a highly sexualized discourse that stirred a mixture of emotions, sometimes on the border of mass hysteria, which raised fear as well as compassion.

In both crusades women, usually from the middle classes, took an active and sometimes the leading part. Women's participation was based on the assumption, like in all philanthropic work of that time,[9] that women had something

---

9. Note that women were involved in different kinds of philanthropic work and were active in various social reform movements. Here, however, I focus only on those areas that led to the formation of international movements and to transnational cooperation.

unique to offer to their fellow women. "An explosion of benevolence toward their own sex" characterized the era (Rendall 1985, 271).This benevolence could, however, be interpreted in different ways and have different meanings. In the abolition campaign there was an attempt to foster a spirit of sisterhood, of shared fate between the prostitutes, the object of the campaign, and all women. State regulation was declared as an assault on all women, practically and symbolically. Any woman walking "aimlessly" in the streets was suspected of being a prostitute and could be subjected immediately to harsh police measures. And men were pointed at as being the source and the cause of this injustice: prostitution existed for their benefit, and they were the ones to punish those who practice it. Therefore, all women, should join forces and fight this horrific injustice. In the fight against trafficking in women, benevolence toward the weak and the fallen was the motivation for women activists and reformers. It was not so much a matter of injustice as much as benevolence mixed with patronizing treatment of young women who had been led astray and were in need of help. Within this framework the involvement of middle-class women in rescuing young women and preventive work only emphasized the differences between themselves and those who were in need of their help. It was through this kind of work that middle-class women reassured themselves of their moral and social superiority over the "poor victims" and reasserted the class system while promoting a rhetoric of sisterhood.

After World War I, with the creation of the first permanent intergovernmental body endowed with a wide jurisdiction—the League of Nations—the crusade against trade in women was expanded, rationalized, and institutionalized. Actually, it would be the only issue concerning women with which the league would deal. Similarly, the foundations for international labor legislation were laid during this period, and women's (and children's) employment featured prominently in the campaign as well.

## "No Night Work for Women and Children": The First Factory Laws

From the second half of the nineteenth century on, attempts were made to get governments to bring about international labor legislation "to improve the lot of the working classes" in general and of women and children in particular. By that time the idea that the state should act on behalf of employed women (and children) as a distinct category of workers was already part of the agenda of various social reformers and was embodied in much of the national legislation of that period. Yet the idea that these matters would be regulated by international agreement was not accepted easily. Labor relations, it was felt, were not an appropriate issue to be regulated by the international community. It was only after many abortive attempts that heads of states agreed to formulate and adopt an international document that concerned labor legislation. Not accidentally, this document was about the principle of "protecting women's employment."

## Employment Policy as Maternity Policy

Most countries at the turn of the century had instituted some forms of labor protection laws that were age and gender specific. These laws regulated the employment of women and children in two main ways. The first declared that women and children were excluded from certain job categories, and their employment was restricted to certain hours of the day. The second type of regulation applied to women only: it specified compulsory time off before and after childbirth, with or without pay, in addition to certain provisions for working mothers.

The first gender-specific labor restriction appeared as early as 1840 in England. Prior to that, protective laws dealt with the employment conditions of children only. The first laws were adopted in 1788 and 1802, but it was not until 1833 that legislation began to be effective and to assume a form that is recognizably the forerunner of modern safety regulation. The movement for a shorter workday and growing public concern over the physical and moral effects factory employment had on women, for example, led to the extension of these protective measures to women as well. The immediate trigger for the passage of these laws was the publication in 1842 of the *Report of the Committee on the Employment of Women and Children in Mines and Collieries,* which caused a public outcry. Objections to the bill came from those who feared that it might expose British industry to unfair competition (Creighton 1979). Claims were made that this was exactly the kind of fear that international legislation would overcome. Imposing the same regulation on all countries was supposed to keep competition fair.

In spite of the opposition, the first laws to protect working women were adopted. Adult women were equated with young persons for all purposes, and the very same restrictions were imposed on both. The first act in 1842 prohibited women, girls, and boys under ten from all underground work. In 1844 the working hours of women and children in industrial employment were limited (Anderson and Zinsser 1988; Creighton 1979). These first laws served as a blueprint for all protective labor laws for more than a century.

It took more than three decades for other countries to follow, and then diffusion occurred rapidly. By the eve of World War I about twenty countries (mostly European but also Australia, Japan, New Zealand, Russia, the United States, and Uruguay) had adopted some form of regulation in regard to women's employment (Blanpain, 1977–90). In most cases a shorter workday was instituted for women and children, and they were prohibited from underground and night work.

To be sure, the laws covered only women working in industry (in big establishments) and excluded retail, domestic services, and agriculture, thus affecting only a minority of the employed women. They were hard to enforce, and many employers avoided them altogether. Still, they paved the way to a differentiated perception of state regulation of labor relations. Whereas regulating the employment of adult males continued to constitute a problem, referred to as "overlegislation," regulating the employment of women was not considered as an "interference" in the same way that regulating children's employment was not considered as such. Thus, the workforce was divided into two groups: one of adult males whose employment was not restricted by state laws and one of women and children to whom state protection was extended.

Protective laws were supported by different groups—conservatives and radicals, Socialists and Catholics, middle-class reformers and trade unionists (Boxer and Quataert 1987). Each group had its own agenda and interests. Working-class men and trade unions were driven by a feeling that limitations on employment would prevent unwelcome competition from women and children, whose wages were far lower than those of adult men; or that protection cloaked male bourgeois anxieties about their manhood threatened by working-class women's independence as wage earners; or that middle-class values, which kept women and children out of the paid labor force, would be imposed on working-class women and children. Others also pointed to groups that were motivated by a Victorian chivalry toward the "weaker" members of society that mobilized the state to intervene in the new domain of labor legislation (Connell 1980; Koven and Michel 1993a). In some European countries the declining birthrate was defined as a national problem, thought to weaken a nation's strength and world position. Thus, in France, for example, limiting women's working hours was one way of tackling the issue of women's increasing economic activity outside the household, believed to lead to the "problem" of shrinking family size (Offen 1987).

Sklar (1993) claimed that it was an instrumental move on the part of trade unions to promote the strategy of "women and children first," the idea being that protective legislation for women was offered as an opening wedge for extending state responsibility to wage-earning men and to other aspects of women's lives. Indeed, protective legislation on women's employment in several countries served as a decisive turning point that signaled and legitimized the state's intervention in labor relations.

In the United States protective legislation took a somewhat different path. There it was only after shortening working hours for all employees, in the 1840s and 1850s, that the use of state power to limit hours and to regulate working conditions was questioned. Then, proponents moved to the position that women in their special capacity as childbearers and rearers served the state's welfare in a special way (Kessler-Harris 1982). The idea that their service to the state entitled women to special protection spread rapidly. The full endorsement was given in the (in)famous 1908 U.S. court decision in *Mueller v. Oregon*.

Shortening the workday was also aimed at safeguarding women's ability to do their domestic work. The German Industrial Code of 1891 limited women's work on holidays and Saturdays so that they could do their housework (Anderson and Zinsser 1988). An 1877 law in Switzerland allowed women with families to take a ninety-minute break in the middle of the day and prohibited their employment on Sunday. Similarly, in Peru, according to a 1918 law, women were prohibited from working on holidays and Sundays. The law stated explicitly that women must have longer "rest" periods to take care of their home and children (Blanpain 1977–90).

Thus, protective legislation was promoted for the advantage of male workers who feared competition, husbands who desired their household chores to be taken care of, and young children in need of parental care, and it was also promoted for the benefit of exploited, overworked women. In any case the rhetoric that was used, by men and women alike, referred to and highlighted women's "natural" attachment to the domestic sphere and to their maternal role.

An article published by officials from the U.S. Bureau of Labor Statistics provides an example of this rhetoric. Endorsing the need for international regulation, the article discussed the reasons why women need greater legal protection. After refuting the argument that shortening the workday would diminish productivity, it went on to point out the benefits that such legislation would bring about. Infant mortality, for example, was lower in those countries where women's employment was regulated, it was argued. And, besides the "necessity from a hygienic point of view" and because "they stand physically in greater need of protection," it was also claimed that long working hours conflicted with women's domestic responsibilities, especially with her duty as a mother and as a potential mother:

Industrial occupations, domestic duties, and motherhood impose very great burden on most women. If, then, it is impossible for a woman with a large family to do her washing and cleaning except on Saturday night, and if her vitality is often prematurely exhausted . . . the excessive strain to which the women in industrial employment are put . . . is bound to result in self-neglect on the part of the mothers and in the neglect of their children . . . the majority of women make use of the additional spare time secured to them . . . to take greater care of their homes . . . Young women are also enabled to cultivate their minds and to obtain domestic instruction. Only when they are employed for short hours is it possible for young women to train themselves for more skilled trades and for the mothers of the next generation of workers to prepare themselves to bring up their children. ("Ten-Hour Maximum . . ." 1913, 49–50)

One could assume that, if the pressing problems of declining birthrates, infant mortality, negligence of housework, the stability of the family, and competition in the labor market were all the result of the increasing rate of women's participation in the workforce, then the obvious solution would have been full state prohibition on the employment of women for wages. Yet there was no country in which such a prohibition was seriously considered. Although women were still not considered "standard" workers, their presence in the labor market had become an irreversible fact that needed to be addressed. At the same time, the solutions to these pressing problems—gender-specific restrictions—highlighted once again women's nonstandard position in the labor market.

Women in various countries were divided sharply on the issue of protective legislation (Boxer and Quataert 1987; Sowerwine 1982). On the one hand, middle-class feminists perceived excessive protectionism as patronizing and potentially harmful to their chances for employment. Working-class and trade unionist women, on the other hand, argued that since women were less organized than men they did not have recourse to unions that men did in their negotiations with employers and had no recourse outside the law (Lipschultz 1991). Therefore, adopting protective laws was seen as a major achievement for working women. Still, in some cases working-class women organized to protest against these laws (Koven and Michel 1993a). This conflict intensified in the interwar era, with the establishment of the International Labour Organization (ILO), which provided an arena for women's movements to express their concerns and to act upon them. In the pre–World War I era, however, with the low level of coherence and institutionalization within the world polity, there were no forums in which to voice such opposition and no international body to lobby.

Note that the rationale for these laws was formulated in universal terms—for the protection of motherhood and for the well-being of the races. Yet since these laws did not apply to a range of jobs that, for example in the United States, employ mostly black working women, such as agriculture and domestic services, they actually referred to white women only. It was white motherhood and the white race that were to be preserved and protected (Boris 1989). Whereas in the United States avoiding including mention of black women was done implicitly, in other countries, such as Australia, it was done explicitly.

Maternity measures gained much wider acceptance. These measures started to spread all over Europe soon after the adoption of the protective laws. Graph 1 shows the adoption of maternity provisions and protective legislation from 1840, when the first such laws were adopted, until 1919. It tells, for each year, how many countries had already adopted either policy. The patterns of adopting these policies look very much alike along a time continuum.

Maternity laws include certain limitations on women's employment after childbirth, usually without benefits (benefits started to be provided only later). On the eve of World War I about twenty countries had adopted such measures. In a few countries, such as France (Cova 1991) and Italy (Buttafuoco 1991), women were opposed to the compulsory nature of the provisions. International women's movements, however, were in favor, as were all the other individuals, movements, and state officials interested in getting countries to adopt an international treaty on that matter.

The early laws forbade women from working for a few weeks after childbirth. Payments in the form of maternity benefits became part of the policy when it turned out that many women could not afford to lose income and were evading the prohibition. These benefits, usually begun as a voluntary insurance system, rapidly became attached to health insurance programs and eventually became compulsory for both women and employers. In some cases compulsory leave and maternity benefits were provided simultaneously.

Most scholarship in this area has emphasized the differences in the circumstances that brought about this policy (Bock and Thane 1991; Koven and Michel 1993b; Ruggie 1984). Thus Germany was the first country to institute maternity allowances for working mothers, in 1883, as part of health insurance for all factory workers and a wide scheme of welfare plans (Quataert 1993).[10] In France

10. Germany was the first industrial country in the West to adopt various welfare measures such as compulsory national pension plans, health insurance, and accident insurance. Adopting such progressive plans, and doing so early, was part of Bismarck's strategy to weaken the Socialists and organized labor (Quataert 1993). Some argue that the same explanation holds for other countries as well (see Klaus 1993, n. 23).

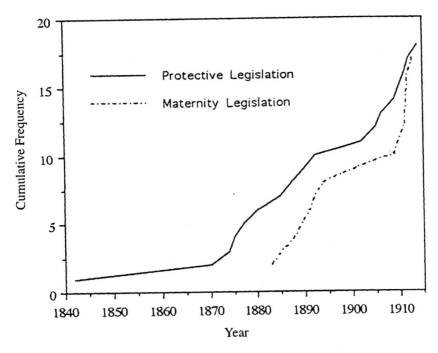

Graph 1.  Adoption of maternity and protective legislation, by year, 1840–1914.

maternity provisions were instituted as a solution to the problem of infant mortality and the larger crisis of "depopulation." These provisions were intended to allow women to take maternity leave without incurring a financial burden and to enable them to breastfeed immediately after childbirth (also a bonus was given to those who breastfed their babies) as well as after return to work (Klaus 1993). Fears of a decreasing birthrate also led France to establish the most generous program of family allowances in Europe, which included domestic workers as well (Pedersen 1993). As in France, anxieties of depopulation in Australia linked motherhood with the "future of the race," which resulted in wide pro-natalist measures to "the (white only) mothers of the race" (Lake 1993). In Italy compulsory leave without pay was first instituted in 1902 as part of protection laws for women and children (Paroli 1953). Later, pay was added in the form of the National Maternity Fund, adopted in 1910 as a result of a long campaign by women's organizations. In Sweden the 1900 law did not provide for pay during the compulsory leave period, tacitly relying on the presence of a husband's wage to ensure the necessary income (Ohlander 1991). Only in the United States was maternity elevated, but "working mothers" were seen as invisible, and thus no provisions were made to enable them to combine maternity with paid employment (Jenson 1988).

These national variations should be considered along with the overarching similarity, too often overlooked. First, most countries followed the same pattern in the sense that the previously discussed protective legislation ushered the way for maternity provisions (in Australia, Belgium, France, Germany, Great Britain, Italy, Russia, Sweden, and some parts of the Austria-Hungarian Empire). Sometimes the maternity measures lagged behind and were not adopted until after World War I (Greece, Japan, Peru, Portugal, and Uruguay). The United States and Switzerland are the exceptions in the sense that they instituted a wide array of restrictions on women's employment, but none of them were in relation to pregnancy and childbirth.

Also, the similarity between the arguments that were used to promote the two policies points to the fact that they were perceived as complementary measures in an overall "maternal policy" aimed not only at the welfare of mothers but more so for the good of the children, the family, the race, and the nation. Maternity protection, in whatever form it was adopted, conceived of motherhood as a matter of state policy. And, since some mothers and potential mothers were engaged in paid employment, it needed to be regulated so that motherhood would be protected. Later, with the emergence of a new ideology about the relations between women, motherhood, and the public sphere, the same road the two had taken diverged: protective legislation declined, and maternity protection expanded, now in the name of equality and not protection.

Thus, since the late nineteenth century gender-specific employment laws had become a standard feature of many countries, including Japan and those of Latin America. At the same time, various steps were taken to bring about international cooperation on labor issues. The widely shared consensus regarding women's protective legislation played an important role in materializing and institutionalizing such international cooperation. In that sense prevailing paradigms regarding women's roles in the domestic and public sphere contributed to and helped shape the emerging world polity.

### Emerging International Labor Policy

One of the reasons that motivated heads of state early on to bring about international labor legislation was the threat posed by the emerging international labor movement. Several decades before states' officials entertained the idea, workers throughout Europe and the United States had begun to organize beyond their national borders. The newly emerging labor movement had an in-

ternational predisposition since its inception; it was international in its ideology, its methods and activities (Hobsbaum 1988). There were about a half-dozen
international workers' organizations around the mid-nineteenth century, yet
most of them were in fact local and short-lived. But one such ephemeral organization, the Democratic Friends of All Nations, led to the formation of the First
International Working Men's Association (later known as the First International), from which the international labor movement was born (Latter 1988).

Organized labor challenged not only employers' authority but the legitimacy
of the system as a whole. The demands of the various organizations—local,
national, and international—ranged from higher wages and shorter working
hours to a transformation of the power relations in industry to uprooting the
wage system and creating a new social order based on the power of the working
classes. A warning sign was a wave of violent strikes and lockouts which spread
all over Europe during the 1860s and 1870s (Van Holthoon and Linden 1988).
Still, the First International, weak in organization and torn by internal conflicts,
dissolved in the 1870s. It was only with the formation of socialist and labor
parties during the last third of the century, and eventually the founding of the
Second International in 1889, that the movement took a firm hold and emerged
in the realm of international politics. With the founding of the International
Federation of Trade Unions in 1899 and the formation of the International
Secretariat in 1900, to provide continuity between the international conferences, the movement gained more coherence and stability (Johnston 1924;
Price 1945).

In spite of the pressure from the labor movements, governments did not
rush to regulate labor relations in support of the workers. Mandating improved
labor conditions by state law was considered an "intervention" in the market,
limiting employers' discretion to determine the organization of work and
working conditions. In addition, with the increasing economic interdependence and intensification of market competition, improving working conditions was thought to threaten the competitiveness of the respective industries,
due to the diminishing productivity that would likely come about. Though
some social reformers in the United States argued that this kind of legislation
would contribute toward increasing productivity by making employers use
labor more effectively (Lehrer 1987), the general consensus was that passing
such laws would have the opposite result. Thus, a country that was willing to
comply with labor demands feared that it would lose in the competition with
the other countries. The optimal solution was to have international standards.
It was argued that the only way a country could neutralize labor agitation was
by passing the appropriate laws. But, to keep international competition fair, it

was necessary that other countries also pass similar laws. This instrumental tone was evident in a letter written by Bismarck to German ambassadors all over Europe (but never sent): "It is not possible to carry out under present-day conditions a legal restriction of the working period in a single country . . . If any country desired to go forward on its own with general introduction of the normal working day then the industry of the same would be compelled . . . whether to . . . raise the cost of production, or to . . . diminish the daily wage of the workmen . . . For the first case if the arrangements were adopted by one state only and not simultaneously and uniformly, the home industry would be damaged or suppressed by the greater difficulty of competing with the foreigner" (qtd. in Shotwell 1934, 459).

This argument, however, was in conflict with the principle of sovereignty—a state's having discretion over its own legislation—which rejected international standards as a source for legislation. The principle would continue to be negotiated for decades.

Early on it was individuals, socialists, social reformers, and industrialists who attempted to influence governments to bring about some kind of governmental cooperation regarding labor. As early as 1818 the British social reformer Robert Owen sent a petition to heads of states convened at the congress of the Holy Alliance in Aix-la-Chapelle declaring that the "prime task for the governments of Europe was the international fixation of the legal limits of the normal working day for the industrial classes of Europe" (qtd. in Johnston 1924, 15). In 1838 the French economist Jerome Blanqui published a book with a similar argument, pointing to the long hours and "starvation wages" in which women and children were employed. Daniel Legrand, an Alsatian manufacturer, in 1847 sent a petition to several European governments, urging them to take steps to enact an international law for improving labor conditions (Follows 1951; Shotwell 1934). Among other matters, proposals included measures that applied specifically to women and children.

Around the same time Edouard Ducpetiaux, a Belgian social reformer, brought up the idea of an international labor organization as part of a larger vision that he had for humanity: "Let Nations unite for social reform . . . Let them summon a general congress to regulate their mutual concerns: commercial and industrial relations and the problems of the workers. All civilized nations should concur in this truly holy alliance which should open to humanity a new era of well-being and universal satisfaction" (qtd. in Follows 1951, 46).

An interest in "international factory legislation" became widespread during the 1860s and 1870s in Austria, Belgium, France, Germany, and Switzerland. There was no public discussion in England, however. England was not threatened by economic competition and held firmly to the belief that "most States would naturally desire to retain the judges of their own interests in this particular field of legislation" (Shotwell 1934). Outside of England political economists, Christian social reformers, intellectual socialists, social philosophers, and some politicians showed great interest and were engaged in public discussions regarding international legislation in general and that concerned with the employment of women and children in particular.

Organized labor held a similar attitude regarding women's employment. The First International, in its first meeting in 1866 in Geneva, adopted resolutions that included the regulation of employment of children and the prohibition of night work for women. In addition, a demand that governments should take steps to bring about international labor legislation was expressed (Johnston 1924; Price 1945).[11] Later the Zurich Congress of the Second International adopted a series of resolutions regarding women's work, including limiting the length of work day; prohibiting night work, employment in hazardous occupations, employment immediately before and after childbirth; and introducing female inspectors in all industries that employ women (Sowerwine 1982).

During the 1860s and 1870s the Swiss government started to take the first semiofficial steps to gather information among the different countries about their willingness to take concerted action. The responses were unfavorable (Shotwell 1934). The unofficial early efforts were replaced by official ones in the 1880s. In 1885 a French bill was submitted to a Committee of the Chamber of Deputies suggesting that a conference be convened to exchange ideas about international cooperation regarding labor laws. The issue had started to raise public interest in Germany following a proposed bill to the German Social Democratic Party and several scholarly publications (Johnston 1924). At that time the strength of German labor had grown enormously, and Bismarck had forestalled its radical tendencies by introducing social insurance legislation.

After an abortive attempt four years earlier, the Swiss government tried again, in 1889, circulating another proposal for a preparatory conference to discuss regulation of Sunday work and employment of women and children (Johnston 1924). The Swiss proposal, though it never materialized, was very telling in regard to the nature of the world polity that existed at the time, the possibilities of creating a global agenda, and ways to act upon it. First, it is clear that the fear of combined revolutionary activities organized by the socialist movement played an important role in this initiative and not altruism, as

11. Follows (1951) disagrees on this point. He claims that the International preferred direct action over "the diplomatic intrigues of bourgeois governments" (58).

argued by Follows (1951). That was the year in which the Second International was formed, and the labor movement, having regained its "subversive" momentum, was now determined to enter politics.

Second, experts were to replace diplomats in an official international meeting. The proposal mentioned political economists, statisticians, hygienists, among others, who would be funded by their governments. The "depoliticization" of the issue by its "scientization" seemed crucial at that point. Scientific experts, as opposed to state representatives, were likely to be perceived as objective with respect to the divergent interests of the states involved and in regard to the conflict between capitalists and workers. And, indeed, this was the way that the first international agreements in 1905 and the whole work of the ILO and other major intergovernmental organizations were conducted since then.

Third, the action to be taken was outlined very carefully. Those issues that could be agreed upon would be circulated to the respective governments as recommendations without binding force. International agreements should then be concluded between those countries that agree on the same points. "These conventions . . . [did not] intend to displace national laws. They would only oblige the contracting parties to introduce into their national legislation certain minimum provisions" (qtd. in Follows 1951, 122).

Fourth, since the participants "recognised the impossibility of obtaining agreement with regard to a comprehensive program in one conference," the agenda included only a few items (Johnston 1924, 20). It proposed that an international conference should be called to deal solely with the question of the international regulation of Sunday work and the work of women and children. It was clear that proposing only these two items was a strategic move on the part of Switzerland, knowing that they were the least contested ones.

The governments of Europe hesitated to respond positively. Britain and Russia refused, and there was no reply from Germany, the Scandinavian countries, and Spain (Follows 1951). All that, in spite of the fact that the task of improving labor conditions through state laws had already been undertaken by many countries. Still, countries were reluctant to codify it internationally. Thus, it is important to distinguish between the legitimacy of a state's regulation of a certain domain and the legitimacy of its international codification. Since sovereignty and setting international standards seemed to be zero-sum terms, a government could embody a certain principle in its body of laws but still refuse to make it into an international binding law.

The Swiss, in the midst of their planning for the already announced conference in Berne, were caught by surprise by the call of the emperor of Germany, William II, for a meeting in Berlin inviting fourteen Western European countries[12] to consider various measures that would "satisfy the needs and desires of the workers which have led to the strikes of recent years and to other forms of unrest." (The emperor took this step one year after the creation of the Second International.) This time the call for international cooperation had tangible results. The meeting in Berlin took place as suggested. Among historiographers the congress of Berlin is considered to "constitute a landmark of the first importance in the history of international labor legislation. It was the first occasion in which accredited official delegates of States had come together to discuss questions of labor legislation" (Johnston 1924, 24).

A series of resolutions were adopted in the congress, among them a detailed proposal that called for the establishment of an International Bureau for the Protection of Labor. Regarding the employment of women and children, one of the questions that was raised was: "How far should states progress on that matter?" and the answer was that women should be completely excluded from mine work, and a series of measures regarding employment of children should be passed.[13] Regarding adult male labor, however, a different question was posed: *should* male workers be protected by law at all?

Indeed, it seems that since the Berlin congress the pace of events started to accelerate. In an unofficial congress that was held in Paris in 1900 it was decided that the International Association for Labor Legislation would be established. And under the direction of its bureau a permanent International Labour Office, with a regular salaried staff, was established in Basel (Johnston 1924; Shotwell 1934).

It was this organization that initiated the conferences that resulted in the first international agreements regarding labor. First, a technical conference of experts was held in Berne in 1905, attended by all European countries except Greece, Turkey, and the Balkan states. At the conference the delegates adopted two draft conventions: the prohibition of the manufacturing, sale, and importation of matches containing white phosphorus and the prohibition on night work for women (alternatively referred to as the introduction of "eleven-hour night's rest"). The basic ideas proposed in the two agreements were not questioned by the majority of states, and the discussions were mainly about details.

---

12. The representatives from the following countries attended: Austria-Hungary, Belgium, Denmark, France, Germany, Great Britain, Holland, Italy, Luxembourg, Norway, Spain, Sweden, and Switzerland. Russia was not invited.

13. Among the other resolutions were: set a minimum age of admission of children to employment; guarantee the safety and health conditions of miners; institute insurance in case of disease, accident, old age, and death; offer arbitration in case of dispute; prohibit Sunday work when possible.

The same held true for the diplomatic conference that took place a year later, in 1906. The agreement concerning white phosphorus was ratified by seven countries, whereas the women's night work agreement was ratified by all fourteen states represented at the conference. Great Britain, despite its previous resistance, signed it as well (Shotwell 1934).

It is clear that at that time the most important and agreed-upon step for improving working conditions was to prohibit women from working at night. Note the array of topics that have been suggested on earlier occasions while discussing international legislation: regulating child labor, prohibiting Sunday work, shortening the length of the workday for all workers, instituting relief measures in cases of inability to work, improving safety conditions, among others. Out of this selection only the night work of women and the issue of white phosphoros were suggested for international conventions, and the former was endorsed by all. The interesting point is that, in the exchange of correspondence among diplomats regarding these conferences, from 1884 to 1906 (published in Shotwell 1934), it was never mentioned why women should be prohibited from night work. Apparently, this issue had already been defined and cleared in previous debates in the different countries.

The same goes for the second convention. A list of issues was proposed to be included: child labor, protection of railway workers, protection of dock workers, the hygiene in the workplace, homework, industrial poisons, the treatment of foreign workers, and many others. Out of the whole list only two were selected: prohibiting employment of young persons at night and establishing a maximum day of ten hours for the employment of women and young persons. Indeed, the two conventions were adopted in a technical conference in 1913, but the outbreak of the war prevented their submission to a diplomatic conference that was scheduled for 1914. It was only after the war, with the establishment of the ILO in 1919, that the two conventions were adopted.

. . . . . . . . .

Thus, nation-states acknowledged women's participation in the labor market and reacted to it by enacting gender-specific protective labor laws. In that way they created gendered workers and labor markets that were differentiated along gender lines. The widely shared consensus of these measures—that is, that the state should intervene in the economy for the sake of women (and children)—facilitated the early stages of forming world bodies and international agreements concerning labor issues. National protective labor laws, a common practice by the turn of the century, were codified into international standards by the eve of World War I. It was only the beginning of an intensive global project in which women's role as workers was negotiated, renegotiated, elaborated, in the interwar era, and totally transformed, in the post–World War II era.

Investigating the global campaign for international labor legislation should be examined alongside the other two campaigns that concerned women: that of abolishing the state regulation of prostitution and trade in women and that of extending suffrage to women. They were all part of the new social reform movements that arose during the nineteenth century and concerned themselves with "social evils" that transcended national boundaries. All three mobilized much world attention and action and, as such, constituted one of the important starting points for the emerging worldwide concern over social problems. All three underscore the nature of the emerging world polity and the prevailing notions of the role of international action vis-à-vis state sovereignty.

All three campaigns reflected and recreated existing paradigms of gender roles in general and that of women's relation to the domestic and public domain in particular. It was women's distinctive, frail, and domestic nature that was underscored in these campaigns. Women (and children) belonged to the domestic sphere. Once they were brought into the public sphere, special action needed to be taken. Women needed to be protected in the workplace and saved from "falling" into prostitution, a danger that confronted all innocent young women. Women needed protection and rescue. The suffrage movement employed the separate sphere doctrine but made it into a powerful resource. Still, the basic assumption regarding the gendered nature of the public and domestic spheres was not challenged.

After World War I world polity gained more authority and coherence, especially with the establishment of several permanent official bodies. These bodies perpetuated, and institutionalized even further, existing images of women and their peculiar position in the public sphere. In addition, women's involvement in the peace movement contributed to the gendered view of women and their role in society.

# CHAPTER THREE

# "For the Protection of Women and Children"

## The Interwar Era Discourse on Women

The world polity after World War I differed from the previous period. Two organizations of a novel type—permanent transnational cooperative bodies— were created: the League of Nations and the International Labour Organization (ILO). Their emergence ushered in a new phase in the construction of world polity. The evolving nature of global political authority and the emerging world agenda, however, were not accompanied by a substantive change in the global discourse regarding women. The activities carried out by these two supranational organizations were a continuation, expansion, and institutionalization of the ways in which women, their place in the public domain, and their association with the domestic sphere were enacted in the prewar era.

In an effort to promote "international co-operation, peace and security" the Paris Peace Conference of 1919 created the first (almost truly) global body, the League of Nations. It was modeled after the Hague conferences (in 1899 and 1907) in the sense that each state, regardless of size and strength, had one vote (Archer 1992). This principle first appeared in the Peace of Westphalia of 1648, which recognized "the coexistence of a multiplicity of states, each sovereign within its own territory, equal to one another and free from any external authority" (Gross 1948). It took almost two centuries for this idea to materialize and to be embodied in a stable organizational infrastructure.

The establishment of the league changed the old system of handling foreign affairs in which heads of states would meet infrequently, on an ad hoc basis, to resolve immediate problems. The mandate of the new organization was to institutionalize arbitration mechanisms among nation-states. Within its framework representatives of nation-states would interact in a formal, ongoing process, enabling interstate linkages to gain a more secure and stable organizational basis.

Also, though still not all inclusive, the membership in the league included nation-states that were outside of the European diplomatic system of the nineteenth century. During the nineteenth century the meetings within the Concert of Europe included only the principal European Powers. The league was open to all sovereign states and only to them; thus, the whole colonized world was excluded (with the exception of India, for which a special provision was made). Thirty-nine states had permanent representatives at league meetings. Nonmember states did take part in some of the league's activities or joined some of its affiliate organizations. For example, Brazil was a member of the ILO, and the United States participated extensively from 1921 onward in almost all league activities, yet neither were official members (Archer 1992; Myres 1935). In that sense it brought together into an institutionalized framework of interactions more of the world than before.

Founded for the purpose of bringing security to a world that had just experienced war on an unprecedented scale, the league was commissioned to secure peaceful cooperation among nation-states. It intended to serve as an umbrella under which a more orderly management of all world affairs—political, economic, financial, cultural—would develop. The league inherited quite an elaborate network of functionally specific international agencies created under the Concert of Europe (e.g., the Universal Postal Union, the International Bureau of Standards). When it was founded, the league expanded the network of agencies and established a wider institutional base to deal with issues such as disarmament and security, communication and transit (e.g., navigation and standardization of road signals), economics and finance (e.g., stamp law and tariffs), intellectual cooperation, international law, and social and humanitarian affairs (Northedge 1988; Siotis 1983). The latter category included matters such as international trafficking in women and children, drugs, and obscene publications. Other concerns were refugees, slaves, native inhabitants of nonindependent territories, and the welfare of children. It was within this humanitarian context that the league's activities regarding women took place.

What shaped the way in which the league dealt with women's issues was its limited mandate regarding the "internal affairs" of nation-states. Its establishment did not mean the founding of a suprastate; rather, it followed the principle of minimum interference with the traditional rights of sovereign states, and its resolutions were to have recommendatory force only (Northedge 1988). Its scope was restricted to regulation of the relations among nation-states (either through creating bodies to resolve conflicts or through standardization of activities and laws) rather than with shaping the relations between nation-states and their respective members.

The result was that the activity that was, for example, under the rubric of humanitarian affairs focused on fighting against traffic in vice and not fighting vice itself. Fighting vice required interference with a state's internal affairs. Similarly, the league concerned itself with protecting categories of people that were *outside* the official relations of nation-states and their respective citizens and did not deal with the way nation-states treated different categories of its own population. No global forum at that time attempted to set global standards for nation-states on the proper treatment of their own citizens, apart from regulating labor conditions. Humanitarian concerns, on the other hand, required action on behalf of children, slaves, refugees, inhabitants of territories, and foreign prostitutes (those who were transported across national borders)— all of which were on the margins of the nation-state system and, as such, fell under the jurisdiction of the league.

Many of these categories of individuals had been on the agenda of the turn-of-the-century transnational reform movements. The league co-opted the problems, which had already been defined, while building an elaborate and rationalized organizational infrastructure for dealing with it; stopping the transport of women across borders for the purpose of prostitution constituted a large part of it.

Women's status and women's rights were not incorporated into the activities of the league, and taking on these issues would have meant stepping outside of its defined boundaries. The rights of individual citizens were not on the official global agenda. And women's rights, more so than rights of any other group, were considered as part of the internal affairs of nation-states and were not the concern of the international community. In this respect the International Labour Organization, the second international organization to be formed after the war, did not differ much from the league. Though the subject of women was part of its agenda to a larger degree than the league's, both organizations were reluctant to act on behalf of "women's rights." Both organizations classified women and children in the same category for most purposes, defining them as requiring special treatment and extra protection.

The ILO was also incorporated in the peace treaty but had a separate constitutional origin. It was one of the more influential organizations established after World War I and the only one to survive the war. Ideas for establishing an international organization for labor legislation and labor affairs in general had already been entertained at the beginning of the century (see chap. 2). But fears of a future class war, stirred by the successful Bolshevik Revolution in Russia, encouraged nation-states to take action. The reorganization of the labor movement, taking place even before the war ended, sent alarming signals. International workers' conferences were held in Leeds, Berne, and Stockholm to make sure labor was represented in the making of the peace treaty. Labor leaders in the United States, France, and England began to communicate and to exchange ideas. The American Federation of Labor, in 1914, passed a resolution proposing the convocation of an international labor conference, with the representatives of organized labor of the different countries scheduled to meet at the same time and place as the peace congress. A special Trade Unions Congress called explicitly for the creation of an international labor organization (Foggon 1988; Johnston 1924).

Heads of states watched these meetings of trade unionists and socialists very carefully. As one observer noted: "It was an interest not devoid of a certain apprehension for fear the internationalism of the Socialists might go too far. Secret service agents were on hand to report to the British government" (Riegelman 1934). The director-general of the ILO, in a lecture given in 1968, explained the circumstances that led to the organization's creation: "Some of the delegates may have thought it rather surprising that one of the first acts of the Peace Conference should relate to labor; but there was general recognition that the ferment and instability which characterized the world of labor and industry in 1918 and 1919, particularly in Europe, called for immediate and constructive action" (Morse 1969, 4).

Thus, the formation of the new organization had a complex mission: to blunt social unrest (by complying with some of the labor demands) and to homogenize labor practices (to counter the problem of economic competition)—and all in the name of promoting a construct new to the official international arena: "social justice." Its unique tripartite structure included representatives of labor, employers, and governments and was intended to facilitate cooperation between the three groups in order to secure the implementation of proposed policies and measures (Luard 1977).

Though the immediate motivation behind the establishment of the ILO might have been the "red scare," once instituted, its wide mandate and organizational dynamics helped shape its mode of action. Mandating an international organization to promote social justice rather than conflict resolution or technical cooperation was a novelty. In the writing of the time the creation of the ILO was presented as a significant historical step. G. A. Johnston, in a history of the ILO published in 1924, wrote: "At the end of a century of endeavor, the International Labor Organization now is . . . to be regarded . . . with Hegel, as the final self-externalization of the spirit of social progress" (36).

In order to attain this new goal of social justice the ILO assumed a new mode of action: setting international standards and instructing nation-states to modify their national legislation to be consistent with world models. No substantive doubts were raised about the ILO's right to take such action. Recalling how many years it took countries to agree to adopt the first international labor conventions in 1906, the change is remarkable.

Having this jurisdiction, the ILO took it upon itself to improve the working conditions of women. The interpretation of social justice, as far as women workers were concerned, was the adoption of measures to guard women from the forces of the market and to protect their "domesticity" even though they were employed in the labor market. In that sense the ILO's activities were a continuation of preliminary efforts made before the war which culminated in the adoption of the 1906 Berne Night Work Convention. When the ILO took charge, however, these measures were extended and expanded to a much larger extent. In the previous period the Hague convention merely codified already existing practice in an attempt to set universal rules. The ILO also set new rules for nation-states. These rules, however, as far as women (always grouped with children) were concerned, were still within the existing paradigm of gender relations. Woman's engagement in paid employment, it was claimed, threatened her specialized roles and familial functions, and thus special measures were required to tackle these risks. The ILO assumed the role of instructing nation-states about what special measures were needed. It adopted a series of measures that included restriction on employment in certain types of jobs (e.g., in the mines), at certain hours (e.g., at night), and at certain periods of a woman's life cycle (e.g., before and after childbirth).

All efforts to take action in regards to women's rights, especially the right to equal pay, failed. The ILO avoided instructing nation-states to make women's status equal to that of male workers. As with the league, rights, such as those demanded by women workers—equal economic rights—were not part of the ILO's discourse. The only type of rights with which it dealt were those of organized labor—that is, the freedom of association. This right, granted to labor as a functional group, was consistent with the corporatist nature of the organization, but rights based on the notion of the individual were not. It was not until the 1930s that the first such resolution was adopted, and an international convention on equal pay was drafted only after World War II.

The transformation in the women's international movements also contributed to and was part of the changing world polity. Women's organizations experienced an expansion in numbers and in organizational activity. Between the years 1915 and 1939 a little less than forty new women's international organizations were created. The creation of the ILO and the League of Nations opened a new arena for nongovernmental organizations, women's included, by offering a central focal point worldwide that theretofore had been lacking. In so doing, they changed the context in which women's organizations operated, consequently prompting changes in their modes of operation as well. Their main effort now targeted the newly created transnational bodies. Many women's organizations moved their headquarters to Geneva to facilitate contacts with the various bodies of the league, while others established specialized bureaus expressly set up to deal with the league (see, e.g., Whittick 1979). In addition, a new type of organization emerged, the multi- or supraorganization consisting of representatives of a number of international organizations in order to coordinate women's international activity. For example, in 1925 the Joint Committee of Representative Organizations was founded, and in 1931 ten of the largest women's groups formed the Liaison Committee of Women's International Organizations. Members of the committee established close contacts with high officials in the league Secretariat, cooperating with the league on various welfare-related and other activities (Miller 1994).

New organizations, representing new groups of women, also emerged. Alongside the socialists and old social reformers, professional organizations were created to foster solidarity and to promote the interests of women in certain professions (e.g., the International Federation of University Women, the Medical Women's International, the International Federation of Business Professional Women, and the International Federation of Women in Legal Careers). Most of them, both the previously established and the newly created ones, argued forcefully for the full incorporation of women into public life while invoking women's image as agents of social improvement. These social feminists constituted the majority within the international women's movement. A minority, though an important one, objected to this strategy, rejected any special treatment and special protection, and claimed women's entitlement to full equal rights, on the basis of justice alone. These included the Open Door International and Equal Rights International. There was a bitter conflict between the two camps: the liberal feminists, who supported action on behalf of women's equality, preferably in the form of an equal rights treaty, and the social feminists, who feared that emphasizing equality might jeopardize protective legislation. Both groups focused their efforts on getting the league and the ILO to take action on women's issues but with quite different emphases.

The horrors of World War I made peace a major issue for the interwar women's movements. Disarmament, arbitration, and conflict resolution were discussed in many of the international conferences held during the period. New peace organizations were established, and new peace coalitions composed of existing organizations were formed. Thus, women from twelve international organizations formed the Peace and Disarmament Committee of Women's International Organizations to work with the League of Nations and with the ILO (Stienstra 1994). In 1921 the Women's Co-operative Guild established the Mother's International to promote security and peace. Other groups, such as the World Union of Women for International Concord (1915) and the International League of Mothers and of Women Teachers for the Promotion of Peace (1928), were also created then. But the most remarkable example of a movement that combined feminism, internationalism, and maternalism was the Women's International League for Peace and Freedom (WILPF), which originated in a peace conference held at the Hague in 1915.

### "Woman Suffrage and Permanent Peace Will Go Together"

The International Congress of Women at the Hague in 1915 was one of the interesting events in the history of the international woman's movement. In some respects it was a continuation of nineteenth-century women's pacifist activities. In other respects it was a product of the twentieth-century suffrage movement, both in ideology and personnel. The congress and its resulting organization dramatize the intersection of the two ideas of peace and suffrage, colored by maternalism and motivated by a diffused notion of internationalism.

Peace was the first cause around which women started to organize internationally. All-women peace societies were active in England and in the United States already in the 1820s and 1830s. During the 1840s a weekly newspaper devoted to international peace was founded by a French feminist. Women's massive participation in the 1848 first international peace congress in Brussels was publicly acknowledged. But the earliest attempts made by women to cooperate internationally were made in the 1850s. During the Crimean War European women formed the Women's Peace League. Frederika Bremer, a Swedish feminist, consistently promoted the idea of an international women's group dedicated to peace work. The idea was realized in 1868, when Marie Geogg, a Swiss woman, founded the International Association of Women. Priscilla Peckover, an activist from England, built up an international network of women for peace with membership in France, Italy, Japan, Polynesia, Portugal, Prussia, Russia, the United States, and Poland. It was probably the first major international women's network. Much inspiration for these peace activities and those to follow came from several publications that emerged from that time. The Olive Leaf Circles (a society formed of women from England and the United States) issued the first women's international publication, *Sisterly Voices*. Later, in 1889, the Austrian Bertha Von Suttner published the book *Lay Down Your Arms*, which became an enormous bestseller whose influence matched that of

Harriet Beecher Stowe's *Uncle Tom's Cabin* (Berkman 1993; Boulding 1977). These pacifist feminists all shared a similar notion of women's role in society. They invoked maternalistic rhetoric that characterized the discourse of the nineteenth-century women's movement (Strange 1990). The 1915 women's peace congress also employed this rhetoric while modifying it to accommodate the demand for suffrage as well.

These early attempts were short-lived. The pacifist energy was not consolidated into a solid organizational basis. The International Association of Women dissolved three years after it was established, and little of the record of other organizations remains. Peace, it seems, was not a central theme of turn-of-the-century international activities. To be sure, many women's peace associations remain active in various countries. Moreover, pacifism and feminism were entwined in many of the European women's movements, so that pacifist beliefs even became a criterion for screening members in some suffrage associations (Berkman 1993). Still, one can find only scarce evidence of international involvement. New organizations were not formed, and veteran organizations became involved in peace activity only to a limited degree.

With the breakup of global order brought about by World War I, the pacifist scene, both international and national, turned very gloomy. Most pacifist organizations were dissolved, due to obvious difficulties but also because of a strong wave of patriotism that swept over Europe. The most telling example is the dissolution of the Second International, as all major socialist parties supported the war policy of their respective governments (Carsten 1982). A deep crisis was experienced by feminist-pacifist organizations as well. Most of them, when their governments entered the war, abandoned their peace politics and got engaged in agitation for the sake of patriotism as well as pro-war activities. Existing charity, reform, and suffrage associations were transformed into war-support agencies (Berkman 1993; Strange 1990). Moreover, some suffragists conceived of their participation in the war effort not only as patriotic but also as a feminist activity: they claimed that it would make women's contribution to society evident and might help in their struggle for the vote (Costin 1982). Just before the war broke out, the IWSA sent a "manifesto" to foreign embassies in London, urging state officials to try to resolve the conflict in peaceful ways (Whittick 1979). But, when the war started, its leadership refrained from taking any antiwar steps. The movement split into two camps, pro-war and antiwar, the former constituting the overwhelming majority. Within this hostile environment only a minority in each country maintained their antiwar views and, despite harsh criticism and social sanctions, managed to keep in contact with women from neutral and belligerent countries.

A small pacifist faction within the socialist movement managed to survive as well, and low-key pacifist activity continued. Rosa Luxemburg, the German socialist leader, was the vivid spirit in a small group of pacifist revolutionaries that came to be called the "Rosa group," and Clara Zetkin, another socialist leader, made efforts to unite women against the war by issuing an appeal to socialist women: "When the men kill, it is up to us women to fight for the preservation of life. When the men are silent, it is our duty to raise our voices on behalf of our ideas" (qtd. in Sowerwine 1987, 419). This appeal was published in a clandestine brochure in France and later in other countries.

An international conference of socialist women, initiated by the Bolsheviks to unite all national antiwar efforts in support of a universal civil war, turned under the leadership of Zetkin into a fully antiwar event. It was held at the beginning of 1915 in Berne and was attended by twenty-eight delegates from six countries (England, France, Germany, Italy, Poland, and Russia). In spite of Lenin's opposition (he tried to act as a shadow leader), the conference demonstrated unity among socialist women in their opposition to all wars. The conference adopted a resolution welcoming all efforts by nonsocialists toward peace and sent a greeting to the liberal pacifist congress due to take place at the Hague (Farnsworth 1980).

Though the two conferences took place in different organizational and political contexts and had no overlapping members, they both advocated women's special connection to pacifism, and both found it appropriate to hold separate all-women antiwar conferences. Yet, whereas the Berne conference was not followed by any further action, the Hague conference did result in the creation of a permanent body.

The first event that marked the onset of the momentum for the liberal pacifists happened toward the end of 1914. The Hungarian socialist suffragist Rosika Schwimmer arrived in the United States to present to President Wilson a plan for a mediation conference of neutral nations and to discuss the prevention of new wars. Some of the ideas included in the plan materialized after World War II: the establishment of a world parliament, a world court, and international nonmilitary sanctions. A petition signed by thousands of women from eleven countries accompanied the program (Bussey and Tims 1980; Snowden 1921). Schwimmer's act was exceptional. It was the first time that women not only had discussed ways to prevent wars within pacifist circles but also presented a practical plan to a head of state. A similar act was to be repeated soon afterward by a group of women who presented a peace plan to fourteen heads of state.

Schwimmer's second objective was to mobilize American women in a worldwide protest against war. She toured the United States, giving talks to groups, clubs, and all gatherings of women. Needless to say, the media coverage that she and the British feminist Emmeline Pethick-Lawrence (who came to the United States for the same purpose) got was very negative. It was the tour by these two European women that inspired the founding of the American Women's Peace Party, headed by Jane Addams, who was later to lead the women's international peace movement (Degen 1972). One should note, however, that when the United States entered the war, membership in the Women's Party declined rapidly, just as it happened within similar European groups (Berkman 1993).

Following the patriotic trend, IWSA canceled its biennial convention, planned before the war to meet in Berlin in 1915, feeling that the time was not appropriate. A minority of women, disappointed by what they saw as a conformist association, expressed the view that at times like this "women have to show that we at least retain our solidarity and that we are able to maintain mutual friendship" (qtd. in Degen 1972, 65). Consequently, a group of feminists from Belgium, England, Germany, and Holland met in Amsterdam in 1915 to call for a Congress of Women to gather at the Hague (Bussey and Tims 1980).

Invitations were sent to women's organizations and those of both men and women as well as to individual women all over the world. One invitation was sent by Aletta Jacobs from the Netherlands to Jane Addams, asking her to preside over the congress. Addams was the perfect candidate to lead the women's campaign for peace. She had earned a worldwide reputation as a pacifist, feminist, and social reformer thinker, writer, and activist and, being an American, had no commitments to either side in the war (Oldfield 1995). In her letter Jacobs wrote, "From many countries appeals have come, asking us to call together an International Women's Congress of the world . . . We feel strongly that . . . we women must show that we can retain our solidarity and that we are able to maintain a mutual friendship . . .The world is looking to them [women], for their contribution towards the solution of the great problems of the day" (qtd. in Degen 1972, 67).

The congress was attended by more than a thousand women (estimates vary from eleven hundred to two thousand) from twelve countries,[1] both neutral and belligerent. Many more women planned to come but were refused passports by their respective countries or detained in the last moment. Out of the 180 British women who were invited, for example, only twenty-four were issued

1. Austria-Hungary, Belgium, Denmark, Germany, Great Britain (British and Scot representatives), Italy, the Netherlands, Norway, Sweden, and the United States. Messages of support came from women in Brazil, India, Poland, Serbia, South Africa, and Spain. Degen (1972) claims that women's groups in France showed no interest. Berkman (1993), however, argues otherwise.

passports, and, eventually, only three succeeded in getting to the event. Considering all the obstacles and the fact that the meeting took place in Europe in the midst of war, these figures are impressive.

At the Hague a series of daring decisions were adopted. First, a comprehensive plan for preventing war and reconciling conflicts was adopted. It included practical points on such issues as the prevention of armed conflicts, cooperative regulation of international commercial trade, open diplomacy, and creating international bodies for arbitration and conciliation. It was decided that two delegations of women would meet personally with the heads of states of all belligerent and neutral countries of Europe and present them with the peace plan that had been adopted at the congress. According to the plan, during May and June the following states were visited: Austria-Hungary, Belgium, England, France, Germany, Italy, Russia, Switzerland, and the Scandinavian countries (Bussey and Tims 1980).[2]

In addition, an International Committee of Women for Permanent Peace was set up, with Jane Addams as the president. At the second congress, which was held in 1919, the Women's International League for Peace and Freedom (WILPF) was formed. At that congress a prophetic criticism was voiced against the punitive clauses of the Treaty of Versailles (Oldfield 1995).[3]

"No," Jane Addams wrote to a friend, "I don't think I have lost my head" (qtd. in Oldfield 1995, 160). Actually, there were at least two possible reasons to suspect that the women at that congress had "lost their heads." First, actually proposing a peace plan and discussing ways of negotiation with "enemies" in times of war and great patriotic zeal did not seem to many to be a reasonable act. Second, international relations and diplomatic missions were not included in the cultural repertoire traditionally assigned to women. In taking these kinds of activities upon themselves, these women had stepped completely out of their normal boundaries and walked into a forbidden territory, one reserved for men. These two points come up repeatedly in the criticism voiced against them and in their own discourse.

The amount and kind of media coverage of the congress also attests to the fact that the whole project seemed outrageous. The women activists themselves were surprised to find how much attention their gathering received: "I imagined that it might very likely simply be ignored. On the contrary, it gives considerable exercise to the minds of various belligerent governments, and the

2. For details on the meetings in each country and the reactions of the officials, see Degen 1972.

3. WILPF has lasted up to the present, though it lost its original strong feminist focus and evolved into a peace organization whose members happened to be women (Foster 1989).

great news agencies have found it worth while to invent all sort of false reports about it" (Addams, Balch, and Hamilton 1915, 18).

Much of the media coverage was negative. One kind of response was directed against the women's "antipatriotism." For example, in England the congress was reported as being managed in the interests of Germany; in Germany the delegates were threatened with social boycott for attending a pro-British meeting (Addams, Balch, and Hamilton 1915). During the war women peace activists in Germany and France were imprisoned, and in the United States they were severely harassed (Berkman 1993). Another typical media response was aimed at ridiculing the whole enterprise by pointing to the mismatch between the women's gender and their activities; it depicted their efforts and aims as either laughable or deplorable. The women had been called foolish and naive; interfering and ill-informed; irresponsible, feminine, and at the same time boldly unwomanly (Bussey and Tims 1980). These responses were similar to those encountered by the American Peace Party, when President Roosevelt announced the party platform to be "both silly and base" and also assailed the motives of the women members. The American public's reaction to the congress was no different; largely, it ranged from the sentiment that "no peace could be made now save one that would favor Germany" to sarcastic remarks about the futility of the whole project (Degen 1972). When Addams, who used to be "the most famous woman in America," returned to the United States, she was called a "silly, vain, impertinent old maid" and "a foolish garrulous woman" (qtd. in Oldfield 1995, 161). When the United States joined the war and Addams continued her activities, she was publicly denounced, ostracized, and even placed under surveillance by the Department of Justice. After the war she was branded as a communist who held "dangerous, destructive, and anarchist sentiments." When she tried to raise money to feed German children, she was called unAmerican and a traitor (Oldfield 1995).

The women involved in this enterprise were aware of how "inappropriate" they were being both on "patriotic" and "gender" grounds, but through their efforts they reclaimed both notions as well as other important symbols. They inverted them and employed them in their rhetoric in such a way as to create an alternative gender discourse, using the existing paradigm of maternalism as a powerful symbolic resource.

First, they reclaimed the notion of "heroism." Heroism is one of the symbols most frequently used in relation to combat and, more specifically, to the death of soldiers during combat. Instead of elevating the heroism of those who kill others, it was the very objection to killing others, the refusal of many of the young men in the trenches "to be absolutely ruthless," which the pacifists held to be truly heroic. Heroines are the women that bless themselves that their sons and husbands did not kill others. Stories about such heroines were a source of inspiration for the women at the congress. Addams, in her opening speech, told of a woman to whom she said: "it must be hard for you and your husband to have lost a son in a battle," and the woman replied quickly: "He did not die in battle, I am happy to say he never engaged in battle. He died of blood poisoning in one of the trenches" (Addams, Balch, and Hamilton 1915, 129).

The dominant gender paradigm of "separate spheres" assigned men and women to different roles in society. The public sphere, which includes politics and, even more so, international politics, are the exclusive domains of men. But during horrible times like war it is not only the case that women should be allowed into politics but it is an actual necessity. It is their duty and obligation to step into politics to save the human race and civilization from the insanity brought on by the current masculine political system. And what qualifies them to be the saviors is exactly their gender—the nurturing qualities *and* reason that are fostered within the domestic sphere.

The very act of holding this congress in the midst of a war was presented both as an act of heroism and of reason. To challenge patriotism, the spirit of the time, and "to appear to differ from those she [the woman who came to the congress] loves in the hour of their affliction" (Addams, Balch, and Hamilton 1915, 125) does not make a woman fall short of heroism. It is also a clear evidence of women's rationality: "the deliberation of the Congress of Women at the Hague was the appeal away from passion and insane hatred to balance of judgment and to truth inspired by reason" (43). Usually, it is the woman who is portrayed as driven by passion and as one who behaves irrationally. Liberal political theories disqualify women from participation in political life on the grounds that they lack reason, a prerequisite for such participation. Now, looking at the world around them, these women argued, one could conclude only the opposite. And in that situation the only ones who remained sane must unite forces: "just because there is this terrible war the women *must* come together somewhere, some way, just to show . . . that when all Europe seems full of hatred they can remain united" (qtd. in Foster 1989, 11).

In contrast to conventional male thinking, it was argued, women's maternal function is relevant for politics. Because of their experience in mothering, women cannot help but enter politics. This task, which they took upon themselves, to end war was not a matter of choice but, rather, a destiny and duty that was assigned to them exactly by their distinctive familial functions. Women's reaction to destruction is shaped by their nature, and motherhood plays a crucial role in shaping this nature. Just as an artist cannot destroy a piece of art, so women, who "have brought men into the world and nurtured them until they reach the age for fighting, must experience a peculiar revulsion when they see them destroyed, irrespective of the country in which these men have been born" (Addams, Balch, and Hamilton 1915, 128). Motherhood not only "forces" them to act in a certain way, but it also equips them with the right traits and skills to become "the custodians of the ages" that cannot consent any longer "to its total destruction."

Motherhood can be used by women in different ways. Already in the nineteenth century it characterized the politics of women's movements. It was mobilized by the temperance and suffrage movements to serve as a rationale for their members to enter the public domain. Like the women social reformers, patriotic women who supported the war effort also saw women's maternal role as extending beyond the family to society. Maternal skills and domestic support are required for a successful war effort, they claimed. Patriotic materialists saw their duty as protecting their sons, their family, and their nation (Strange 1990).

The pacifists defined maternalism and their motherly role in a much wider sense. Motherhood meant protecting all sons, and all children, regardless of nationality. They gave maternalism a universal rather than national sense. Addams quoted the painful and incredible words of a woman who said: "Yes, I lost my son in the first three months of the war and I am thankful he died early before he harmed the sons of any other woman called an enemy" (Addams, Balch, and Hamilton 1915, 129). Woman's assigned maternal role and nature entrusted her with a role that extended far beyond the boundaries of the private individual family to the realm of protection of civilization as a whole. As the German representative said at the congress: "the women are here . . . to do their duty as wives and mothers, to protect life, to fight against national hatred, to guard civilization, to further justice—justice not only for their own country but for all countries of the world" (45).

Note that these women's sense of internationalism does not have an instrumental tone to it, as does the internationalism advocated by the socialists, for example. It is, rather, a more diffused notion of humanity that people share above and beyond their national borders. Internationalism is equated with humanity, whereas nationalism brings about its destruction: "If we can bring women to feel that internationalism is higher than nationalism, then they won't stand by governments, they will stand by humanity" (qtd. in Foster 1989, 16).

Suffrage was an integral part of these women's worldview and agenda. As "the guardianship and nurture of the human race," women were responsible for stopping the present war and all future wars. But, for that goal to be realized, it was their *duty* to demand suffrage: "Since the combined influence of women of all countries is one of the strongest forces for the prevention of war, and since women can only have full responsibility and effective influence when they have equal political rights with men, this International Congress of Women demands their political enfranchisement" (Addams, Balch, and Hamilton 1915, 154).

Indeed, suffrage and pacifism were portrayed as being twin principles, one enabling the other. This was the motto of the 1915 congress, and these were the only two principles women had to commit themselves to in order to attend the congress. The conclusion that enfranchised women would stop wars was derived logically from the way in which the feminist-pacifists constructed women's assigned roles in society and history and in light of what had been done by men so far. In the words of Aletta Jacobs: "Woman suffrage and permanent peace will go together" (qtd. in Foster 1989, 16).

The feminist-pacifists' conception of both motherhood and suffrage was truly universal. The suffrage movement demanded political rights so that women would have an impact on national politics. The peace movement demanded political rights so that women could influence global politics, especially decisions concerning the waging of war and the brokering of peace—an area in which the presence of women was even rarer. Women demanded a voice in the exclusive male territory of international affairs. This voice, however, expressed a deviant "antipatriotism" that bordered on treason. Moreover, what used to disqualify women from participating in politics, their gender identity, was invoked, inverted, and redefined in such a way as to be their main qualification for entry. "Feminizing" global politics also went hand in hand with a romantic notion of internationalism in which national borders lose their significance and nationalism is replaced with humanity.

## "Mothers of the World" and the League of Nations

Historical accounts of the interwar period focus on the campaign led by women's groups to mobilize the League of Nations to promote the issue of women's status (Becker 1981, 1983; Miller 1994; Pfeffer 1985). Economic rights, nationality, and suffrage were the issues most frequently discussed in this context. The studies also show the limited success of this project ultimately and point to the fact that the league did not respond to demands to adopt an equal rights treaty nor to enact the principle of equality between the sexes in nationality laws. This focus, however, overlooks a whole array of the league's activities that did deal with women though not with their status and rights. I refer to the elaborate project, developed under the auspices of the league, which was designed mainly to rescue women in various distressing situations and to fight against trafficking in women. The very fact that the league concerned itself with this kind of activity and at the same time refrained from anything that had to do with "women's rights" per se indicates the nature of the world polity at the time as well as the gender images that underlined its action or lack thereof.

## Setting the Stage: The 1919 Peace Conference

The Peace Conference in Paris in 1919 served as a setting not only for the creation of the first official global organizations—the League of Nations and the International Labour Organization—but also for the consolidation of the women's movement. Representatives of many different women's movements came to Paris to try to mobilize the newly created organizations for their cause and to carve out a space for themselves within the emerging agenda. The conference served as a forum for the various groups to define themselves vis-à-vis one another; to form initial contacts that would later be formalized and result in new alliances, and, most important, to constitute themselves as a group with distinct interests that should be represented in the new world arena.

The lobbying efforts intensified when it turned out that women were not going to be represented in the Paris conference at all. Women's groups, mainly the International Woman Suffrage Alliance (IWSA) and the International Council of Women (ICW), lobbied heads of states and the organizers of the Peace Conference via official and unofficial channels. President Wilson, referring to the delegation as "representatives of the mothers of the world," eventually approved of the "representation of women's interests" at the peace conference. The French representative, Clemenceau, thought that women could best represent "women's interests" and, therefore, women themselves should be included in the Commission of the Peace Conference. Wilson, on the other hand, meant to appoint a special commission (of men) who could hear suggestions from women's organizations about "questions of interest to women which were of international importance." The Supreme War Council of the Allies ruled that neither was necessary; instead, all commissions relevant to women's issues could receive delegations from women's organizations (International Council of Women 1966; Whittick 1979).

It was decided that two such commissions would receive women's delegations: the Commission on International Labour Legislation and the Commission on the League of Nations. The women's delegation to the Commission on the League of Nations presented seven resolutions covering the moral, political, and educational domains. None of the resolutions were "radical" even in the terms of the period. Even the political resolution on suffrage was formulated with caution: "The principle of woman suffrage should be proclaimed by the Peace conference and the League of Nations so that it may be applied all over the world as soon as the degree of civilization and democratic development of each nation shall permit" (qtd. in Whittick 1979, 71–72).

No resolution, however, was adopted. Instead, there were three references made to women in the league's charter. The first reference concerned women's representation: "all positions under or in connection with the League, including the secretariat, shall be open equally to men and women" (Art. 7). Nevertheless, the representation of women was minuscule in most of the league's institutions, except the ones that dealt with humanitarian affairs. This underrepresentation of women served as a rallying point for women's organizations throughout the interwar period (Miller 1991). The second reference concerned working conditions: "fair and human condition of labour for men, women and children" (Art. 23). Indeed, the International Labour Organization was very active in the area of women's employment, interpreting "fair and human condition" to mean requiring an elaborate set of protective legislation.

The third reference dealt with traffic in women and children and was very mildly put: "supervision over the execution of agreement with regard to the traffic in women and children." One of the "moral" resolutions that the women's delegation presented to the commission involved the same matter. Incorporation of this issue in the charter had nothing to do, however, with the women's proposal. This issue was already an established international concern; it was compatible with the league's humanitarian mission and did not relate to matters of sovereignty. Indeed, this became the major preoccupation of the league. Women who worked abroad as prostitutes and women who were dislocated by various military and political circumstances (always classified with children) were the only categories of women with which the League of Nations dealt extensively.

## The Humanitarian Agenda: Prostitutes, Refugees, and Deported Women and Children

The League of Nations was founded at a time in which the antiprostitution crusade was already a full-fledged international campaign (see chap. 2). There were already two international agreements in place; several international conferences had been held; an international bureau made up of representatives of various organizations was formed; and a large number of nongovernmental organizations were already active in the field of fighting traffic in women (and children). The arena was ready for the league to jump in.

Indeed, the league immediately picked up the issue, incorporated it into its covenant (Art. 23), and acted on it shortly after its inception. First, it sent a questionnaire to all governments, inquiring what legislative measures they had taken to combat traffic in women and children and what additional measures, if any, they were proposing. The questionnaires were sent out in 1921. A year later ninety replies (including some from mandate territories such as Syria and Lebanon) had been received. This high return rate indicates beyond any doubt that states acknowledged the right of an international body to initiate action in this domain. Nongovernmental organizations that were active in the field got involved in the project as well and sent questionnaires too.

Based on the replies and proposals, the league set in motion a plan to build a whole bureaucratic apparatus to set procedures to operate and define the appropriate lines of action. In 1921 an International Conference on White Slave Traffic was held, attended by delegations from the thirty-four countries that adhered to the conventions of 1901 and 1904. This conference resulted in a convention (the International Convention on Traffic in Women and Children) and several resolutions that set the path for how to deal with these issues. By setting up a bureaucratic unit made up of states' representatives, with a method of annual reports, to be compiled and sent periodically to all governments, the importance of establishing central national authorities (first mentioned in the 1904 convention) was reaffirmed, and a system of coordination among all bodies was suggested.

A permanent body—the Advisory Committee on Traffic in Women and Children—consisting of representatives of nine countries[4] and of international nongovernmental organizations, was established. The organizations were given the official status of "assessors." The system of annual reports, submitted by states on their actions regarding traffic, as well as proposals of new means to be taken, were considered a key to the success of the operation. This system of social control, to which countries that ratified the convention submitted themselves, was relatively successful at least in eliciting the requested information. As stated in a 1949 lecture reviewing the work of the league, "I was impressed with the readiness with which these reports were usually supplied, and the regularity with which they were continued once the practice had been established. Once you get government machinery into action, very little can stop it" (International Bureau 1949, 14).

Another commitment that governments took upon themselves was to establish central authorities (what in the postwar era will be called "national ma-

4. Denmark, France, Great Britain, Italy, Japan, Poland, Romania, Spain, and Uruguay.

chinery") to coordinate all information regarding procuration of women and girls "for immoral purposes abroad." It was considered of the "utmost importance" also that the Secretariat of the League should maintain close contact with these authorities (League of Nations 1922, 74). These central authorities constituted a direct link between nation-states and the international body. They functioned on a regular basis rather than in ad hoc fashion, thereby giving the system a stable bureaucratic basis. Though the central authorities were part of the administrative structure of the respective governments, they also enjoyed some discretion stemming from their contact with the league and from the authority of the expert members.

A few years later some steps were taken toward scientization and rationalization of this global bureaucratic apparatus. A major step in that direction was the decision taken in 1923 to appoint a group of experts to conduct what today we would call an evaluation study—that is, to see how effective are the measures that have been hitherto taken to suppress the traffic and to understand what were the conditions under which traffic was carried. The idea for this study came from an American delegate and was funded by the well-known philanthropist John D. Rockefeller Jr. through the American Bureau of Social Hygiene. This well-funded bureau, which commissioned and supported several important investigations in the United States and in Europe, seemed to be the perfect answer for the "spirit of fact finding" that characterized the field at that time (Winick and Kinsie 1971). The committee was headed by an American physician with extensive public health experience and staffed mainly by members from the Social Hygiene Bureau. It spent two years compiling material from twenty-eight countries, using about five thousand informants and corroborating all pieces of information (Bristow 1982). Commentary about this report indicated that "this impressive report made a considerable stir, as this was the first time in which the character of the traffic in women and children in its most blatant form, the methods by which it was carried on, and the inadequacy of the measures taken to prevent it, were described in detail in a report published with official authority" (International Bureau 1949, 10).

Recognizing the need for coordination, the committee also decided to compile a list of the laws passed by each country to be circulated among the various countries. Links between the secretariat, the central authorities appointed by the state, as well as the voluntary organizations were established "in order that there may be a free exchange of information, and that complaints and reports may be forwarded without delay to the proper quarter for investigation and action" (League of Nations 1923, 82). Thus, a highly structured, rationalized, well-monitored, and scientifically informed system for fighting the "social evil" was put in place. This elaborate system was supposed to be organized in conjunction with a "public relations" campaign that aimed at "the maintenance in all countries of an informed and active public opinion" (League of Nations 1925, 106). This system was able to mobilize countries for a concerted effort and to reach distant geographical parts of the world.

How involved were the different countries in league activities? There is no available information about the actual effort made by individual countries to follow the recommendations of the league. One loose indicator of states' involvement, however, is the degree of compliance with the 1904 and 1922 conventions requirement that all states that ratified those conventions submit annual reports on their activities regarding traffic in women and children. In 1931 it was indicated that an average of twenty-one annual reports had been received each year since 1924, which is about 35 percent of the total number of states members in the league. In 1929 the return rate rose to 46 percent, in 1933 to 52 percent, and in 1934 to 61 percent. These reports included also the British colonies, protectorates, and mandated territories.

The league also extended the boundaries of its activities beyond Europe and the United States. Whereas at first the Special Body of Experts conducted its inquiry in Europe and the United States, in 1929 it was recommended that the inquiry should be extended to cover the eastern countries (Near, Middle, and Far East), "realizing that the conditions in those countries were widely different from those in Europe or America" (League of Nations 1929, 107). Thus, the "Orient" came under the surveillance of league experts as well, and reports on the situation there started to flow in. In addition, an international conference of central authorities in the East was planned for 1937. This conference recommended that a regional office of the league should be established at Singapore whose purpose was to establish closer cooperation and fuller exchange of information between the authorities in the East and those in the West. It is also true that in the prewar era the various international organizations that were active in the field reached out and conducted their work in non-European areas as well. This time, however, the establishment of "central authorities" in the East meant that the Eastern *states* got involved as well. Not only were traffickers and immigration paths being traced, but, moreover, permanent bureaucratic links were being established which embraced the Eastern states as well.

A further specialization took place when in 1925 the Advisory Committee on Traffic in Women and Children was split up and reconstituted under two separate bodies with different functions: the Traffic in Women and Children Committee and the Child Welfare Committee, now with the participation of the United States. Cooperation with other organizations expanded when the ILO and the Health Organization were invited to nominate representatives on these committees. Later, in 1933, a resolution to convene a diplomatic conference was passed, and another international Convention was adopted—the International Convention for the Suppression of the Traffic in Women of Full Age. The new committee followed the same line of work as set by the previous committee, and no major changes took place during the second half of the 1930s.

Overall, the organizational infrastructure and procedures that had been put in place to deal with the problem of international trafficking in women signaled a new phase in this international effort. The moral passion that characterized the previous era had been replaced by a rationalized and coordinated global activity in which states and international organizations took part. The purity crusaders were replaced by state officials and, more importantly, by experts specializing in "social hygiene" and "public health." The field was scientized and psychologized. Thus, for example, in a report that was submitted in 1927 structural factors such as the economic situation and low wages paid to women were discussed as possible causes driving women to prostitution. A report from 1936 pointed at the mental state and cognitive level of women prostitutes; it concluded that there was a "need for a psychological and psychiatric study of prostitutes at an early stage and for a system of care of the feebleminded and insane which should result in reducing the number of such cases among prostitutes" (League of Nations 1936, 164).

Certain situations were defined by the league as being especially prone to drive women to "ruin." Accordingly, certain groups of women (all "dislocated" women) were targeted as potential prostitutes if specific measures were not taken to protect them. One such group, which continued to draw the attention of the league for many years, included "women and girls seeking theatrical engagement abroad." Therefore, "governments should exercise supervision over the employment of girls in theaters and music halls, in order to secure that no attempt should be made to induce them to lead immoral lives" (League of Nations 1922, 74). But it was not only women in show business who were thought to be at risk. Women immigrant workers, and actually all traveling women, were at such risk. Note the following resolution: "certain precautionary measures should be taken to protect emigrant or immigrant women and women traveling alone, and that there should be a special licensing and supervision of employment agencies" (League of Nations 1921, 74).

The focus on women who cross national boundaries in the context of prostitution is not only an indication of the anti-immigrant feeling that prevailed at that time, as Connelly (1980) has argued, but also evidence that women's "moral fabric" was perceived as frail, which put them at risk when they were removed from their natural surroundings. Furthermore, it was consistent with the league's prudence not to initiate any action regarding the system of "licensed houses" (legal brothels). The league dealt with the issue of trafficking and not with prostitution per se, with coercion of women across national borders but not within national borders. "Local" prostitutes were not part of the league's concern. State regulation of prostitution and the existence of licensed houses, the main target of the abolitionists, were considered as falling outside the jurisdiction of the league.

Only later, and after a long debate, the Committee on the Traffic in Women and Children adopted a resolution calling for the elimination of licensed houses in all countries. In 1937 the league prepared a draft convention for this purpose, but World War II interfered before an international conference could convene (Winick and Kinsie 1971).

Another domain that the league got itself involved in was rescue work of dislocated women and children and of refugees. In 1921 the league decided to intervene in Turkey in order to prevent the deportation of women and children for political and military purposes, which it found to be "contrary to the laws of humanity." Two commissions were established: a Commission of Enquiry on Deported Women and Children and a Commission for the Reclamation of Women and Children. Both commissions worked especially in Constantinople, Turkey, rescuing Armenians and providing "temporary accommodation for deported women and children *not accompanied by adult male relatives,* who are in the process of being evacuated from Turkey" (League of Nations 1923, 85; emph. added).

In both cases, that of "transported prostitutes" and that of women refugees, the league singled out special categories of women that either posed a threat to the "good health and public order" or needed to be protected and rescued from "immoral life" or devastation and destitution. In addition, in both cases these two groups of women did not reside within their respective countries. The league could deal directly with persons who were outside the protection of their own states, but it was reluctant to instruct or even advise nation-states about how to deal with their own members. Therefore, the league could devote resources to dealing with foreign prostitutes while avoiding the issue of women's rights.

## Humanitarian Agenda and Not Women's Rights

The humanitarian activity of the league provided an arena in which women's organizations could operate. The league encouraged the active participation of women's groups in these matters, giving some of them the official status of "assessors" and seeking their help in collecting relevant information and soliciting ideas and proposals. Indeed, during the whole interwar era women's organizations cooperated with the league in fighting against trafficking in women and children, monitoring the welfare of children, and doing peace work.

But in the 1930s some of the women's international organizations became involved in another type of activity—lobbying the league to take action with regard to women's rights, mainly to adopt an international equal rights treaty. Most of the women's groups at that time objected to the idea of the convention, fearing that it might jeopardize achievement in the area of employment legislation, particularly protective legislation. This conflict between the two camps, the social reformers and the liberal feminists, was as old as protective legislation, but it intensified during the interwar era. This struggle was preceded by the campaign for an equal nationality law, giving married women the same right as men to change or retain their nationality, which, while much less controversial then the idea of the equal rights treaty, was not any more successful as far as the league was concerned.

The end of World War I brought the issue of nationality to the forefront, especially with the collapse of old empires and the emergence of numerous nation-states in Europe and Asia. New borders and national boundaries were drawn in the postwar settlements, and nationality laws began gaining greater symbolic and practical importance than ever before. At the same time, the suffrage movement first started to expand the notion of equality between the sexes beyond political equality and nationality rights featured in its new expanding agenda.

The league acknowledged the importance of nationality law and decided to include this matter on the agenda of the Conference for the Codification of International Law to be held in 1930 at The Hague. Several women's movements lobbied the preparatory committee for the conference so that the principle of equality between husband and wife in regard to nationality would be recognized. Bowing to this pressure, the committee agreed to consider nationality laws as they affected married women (Miller 1994). After consideration, the committee recommended that the principle of the unity of the family and not that of equality between the sexes be included in the proposed convention. The distinction between women based on their marital status was retained. The committee members echoed the often repeated argument that it is not their role but the state's to deal with equality between men and women (Stienstra 1994).

A more coordinated protest was held during the conference. A joint conference and demonstration, attended by delegates from thirty-five countries, was held to support the principle that "every woman, whether married or unmarried, shall have the same right as a man to retain or change her nationality" (International Council of Women 1966, 60). An international committee of women was set up which addressed a set of memoranda to governments and to the League of Nations. A memorandum was also presented to the chairman of the codification conference. The requests were not granted. Instead of drafting a binding international convention on the matter, the conference settled for a recommendation to governments that the principle of equality between the sexes be embodied in their respective laws regarding nationality (Bussey and Tims 1980).

Women's groups, especially the IWSA, decided to continue the campaign. They organized an intensive telegram campaign during the league council meeting in 1931. Women from all over the world sent telegrams and cables to council members; the president of the council alone received 210 telegrams (Miller 1994). The result was compliance with the women's groups request, and a Consultative Committee on Nationality of Women was appointed, but no funds were allocated to its work: "the Secretary-General pointed out that there was no credit in the budget out of which this resolution could be met. Any steps, therefore, which the secretary-general might take to give effect to this resolution must not involve any expense under the League budget" (League of Nations 1931, 232).

Apparently, budgetary constraints were never mentioned in connection with the work of the league on issues such as trafficking in women. The Nationality Committee asked the league to reconsider the Hague Convention on Nationality and expressed the view that a new agreement, in which the principle of equality would be embedded, should be adopted. The league responded evasively again, asking for more information from nation-states and women's organizations.

During the same time regional organizing in the Latin American countries began to respond favorably to the demands of women's movements. Due to heavy lobbying efforts, during the Pan American Conference in 1928 in Havana the first intergovernmental body to deal with women's issues was established— the Inter-American Commission of Women (Comisión de Interamericano Mujeres [CIM]). This commission brought about the adoption of two major documents by the Pan American Conference in Montevideo in 1933: the Convention on the Nationality of Women and the Treaty on the Equality of Rights between Men and Women (CIM 1974). These were the first two official international conventions that explicitly set sexual equality as a principle to be incorporated into national legislation. These documents indeed remained unique during the whole interwar era; neither the League of Nations nor the ILO adopted similar documents. Bringing the existence of the Pan American nationality convention to the attention of the league had no tangible effect. The league put it on its official agenda but settled for issuing a recommendation that states modify their nationality laws accordingly and announcing that the convention was open to accession by all states (League of Nations 1934).

Thus, beside discussions, recommendations, "collection of opinions," and solicitations of proposals from various sources, the league did not take any decisive steps to remedy the inequality between men and women regarding nationality. This issue was one of the first to reemerge after the war on the agenda of the United Nations Commission of the Status of Women. This time the current world agenda and the commission's mandate enabled it to take some definitive steps, in time passing various resolutions and eventually adopting an international convention—the 1957 Convention on the Nationality of Married Women.

Becker (1981) argues that the establishment of the Inter-American Commission and the adoption of the two conventions were the result of the work of the American National Women's Party. Stienstra (1994) holds that the suffrage and the existence of a vivid feminist movement in the Latin American countries are responsible for these pioneering steps. Whether they were an authentic expression of Latin American feminism or not, the two Pan American treaties did serve as a point of reference for the international women's movement—both as a source of inspiration and a cause for conflict and controversy, especially around the issue of the equal rights treaty.

The idea for such a treaty originated in England in 1926, was communicated to American feminist groups, and was then picked up by various women's international organizations (Miller 1994). For more than a decade the issue divided the international women's movement, the conflict intensifying when some groups launched an extensive effort to get the League of Nations to draft a treaty. Equal Rights International (ERI), founded in 1930, was the leading force in this campaign. The International Woman Suffrage Alliance, the St. Joan Social and Political Alliance, the Women's International League for Peace and Freedom, and many professional women's organizations joined the campaign. It was believed that international legislation in the form of a treaty was a more effective strategy than incremental national legislation.

Many of the supporters of the treaty emphasized not only its moral implication but also its benefit for society as a whole. Much like the suffrage argument of the previous era, it was claimed that women's contribution was urgently needed, because "on it depends the release of the full service of women, half of humanity, for work in solving the problems and suffering of the world" (League of Nations 1935, 47–48). And it was not only the case that more power would be harnessed now to solve the problems of the world; women would bring with them their unique experience, skills, and talents, which are essential for bringing about a better future. The key for their entrance into the public sphere as equals was again their motherly nature, experience, and character. Note how the IWSA continued this nineteenth-century discourse as manifested in its communication to the league concerning suffrage: "Moreover, the exclusion of women must often mean the exclusion of highly gifted individuals; it means the exclusion of the direct experience of maternity, with its consequent concern with youth . . . it is essential to utilise her experience in planning for the child's life, which enables her to see how the laws of the State may be best adjusted to meet the needs of the new generation" (qtd. in League of Nations 1935, 8).

The idea of the treaty was highly divisive because of its possible implications for protective labor legislation as developed by the ILO. The women's organizations that supported an equal rights treaty opposed the expansive nature of ILO's legislation carried in the name of protection. Those who objected to the treaty saw labor legislation as promising a major improvement in women's working conditions and feared that such a treaty might jeopardize that development. Note the following statement made by the World's Young Women's Christian Association to the league's secretary-general in reference to the possibility of drafting an equal rights treaty: "It has been ascertained from experts in international law that an international draft convention introducing equality as between men and women in general terms . . . would override the existing International Labour Conventions applying to women and so deprive women in industry of their protection. This reason alone would make it impossible for the Association to support a draft convention covering the whole status of women" (qtd. in League of Nations 1935, 10).

During the 1930s the campaign for an international action intensified. What gave the issue greater urgency was the economic crisis of the 1930s, which brought about major reactionary steps against women's employment, coupled with the emergence of fascist regimes in Europe. An international treaty that expressly affirmed equality of rights between men and women in all areas of life, including economic activity, seemed imperative: "the time has come to move from national to the international sphere, and to endeavor to obtain an international agreement what national legislation has failed to accomplish" (qtd. in Miller 1994, 221).

Due to demands put forth by members of the Inter-American Commission, delegates from Latin American countries requested that the league put the question of the status of women on its agenda. In 1935, for the first time, the issue was discussed by the league and once again in 1937 (League of Nations 1937). The league addressed "the question of the status of women in all its aspects," and the possibility of adopting an international treaty was discussed. The official report stated that the league expressed appreciation for the "strength and extent of the movement for the removal of differences in the legal position of the sexes"; "sympathy was felt for the ideas underlying this movement" (League of Nations 1938, 178). But a series of reasons were given to explain why no action could be taken and no such treaty could be adopted. The first obstacle resulted from the differences in "social and legal habits and structure of different countries." Second, and more important: "No delegation proposed that the League should at present attempt to have such a convention negotiated under its auspices, and certain delegations declared that, in the opinion of their Governments, the status of women was so essentially a matter of domestic jurisdiction that it ought not be considered to fall within the field of action of the League" (League of Nations 1937, 3).

These arguments were brought up repeatedly throughout the years of the league to explain what prevented it from dealing with the issue of the status of women more extensively. It is interesting to note that this attitude disappeared in the years after World War II, replaced by the notion that it is the *duty* of the major intergovernmental body at the time, the United Nations, to create "progressive" norms and standards for all nation-states to follow.

The only affirmative step was taken in 1937, when the league decided to conduct "a comprehensive study . . . giving full information on the legal status enjoyed by women in the various countries of the world" (League of Nations 1945, 135). Objection of some league officials on the grounds that this move might raise questions about "the internal political and social organization of states which have no international character" was rejected (qtd. in Miller 1994, 235). Framing the study as preparation for an international convention, the assembly decided to set up a committee of experts to work closely with representatives of women's organizations and legal scholars to produce a plan of the domain and geographical scope of the survey. The International Institute of Rome for the Unification of Private Law and the International Bureau for the Unification of Penal law were appointed to carry out this project.

This was not the first endeavor to gather information on a worldwide scale about women's status. The suffrage movement started early on to collect information on the legal status of women in different countries. Already in 1902, the IWSA published such a survey with data on nineteen countries (National

American Woman Suffrage Association 1902). The ICW decided in 1909 to ask the various national councils to write reports on the "existing unequal laws in their respective countries which deal with the relations of women in the home, the family, the municipality, and the state" (International Council of Women 1912, 3). It resulted in a somewhat standardized report on seventeen countries, written in different languages and covering a priori specified legal areas. The idea that underlined these early cross-national studies is the comparability of the situation of women in different political, social, and economic contexts. These early efforts toward the scientization and standardization of "women's status" would mature into a full-scale project several decades later, during the UN Decade for Women, with the help of officials and experts of all disciplines.

The 1936 study, however, was the first to be initiated by an official world body and to be carried out by state governments. Indeed, it was defined as a historical event. At the public meeting of the league the chairman declared that, "even as it stood, the programme of work is vast . . . Nothing of the kind had ever before been attempted on such scale" (League of Nations 1938, 180). Similarly, a member of the International Woman Suffrage Alliance commented: "In 1937 we shall know what is the civil and political status of women in all countries, through an inquiry by the League. It is the first time in human history that a world assembly has wanted to get a clear picture of the rights and disabilities, the triumphs and the defeats of women" (qtd. in Whittick 1979, 129).

In spite of all the enthusiasm, the result was much less than expected. First, the study was not as comprehensive as planned. Second, it was never completed. And, third, the number of countries that responded was low. As for the first limitation, it turned out that the committee was unable to study the situation of women "of the primitive people" and in countries ruled by laws not of the "Western type, such as Mohammedan law and Hindu law" (League of Nations 1939, 160–61). The outbreak of the war prevented publication of the full report, originally intended to be completed by 1941. Only one part of it was published. In addition, some of the governments refused to supply any information, arguing that the question of the status of women was one of internal national policy, unsuitable for international regulation. (Unfortunately, exact figures of the return rate were not provided.)

Still, one cannot downplay this achievement altogether. Women's movements managed to get the league to expand its agenda to include matters such as women's status. What used to be promoted by women's organizations alone was now picked up by an official world body. It was the first step in transforming the issue of women's status and rights from an internal affair to an international one. It is true that women's issues and women's welfare were on the international agenda before; the novelty here, however, is the explicit reference to the principle of women's rights.

The international organization to be formed after the war, the United Nations, not only continued the work of the league but also created a whole new global agenda, different qualitatively and quantitatively from that of the prewar era and one that had an enormous impact worldwide.

## "Working Mothers" and the International Labour Organization

### Setting the Stage: The 1919 Paris and Washington Conferences

The first commission to receive women's delegations at the Peace Conference in Paris was the International Labour Legislation Commission. Many women activists made their way to Paris and obtained interviews with members of the commission to present their approach to issues related to women's employment, broadly defined. The first International Labour Conference took place in Washington, D.C., focusing the attention of the women's movement once again. These two conferences, especially the latter, were formative in shaping the global discourse on women's position in the public sphere in general and in paid employment in particular. They were also formative in defining the pattern of interactions between the women's movements and new official world organization for the interwar era.

A wide range of views and topics were expressed by the women's delegates to the commission. The resolutions presented included matters such as expansion of women's protective legislation (e.g., prohibition of all nightwork for women, paid maternity leave, part-time work for married women); equality between men and women in employment (e.g., equality in pay, in the right to enter and practice all professions, in technical training); general welfare reforms (e.g., abolition of child labor, compulsory education until the age of eighteen, one day of rest in seven, social insurance, shortening the workday); and representation of women in the ILO's bodies. Lubin and Winslow (1990) have described how, thanks to these efforts, the part of the Paris treaty that provided for the establishment of the International Labour Organization was amended to include the following: (1) when any question regarding women's labor was to be considered, a member of each delegation would be a woman (Art. 3); and (2) the director of the International Labour Office should employ a certain number of women on his staff (Art. 9).

In these amendments two major principles were recognized. The first is that women, as a group, have needs and interests that can be best understood and served by their own kind. The second is that women constitute a category that is entitled to representation in positions of power. The importance of the amendments is not that it guarantees their implementation. Rather, they are significant in the sense that, when they are not respected, this can serve as a symbolic message and a cause for mobilizing and for taking action. In fact, the ILO enabled women's participation in decisions regarding women's employment. It was done, however, only in an indirect way. Through the years it became a standard procedure for the ILO bodies to consult with women's organizations in matters regarding women's employment and to request their advice and assistance on various issues. As noted in a report of the director to the ILO conference: "No steps would be taken in connection with women's protective legislation without previous consultation with the working women's organization concerned" (International Labour Conference 1928, 60–61). Thus, women were mobilized, their representatives were recognized, but they were granted no official power nor any office within the formal structure of decision making. Though the ILO solicited their views, it did not yield to any demand that was not consistent with its own course of action.

Some of the other demands that were presented to the labor commission, especially those that favored the expansion of protective legislation, stirred controversy among the different women's groups. Women's groups had expressed different views regarding gender-based labor laws in earlier periods as well, yet these differences in opinions gained a new meaning in the present context. With the opportunity to present their demands to the newly formed official organization, and the fact that doing so might have some real consequences, this controversy became more acute. The previously amorphous divergence of opinions crystallized into two opposing strategies, with each side trying to get the ear of the international labor organization.

Under the terms of the Treaty of Paris the first conference of the new labor organization was to be held in Washington, D.C. Since, as with the Paris conference, no provisions were made for women delegates, those within the women's movement decided to take action. The National Women's Trade Union League of America decided to call an international congress of working women to meet immediately preceding the labor conference. The preparation for this meeting had taken place already in Paris, during the peace conference, and it was there that initial contacts were made (Schneiderman and Goldthwaite 1967). The plan was to develop a unified women's approach to the new organization's first meeting. The longer-term aims were to monitor the ILO and to examine all of its legislative projects; to develop the congress's own international policy to be presented to the organization; and, finally, to promote the appointment of women to organizations affecting the welfare of women (Foner 1980; Lubin and Winslow 1990; Waggaman 1919).

Representatives of trade unions from nineteen countries attended the congress. Most of these women later participated also as delegates to the International Labour Conference. The agenda for the 1919 congress included mainly the items that concerned women and that were to be discussed later at the ILO conference. Eventually, they submitted two resolutions requesting changes in the proposals concerning hours of work and the employment of young persons. The resolutions were brought to the attention of the respective committees, but none were adopted (Lubin and Winslow 1990). Not discouraged by this first abortive attempt, members of the congress decided that a permanent organization was needed and formed the International Federation of Working Women, the first international organization of women's trade unions. For the next few years of its existence the organization held meetings in conjunction with the International Labour Conference, discussing items for the conference agenda as well as broader issues.[5]

One can see how the creation of the two new official organizations—the ILO and the League of Nations—energized the global arena and reshaped the international women's movement. In both the first conference of the ILO and the Paris conference there was a clear impetus for women to voice their demands. But the need to interact with the official organization required a more stable and coordinated structure in order for negotiations to carry on. Thus, as a result, more permanent bodies were created, furthering the coherence of the women's movement as well as opening new domains for disagreements.

Women's employment, more specifically women's employment at night and women's employment before and after childbirth, was on the agenda of the first session of the International Labour Conference. A committee of experts, already nominated in Paris to conduct a study and to draft two conventions on these issues, submitted its reports. The two proposed conventions—the Convention Concerning the Employment of Women before and after Childbirth and the Convention Concerning the Employment of Women during the Night—were adopted.

This first session set the path for the following years for the ILO to operate both substantively and procedurally. First, protective legislation enacted by

---

5. In 1925 the International Federation of Working Women ceased to exist as an independent organization and merged with the International Federation of Trade Unions.

drafting these two specific conventions, to be joined later by similar and more comprehensive measures, constituted the only aspect of women's employment on which the ILO would focus. This path, set already at the turn of the century, was expanded and extended with the creation of the new labor organization. For example, the prohibition that was specified by the Berne convention exempted small industrial firms (of ten employees and less). But the approach of the 1919 committee of experts was that since "night work for women is undesirable . . . this prohibition should be as far as possible universal" (International Labour Conference 1919, 102). As a result, the new convention applied to all employers, regardless of the number of their employees.

On the whole there was an agreement between all the participants about the need for such measures. Only the Norwegian representative opposed a special prohibition for women and, instead, advocated prohibition of night work for all workers. This agreement was reiterated in subsequent discussions as well, emphasizing the great worldwide consensus for these kinds of standards. For example, in 1935, when the Committee on the Employment of Women presented its report on the draft convention on employment of women in the mines, it was happy to announce that "it would not be an exaggeration to say that" total exclusion of women from underground work "is perhaps one of the few questions where there is no conflict of opinion" (International Labour Conference 1935, 374).

In the 1919 discussions not only agreement but also a sense of enthusiasm emerge from the text of the proceedings. The delegates expressed a feeling of being a part of an important historical process in which they had a special role. Progress was in the making, and they, as members of the new international organizations, had a mission to make it work. In the words of the president of the conference: "The Berne convention represents the first step in international labor legislation. It was a valuable step. It was a step which has carried us some way along the road of the better protection of our working womanhood. It is for this conference to go a step further to complete the work of those pioneers of 1906 and, in its much greater strength, in its far more representative character than any conference those days, to carry on the effort to come closer to the goal" (International Labour Conference 1919, 103).

This self-conception of "history in the making" was not evident in the documents of the 1904 Berne conference. The latter was characterized by a much more instrumental tone, which stands in sharp contrast to the spirit of "mission" and "responsibility" that the ILO members were expressing in 1919. Second, introducing experts to the realm of international work had been done already with the preparation of the Berne convention of 1906. This precedent had been extended and institutionalized so that using experts became a permanent feature of the work of the ILO. In years to come experts would play an increasingly important role in the ongoing work of international bodies. Third, the perception that children and women "go hand in hand" dominated the discourse in this first session, as it would for several decades to come. This image was not new and had already featured in the first labor reforms of the nineteenth century. This time, however, it was endorsed by an official world organization, incorporated into world documents, and underscored much of national and international employment legislation of that period.

Women and children historically have gone together in very many ways. In most protective legislative measures adopted in the various countries, children (and sometimes young persons too) and women were included in the same category. Whenever night work, underground work, and hazardous occupations were discussed, it was usually in reference to both women and children. The category "women and children" was the only category of workers to be singled out as requiring special measures. On some occasions the elderly were brought in as well: "The test of a great nation might be divided into three categories: how a nation treats its young; how a nation treats its aged; and, not of least importance, how a nation treats its women" (International Labour Conference 1935, 378). Including women in this list emphasized once again the peculiar symbolic and concrete location of the category of women, located on the margins of the "great nation." Only later would additional special groups appear to be added to those having distinct characters and needs.

Women and children were not only considered similarly as far as employment was concerned, but they were also seen as having similar needs in times of distress. For example, in reference to supervision of immigration it was recommended that "where 15 or more women or young persons are carried as emigrants on board of an emigrant vessel, a properly qualified woman . . . should be carried who could give such emigrants any material or moral assistance of which they may stand in need" (International Labour Office 1926, 67).

On the one hand, women and children had the same status in regard to employment, but, on the other hand, women's status was also determined by the very fact that the responsibility for children fell exclusively to them. All protective employment laws were based on this assumption. One such example was that the length of a woman's confinement before and after childbirth was determined by the need to care for her new child. Women themselves embraced this notion; whenever they put forward demands for social or labor reform, it always included the welfare of the child. Whenever employment of minors was discussed in the meetings of the ILO, women's organizations expressed interest and were consulted.

Whereas the maternal roles of women would continue to be enacted in international labor law, as will be evident in the continuous expansion of maternity provisions, "working women" will change their location and switch to a different category. With the emerging emphasis on equality of wages and opportunities, women will make the transition from being included in the same category with children to be compared to a category of adult male workers, and "discrimination" will replace "exploitation."

Thus, in the first session of the new organization the parameters of the discourse regarding women and employment were determined, and women's issues were defined. Maternity provisions and the prohibition of certain types of work and, at certain times, their expansion or relaxation would be the only women's issues to be discussed and to produce international agreements. Several women's organizations, doubting the benefits of protective legislation, pointed to its discriminatory effects. They put forward the demand for an international convention regarding equal pay for men and women and pushed to put the issue of the status of women on the ILO's agenda. Until the late 1930s the ILO did not endorse these issues, and it was not until after World War II that proposals for an international convention on the matter were discussed seriously and accepted.

## The International Labour Organization:
## "A Menace to Women All over the World"

At the annual International Labour Conference of 1930 delegates decided to revise the 1919 convention on women's employment during the night on two specific points: to exclude from its application women employed in a supervisory capacity and to allow latitude in fixing the beginning and the end of the night period in which women's employment was prohibited. This attempt somehow to narrow the application of protective measures brought to the surface again the old controversy within the women's movement. The women trade unionists categorically opposed any revision that resulted in limiting the application of the protective measures. In their view doing so was a dangerous precedent (International Labour Office 1931). Similarly, the International Council of Women demanded an expansion of protective measures, pointing out that women's organizations opposing protection generally had few working women members (International Council of Women 1966, 59).

On the other hand, the opposition to all-inclusive protective measures intensified as well. A British group of radical opponents to protective legislation formed, in 1927, the Open Door Council. But acting nationally was not enough. In light of action taken by the ILO, they decided to join forces with similar groups abroad, and in 1929, in Berlin, they created the Open Door International for the Economic Emancipation of the Woman Worker. "The struggle has become international," declared their manifesto (qtd. in Becker 1983). As suffrage had been the most important issue in the past, so, though it might be even harder, economic equality should be the most pressing issue that women should fight for now. The first obstacle for obtaining full economic equality was the ILO itself. "War" was declared on this "enemy of women": "The time has come to promote the formation of [an] international body . . . as it became daily clearer that the problems created by the work and influence of the International Labour Organization was a menace to women all over the world, and that nothing but an international organization would be in a position to combat its attack on women workers . . . the International Labour Organization . . . becomes an international danger when it proposes special restrictions on the work of women. It may be likened to a factory where proposals for limiting the freedom of woman as a worker are turned out by mass production methods" (Open Door International 1929, 6).

Protective measures based on the "sex of the worker" were equated with "tyranny" that "denies her [the woman] status as an adult human being" (Open Door International 1929, 7). The group advocated "true protection" for all workers based on "the nature of the work and demanded an international convention on equal pay for "work of equal value." Their argument was simple: the right to work is a basic human right. Protective measures constitute a violation of human rights since they restrict women's complete access to employment of her choosing.

Though the main propaganda effort was directed at the ILO, its members invested energy also in traveling to different countries (including Egypt, Iraq, Russia, Syria, and Turkey) to spread the message among working women and to try to fight the limitations posed for married women in terms of employment due to rising rates of unemployment (Open Door International 1931). Restrictions on married women's employment, they argued, "taken to provide work for men, do not reduce unemployment but merely shift its incidence from male to female workers" (League of Nations 1936, 44). The group viewed employed women as workers in the same sense as men. Unemployed women raise figures of unemployment in the same way that men do. Employed women support themselves and their families, and lower unemployment figures also in the same way that men do. Clearly, their views differed largely from the dominant approach of the time.

Their opposition to discrimination of employed married women earned them a favorable reputation, but their position against all protective measures did not. Open Door International represented an extreme case in this controversy. Although there were other organizations that maintained that protective legislation might, in some cases, restrict the opportunities of working women, none was willing to give up *all* special provisions as Open Door did. Open Door drew the only logical conclusion it saw fit: elimination of all gender-specific measures, including maternity provisions. What triggered the group's objection was the compulsory leave that became part of these provisions. "That a woman has borne a child, or is about to bear a child, is no reason for depriving her of any inherent human right. Such a right is the right to decide for herself whether or not she will engage in paid work. Deprived of this right, the woman inevitably suffers loss of her status . . . Such a loss of status has repercussions not only on the childbearing woman, but on all women wage earners" (Open Door International 1937, 12).

Open Door even opposed the proposed equal rights treaty on the ground that it was not radical enough and that it was too vague to bring about the repeal of existing discriminatory laws (Miller 1994). According to its own reports, the group's ideas were "ridiculed" and "met with spirit of hysteria." Descriptions of how their principles and proposals were being studied carefully by their opponents so that good counterarguments could be provided were brought up as evidence of the group's potential impact. It is hard to assess how much support it got. According to its reports, in 1936 Open Door had national branches and affiliated societies in thirteen countries, and about five women's international groups kept official contacts with it (League of Nations 1936).[6] Still, it is clear that Open Door was located far along the margins, signaling the boundaries of the legitimate debate of the period.

## Married Women and the Male Breadwinner during the Depression

The worldwide economic crisis and the unemployment that followed it brought to the forefront the question of married women's participation within

6. Observers were appointed by the following international organizations: International Woman Suffrage Alliance (IWSA), International Council of Women (ICW), the International Federation of University Women (IFUW), the Women's International League of Peace and Freedom (WILPF), and the Medical Women's International Association (MWIA).

the labor force. My argument in this book has been that woman's incorporation into the public sphere was done through the renegotiation of her assigned role in the private sphere. Her access to the public sphere was affected, to a large degree, by her status in the domestic sphere. The 1930s public debate and states' action regarding married women's employment dramatized once again the peculiar status of women in the public sphere as compared to men's—the standard worker.

As long as there was a labor shortage, the question of women's role in paid employment, whether they were married or unmarried, was suppressed, though never completely. But when the time of severe unemployment came about, the issue surfaced forcefully and moved to the forefront. All over Europe the employment of married women was "under attack." The ILO *Year-Book* for the years 1930–37 documented two opposing trends regarding the "place of woman's worker in the economic system." In Russia and in countries that were not hit by the Depression there was an increase in women's participation in the economy. But this trend was shadowed by an opposite one. Wherever there was a fall in the demand for labor, a "campaign against double earning" was launched. The gender-neutral term *attack on double earning* masked actual measures that were very much gender specific.

During the 1930s more and more countries adopted measures aimed at restricting or forbidding altogether the employment of married women (Sweden being the only exception). The Netherlands refused unemployment benefits to married women, and Great Britain made the conditions for such benefits harder for married women. In Germany and Austria married women were dismissed from the civil service (Open Door International 1933).

The offensive that was initially aimed at married women soon turned into a more inclusive one when applied to all women. In Italy various public departments defined a quota of women to be employed at the various levels—the higher the level, the smaller the quota.[7] In Belgium the Council of Ministers decided that all posts in public administrative departments must in the future be reserved for men as long as a sufficient number of qualified male candidates were available. In the Netherlands local authorities were instructed to replace women by men in posts not specifically requiring female labor. Similar measures were adopted also in Australia, Czechoslovakia, France, and New Zealand (International Labour Office 1934–35).

There were no restrictions on employment of single men to protect the jobs

---

7. The prohibition to recruit women did not, however, cover staff employment in cleaning offices. These jobs were kept for women only.

of women who were the sole providers for their dependents. Nowhere was there a distinction between married and unmarried men in respect to the protection of jobs. Even at times like that, or maybe more so at times like that, all men were considered to assume the role of the provider and all woman to be the dependents. The notion that women took men's jobs demonstrates clearly that the labor market has been conceived as men's terrain; at times women are allowed in, and at other times they are excluded.

This trend was consistent with the growth of the "back to the home" movement for working mothers, promoted especially by Catholic organizations (Pedersen 1993). They advocated "indirect measures that would make it unnecessary for the mother to go out to earn (such as higher family wages paid to men, family allowances) and would act as an inducement to her to devote herself to the home of her own free will," rather than legislative prohibition (International Labour Office 1933, 151). Countries like France instituted the "Medal for the French family" for a certain number of legitimate children (Anderson and Zinsser 1988, 209). International conferences were held to discuss and propose ideas about how to keep mothers at home. One such example was the 1933 International Congress on Industrial Work of the Mother and the Worker's Home. The point was that market necessity drives women to seek employment outside; the state should step in and, in the name of the family and the next generation, should take all steps necessary to counteract market forces and to bring women back home. "Until the family wage become general, the Congress hope that use will be made of forms of work which are less destructive of family life than paid work for mothers outside the home, such as . . . handicrafts, domestic industry . . . national legislation and international conventions should make for the unity, stability and safety of the home . . . The committee also recommended that committees for the mother in the home should be set up in all countries" (League of Nations 1933, 141–42).

An unexpected development arose, however, from the increasing competition in the labor market. It turned out that at times like that the principle of equal wages could serve men too. "The economic depression is making it all the more urgent to counteract the insufficient remuneration of women, both in their own interests and in that of men, whose wage level may be unfavorably affected by the competition of low-paid women workers" (International Labour Office 1931, 248).

Once the negative effects on man's wages and employment were "discovered," measures to correct women's "insufficient remuneration" were proposed. Note that the term *unemployment* actually meant *men's unemployment*. Equal pay and minimum wages for women started to be discussed as two alternative solutions to the problem of protecting male workers from the existence of a low-paid class of workers. Raising women's wages cannot lower their rates of unemployment. It can only make them a less attractive workforce under conditions of high labor supply. Legislating universal minimum wages were postponed until "the time will be ripe." Though the principle seemed logical, very few countries passed equal pay measures at that period. The only ones to do so were some of the Latin American countries. Others legislated minimum wages for women. In some cases, such as in the five Australian states, a court decision from 1933 fixed the basic wage for women at 52 percent of that of men (Open Door International 1935). But the overwhelming majority of countries preferred either administrative or legal measures that restricted the employment of married women altogether.

Alarmed by this situation, women's organizations tried to raise the world's consciousness. Many of them held discussions and adopted resolutions on the matter, "proclaiming the right to work to be a fundamental and inalienable human right, also for women, married or unmarried" (International Labour Office 1933). Considering the general atmosphere, the fact that the International Congress of Trade Union Women managed to get its "parent" organization, the International Federation of Trade Unions, to adopt also a similar stand is notable.

Efforts were made to mobilize the ILO on both sides. Two opposite petitions were submitted in 1935 to the International Labour Conference. One petition was submitted by the Christian Associations of Young Workers which recommended limiting women's work as a solution for unemployment among young persons (i.e., young men). Women's organizations, in turn, petitioned the conference "to respect the right to work of married and unmarried women" (International Labour Office 1935–36, 189). There was no report of an official response to these petitions.

Indeed, the ILO did not endorse the policy of replacing women by men workers. All its unemployment measures applied to men and women equally. But, at the same time, there is no evidence that it took a firm position against it, nor did it condemn countries that did adopt such measures. Thus, in the standard reports published in the ILO *Year-Book* all through the 1930s there was no expression of condemnation of any sort nor any reference to the "right to work," which is supposed to be fundamental to the ILO's work. Still, after the war, in a report published in 1944, the ILO prided itself for not following the trend, even "when in many countries thinking was confused by the panic caused by the economic depression" (International Labour Conference 1944, 95).

It was only with the improvement of the economic situation that the objection to married women's employment weakened. States began to remove some of the restrictions and even to adopt measures that intended to support the extension of women's employment (International Labour Office 1936–37). And in the second half of the 1930s the ILO got involved with women's status and employment rights, though to a very limited degree.

### The ILO and the Status of Women

As with the league, the ILO's involvement with the question of the status of women was very much the result of the activity of women's movements. Its first action was conducting research according to the league's request. In 1935 the issue was put on the league's agenda, with a special reference to the 1933 Equal Rights Treaty signed at Montevideo. This discussion triggered women's organizations to request that the league conduct a comprehensive study. The league responded positively. It asked the ILO "in accordance with its normal procedure to undertake an examination of those aspects of the problem within its competence—the question of equality under labor legislation—and that it would in the first place examine the question of legislation which affects discrimination." Thus, for the first time equality and discrimination, and not protection, were the topics to be studied. Consequently, the ILO decided to "develop to the greatest possible extent its studies of the question of the actual economic position of women workers as shown by the facts" (International Labour Office 1935–36, 189).

A plan of study was drawn up, and women's organizations were mobilized to help with collecting data. For example, at the request of the International Conference of Women Trade Unionists, the International Federation of Trade Unions called upon its national sections to send any relevant information that they might have. As a result, "data are now reaching the office from all over the world" (International Labour Office 1936–37, 209). In addition, with a small staff of research assistants, several special studies on women's issues, including a survey of the protective legislation for women throughout the world, had been published. This study had been stimulated by suggestions from a number of women's organizations. Later the study was updated, expanded, published under the title *The Law and Women's Work*, and given wide circulation (Lubin and Winslow 1990).

In 1936, for the first time, the principle of equality between men and women in employment was pronounced by an international governmental organization—the Latin American section of the ILO. The Conference of American States members of the ILO, at their meeting at Santiago de Chile, submitted the following resolutions to the Governing Body of the International Labour Office: "Equal pay should be paid to men and women for the same work. Wages should be fixed according to the nature of the work irrespective of the sex of the worker . . . The maximum working day of women should be the same as that of men" (International Labour Office 1936, 45–46). And to implement the resolutions they appointed a Committee on the Work of Women and Juveniles. Note that, even when in the context of equalizing the conditions of women's work with that of men's, the machinery that was established to deal with these issues was for women *and* children. The conference also recommended that, in order to bring about "socially desirable development of women's work," special divisions and women's bureaus should be set up within the Department of Labor. Indeed, the Latin American countries were the first to form state agencies designated to supervise women's issues as they relate to employment. Later, the United Nations will adopt this strategy and expand it to a large degree, recommending establishing national machinery "for promoting the status of women" in all areas of life.

One year later, in 1937, the International Labour Conference, for the first time, adopted a resolution affirming the importance of women's economic rights and especially the right to work and to equal pay: "It is for the best interests of society that in addition to full political and civil rights and full opportunity for education, women should have full opportunity to work and should receive remuneration without discrimination because of sex, and be protected by legislative safeguards against economic exploitation, including the safeguards of motherhood" (146).

The American delegates, when presenting the resolution, emphasized the larger benefit that equality would bring to society as a whole and downplayed any moral or justice justification. They made a link between women's full civil, political, and economic rights and progress, the former being a precondition for the latter. This argument will be elaborated much further in subsequent decades, especially in the 1970s, with the emergence of the development discourse. Another argument, reiterating past arguments, was that women's low wages were detrimental to men's as well: "discrimination in the wage-scale is a two-edged sword . . . wage differentials between men and women prove in the long run to be unfair to both" (International Labour Conference 1937, 463).

Two years later, just before the war broke out, the ILO took another step in that direction when announcing, for the first time, that its role was not only to protect "our working womanhood," as was declared in all its years of existence, but also to raise its position "throughout the world." It does not say that women's position, in general, should be equal to that of men's in all aspects, but it does acknowledge again that women should be paid equal to men, when performing the same work. All that, without yet doubting the benefit of protective legislation. All that was to change in the post–world war era.

# CHAPTER FOUR

# Human Rights and Working Women
## The Global Campaign and State Action

Women's issues and women's presence in the public sphere were acknowledged and discussed in the small-scale world institutions of the prewar period. Yet it was always their familial roles, maternal functions, and distinctive character that shaped what was then defined as "women's issues," from the special protection they needed as workers to special measures they needed to save them from falling into "white slavery." In such cases states were called upon to take action to protect women from the harshness of the public sphere. Women were placed in the same category as children, a distinct social category, more exploitable and more fragile than adult men. In the spirit of benevolent social reforms, these women required special attention and action. In the two campaigns for women's involvement in the political sphere—the campaign for suffrage and for world peace, both led by women activists—it was women's distinctive character, nurtured in the domestic sphere, that was highlighted. Women should have a say in politics, both domestic and international, it was argued, because their potential contribution was unique from that of men.

With the end of World War II the discourse that shaped "women" and women's issues changed dramatically. To put it briefly, the "natural" attachment drawn between women and the family diminished, and women's distinctive character was modified. The old ground for women's rights was dismissed. In the new ideology of "rights" and "equality" that invaded most major world institutions of the postwar era, women were transformed from a distinct category that required protection to a category of individuals that needed to be incorporated into all domains of public sphere. The eighteenth-century language of "natural rights" that once served men in gaining equality was revived under the notion of "human rights" to enable additional groups, women among them, to gain equal protection and equal rights from their respective governments.

In addition, world polity become more authoritative and "intrusive," as far as nation-states were concerned. The hesitant efforts to set international standards and the caution of the previously existing transnational bodies were replaced by instructions delivered to nation-states concerning the specific steps they ought to take for the sake of their women members—for example, modifying existing laws, creating new organizational structures, undertaking research activities, and reprioritizing national development plans. These changes in world polity—putting women's rights on the agenda and assigning nation-states the task to make their respective women's citizens into full members—ought to be considered in the wider context of the following three processes that have taken place in the post–World War II era: the changing nature of world polity; the expansion of the state system; and the emergence of human rights on the international agenda.

After World War II the world polity expanded dramatically. New governmental organizations were established—chief among them the United Nations and its associated agencies—each with a comprehensive mandate and a universal membership. A variety of organizations with a more limited membership also sprung up. Some of them were confined to particular geographical areas, while sharing a political and ideological orientation (e.g., the Organization of African Unity or the North Atlantic Treaty Organization [NATO]), while others focus on technological and economic cooperation (e.g., the Organization for Economic Cooperation and Development [OECD] or the International Telecommunication Union [ITU]). In addition, nongovernmental organizations, in every conceivable field, mushroomed after the war at an unprecedented rate (Boli and Thomas 1997).

Cooperation between the nonofficial and official organizations was enhanced too. In the early 1990s there were 640 nongovernmental organizations that have formed official relations—that is, they have been granted "consultative" status—with the United Nations (Archer 1992). It is also the case that the United Nations has been involved, directly and indirectly, with the founding of various nongovernmental organizations. Mechanisms of coordination among organizations within similar functional areas have been created. These activities have resulted in a more coherent and rationalized world polity, with the authority to regulate many more domains and the organizational infrastructure to carry it out.

The expansion of world polity did not result in the diminished authority of the nation-state. State authority and global authority should not be seen in zero-sum terms but, rather, in a mutually constitutive way. The expansion of the world polity led to the extension of state authority into new domains as well as to the extension of the state system. "The authority of the state and the extension of the state system derive from a wider world polity, which both provides a necessary legitimacy and defines appropriate and necessary areas of jurisdiction and form for the state" (Thomas et al. 1987). The model of independent nation-state which was adopted worldwide is the liberal one in which all members have equal (formally defined) citizenship status. Hence, members are incorporated as individuals—not via membership in a clan, trade, or race—into the political body, that of the nation-state.

In addition, the process of decolonization which gained momentum after the war and "exploded" in the 1960s resulted in the triumph of the nation-state as the only model for political units to organize (Meyer 1987). The extent of the phenomenon is striking: 130 colonial dependencies of Western states became recognized independent states or were fully integrated as parts of sovereign states during the twentieth century, the overwhelming majority of them after World War II (Strang 1990). McNeely's study (1995) illustrates the impact of global authority as embodied in the United Nations on the principles of statehood and sovereignty as manifested in the process of formation of new nation-states.

Another significant transformation that took place after World War II was the emergence of human rights as a concern for the international community. Previously, international bodies had been engaged in political, economic, and technological cooperation. The international movements that promoted social reforms were motivated by humanitarian concerns and usually dealt with fighting "social evils" of various kinds. Notable examples are the movement for abolishing slavery and the crusade against trafficking in women and children. No movement and no official body promoted setting international standards that defined for nation-states the rights of its members. The sovereignty of states precluded the international community from being in any way responsible for the rights of individuals or from taking on any role with regard to a state's treatment of its own citizens (Armstrong 1982; Donnelly 1986).

The horrors of World War II and the atrocities committed by the Nazis and their allies were the trigger that brought the issue of human rights to the agenda. The scope of the new international bodies that were created after the war included the relations between nation-states and their respective citizens in their domain. The new ideological construct of human rights signified the new relationships between world polity, nation-states, and the individual. The concept implied that each individual is vested with a set of "rights" that are independent of their citizenship status. Global polity was to establish what these rights are and to supervise nation-states in respecting them.

This idea was embodied in various human rights documents that were formulated and adopted by the United Nations and other official organizations as well as in several bodies that were commissioned to monitor the implementation of the documents (Armstrong 1982; Donnelly 1986; Gibson 1991; Szego-Bokor 1978). The most important documents were the UN Charter and the 1948 Universal Declaration of Human Rights. The central UN-designated body since 1945 is the Human Rights Commission. It has received tens of thousands of individual petitions, asking the United Nations to protect individual rights (Haas 1964).[1] By 1982 the number of human rights documents (conventions and declaration) adopted by the United Nations was above sixty (United Nations 1982). The significance of major world events such as the 1968 Teheran International Human Rights Conference and documents such as the UN Charter and the Universal Declaration of Human Rights cannot be exaggerated as far as their effects on legitimizing the issue. As one observer noted: "[The] organizational ideology of the U.N. . . . largely determines the legitimate concerns for the international community and gives guidance to the selection of organizational activities" (Mogami 1990, 180). Concern over maltreatment of persons in all parts of the world mobilized thousands of individuals. A multiplicity of nongovernmental organizations, some of them old but most of them new, played an active role in this emerging field of global human rights (Thoolen and Verstappen 1986).

These three processes—the transformation of world polity, the expansion of the state system, and the emergence of human rights as a global issue—gave rise to a world in which supranational institutions were expected to set standardized guidelines to be followed and implemented by all nation-states as far as the well-being and the rights of their respective citizens were concerned. What used to fall under the sole jurisdiction of nation-states—the rights of their inhabitants—now became a concern for the international community. This context enabled women's rights to be placed on the world agenda. Now the required international organizations came into existence, the appropriate ideology was in place, and the political units were invested with the authority and equipped

---

1. Regional bodies are active in the field as well: The Inter-American system is based upon the 1948 American Declaration on the Rights and Duties of Man. This was followed by the formation of an Inter-American Commission on Human Rights in 1959. In 1968 an American Convention on Human Rights was set up. The Council of Europe drew up a European Convention of Human Rights that came into effect in 1953. In addition the European Commission for Human Rights and the European Human Rights Court were established (Armstrong 1982).

with the machinery to carry out the ideological priorities that had been formulated on the global level.

These new ideological and organizational transformations in world polity were the parameters that shaped the ways in which women's issues, now defined as women's rights, were acted upon in the early decades after World War II. The establishment of the Commission on the Status of Women embodied this spirit and, through its activities, helped institutionalize it further. The commission was in constant dialogue with the ILO and watched closely its policy regarding women. Looking at the changes that took place in the ILO's women's employment policy can serve as a lens to examine the processes of change that were taking place in international politics.

International employment policy has been a prominent issue with a long enough history so that its examination can provide insights into the changes in the relations between global authority, the state, and women as well as into the changing conception of the role of women in the public sphere. Employment policy regarding women was one of the first women's issues to become an international concern. Likewise, the first negotiations among heads of states at the turn of the century to pass international labor laws concerned protective measures for women. After World War I the ILO took upon itself the mission to "protect the working woman" and adopted a series of international standards to implement this task. In addition, economic rights for women were always on the agenda of women's organizations, more so with the decline of suffrage as a mobilizing issue. (Suffrage was extended to women in many countries in the postwar period.)

Three changes took place and transformed global employment policy (women's): the principle of equality in employment emerged on the agenda and was incorporated into two international conventions. Protective legislation declined. Maternity protection expanded within a framework of a new context and was accompanied by the new idea of providing parental leave time. All three reflected and enacted the new world model of women as articulated and promoted as *the* model for nation-states to follow. Women's incorporation into employment was to be compared and equalized with that of men (equal pay) and not be affected by their familial functions, which now have been degendered (parental leave).

Indeed, this model was followed by nation-states worldwide. In the postwar period most nation-states embodied the principle of equality-in-employment in their national legislation and revised both protective legislation and maternity provisions. Global models shaped, to a large degree, states' modes of incorporation into paid employment, as manifested in their respective employment laws. This stands in contrast to previous periods. Around the turn of the century and before World War I, state officials, supported by social reformers, made the first steps in creating international labor laws. Then there were no authoritative world bodies and no supranational organizations to set models for nation-states to follow. The treaty that was agreed upon and signed, the 1906 Prohibition of Night Work for Women, did not contain any element that was new to nation-states. In the post–World War II era, with the growing authority and coherence of world polity, things changed. World polity became a source of innovation for most countries in the world; nation-states followed the models promoted by world organizations and incorporated the appropriate policies into their national legislation systems. This phenomenon is evident when tracing the history of the three global trends (emergence of equal pay laws, decline of protective laws, and expansion of maternity provisions) and examining their effects on nation-states' policies. The United Nations Commission on the Status of Women (CSW) played an important part in changing conceptions of the role of world polity and in the model of women it promoted.

## New Arena for Women: The Commission on the Status of Women

The controversy that arose within the United Nations in 1944 around the proper framework and status of the Commission on the Status of Women reflected a long and continuing debate: should women's rights be dealt with by a designated body or by the Commission on Human Rights? Initially, it was agreed that it would be the latter. Yet, after a delegation of women's groups presented its position to the Economic and Social Council that it was appropriate to have a separate body, the council decided to establish a subcommission within the framework of the Commission on Human Rights. This step reflected a compromise between those who preferred full incorporation into the existing human rights body and those who insisted on a separate body. One year later, upon a request from the new subcommission, the Economic and Social Council raised its status into a full-fledged commission (Stienstra 1994). This was done despite various objections even from those who did favor the women's cause. For example, Eleanor Roosevelt, the chairwoman of the Commission on Human Rights, put it very clearly: "women should come in on equal basis—not even as specialized groups unless they are representing some particular objective (qtd. in Pfeffer 1985, 468).

Though the commission's mandate was much wider than any other women's committees that acted within the framework of the League of Nations, still it was much narrower than envisioned. The original ambitious plan of the nuclear subcommission for the future body was drastically modified and narrowed down by the Economic and Social Council. The commission's role has been defined as one of general policy development, data gathering, evaluation, inspiration, and education (Reanda 1992). Thus, without downplaying the significance of the fact that women's issues were considered worthy of designating a specific body within the United Nations system, one should also note that this body had to operate with limited jurisdiction, lack of sufficient resources, and tight scrutiny by the Economic and Social Council (Coliver 1989; Galey 1979).

Since its inception until the early 1970s the principle of equality (between women and men) and human rights shaped much of the commission's activities. Note that this principle, though old, was quite novel for any official world body. Motivated by the idea that women should enjoy equality with men in all spheres of life, it concerned itself with mapping domains and areas of social life in which women, when compared to men, were discriminated against. Reviewing the items on the commission's agenda (from the various United Nations *Yearbooks*) reveals that, even though the major emphasis was on political, educational, and economic rights, a wide range of topics was added during the years (e.g., status of women in public law, in private law, penal law, tax legislation, nationality and property rights of married women). By emphasizing women's equality with men, more and more areas of social and economic life were targeted as possible sources of discrimination to be eliminated by introducing "sameness." Note, for example, the expansive nature of possible discrimination in the area of education and the proliferation of means for its remedy which were discovered throughout the years: if all children were to have an equal chance of really benefiting from educational opportunities, then boys and girls should have the same curricula and programs, the same facilities, the same financial assistance, the same choice of courses, the same examinations, and the same teaching staff with the same qualifications. More areas and types of education were targeted: basic education, higher education, adult education, continuing education, extracurricular education, and remote education (Berkovitch and Bradley 1994). This process expanded even further during the 1970s, with the intensification of global activities on women's issues within the framework of the United Nations Decade for Women.

One way of mobilizing nation-states to take action against the various types of discrimination that women suffer in their respective countries was by "standard setting," that is, drafting and adopting international conventions, encouraging nation-states to ratify them, and establishing a reporting system to monitor their implementation. Even though at its inception the commission was not vested with such a mandate, early on it started initiating various conventions that dealt exclusively with discrimination against women (Reanda 1992).[2] In addition, the commission issued declarations—though they were without binding power, still they held moral force—the most important of which was the 1967 Declaration on the Elimination of Discrimination against Women.

This declaration set the basis for the most important and most inclusive convention, the 1979 Convention on the Elimination of All Forms of Discrimination against Women (CEDAW). It incorporated most of the provisions in previous women's rights conventions and added new issues, mainly those that refer to the "integration of women in development," the new theme of the 1970s. It took seven long years since the first mention of such a comprehensive convention until it materialized (Jacobson 1992). But, once drafted, it was quickly endorsed worldwide. Despite its broad reach over individual nation-states, including a relatively highly specified reporting and review system, its ratification rate was impressive. By 1990 it was ratified by one hundred countries (see graph 2). Its visibility and contribution to the global effort of putting the issue of women's rights on the agenda of nation-states worldwide cannot be overemphasized, as was noted by Jacobson (in an otherwise quite critical article): "Many countries that had focused little if any attention on women's rights in the past do so today in large part because of the treaty" (1992, 444).

The creation of the United Nations and the commission also affected the ways in which women's international movements operated. As with the league, the new bodies provided an arena in which to act, to lobby, and to mobilize for various campaigns. But, since the mandate of the new bodies was much wider, the attention they received from women's organizations was greater, and the level of formal and informal cooperation between them and women's groups increased. Many of the mainstream women's organizations devoted most of their time and energy working cooperatively with the United Nations–affiliated bodies in general and with the commission in particular. In contrast to the league, the United Nations provided a structured format for cooperation with nongovernmental organizations. It conferred consultative status to certain organizations "to secure expert information or advice and, on the other hand to enable organizations which represented important elements of public opinion

---

2. These conventions are: Convention on the Political Rights of Women (1952); Convention on the Nationality of Married Women (1957); Convention on the Consent to Marriage, Minimum Age for Marriage and Registration of Marriages (1962); Covenant on Economic, Social and Cultural Rights (1966); International Covenant on Civil and Political Rights (1966). On the debates that accompanied the ratification of each, see Reanda 1992. For an analysis of each convention, see Hevener 1983.

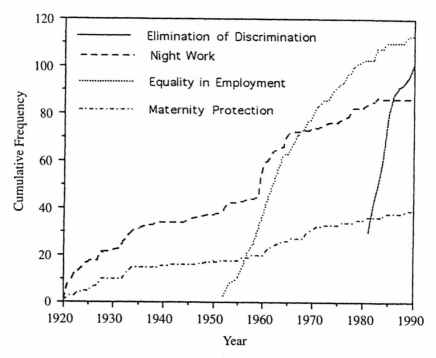

Graph 2. Ratification of conventions: Equality in employment, maternity protection, elimination of discrimination, and night work, 1920–1990.

to express their views" (United Nations 1947–48, 551). Already in the first decade, twenty women's organizations were granted this status (constituting 18 percent of all such organizations). In 1985 six organizations (constituting 17 percent of all organizations in this category) were granted the more privileged status (category A) which permits more direct access to the council.[3]

As was shown in chapter 3, all through the interwar period extensive efforts were made by various women's groups to get the ILO to acknowledge their demands publicly and to take action for the sake of women's rights. The ILO

3. Organizations in category A can send observers to all public meetings of the council and circulate written communications to members of the council; they can consult any standing committee, and they can present their views to the council (United Nations 1946–47). The figures are calculated from United Nations *Yearbook,* various years. The six women's organizations that were granted category A status were: International Alliance of Women, International Council of Women, International Federation of Business and Professional Women, Soroptomist International, Women's International Democratic Federation, and Zonta International–International Service Organization of Executive and Professional Women.

responded very hesitantly and very late. In the postwar period a major shift took place. The ILO, changing its whole approach, endorsed and started actively promoting the principle of equal economic rights for women.

## The ILO Introduces the Principle of Equality

While still in Montreal (the ILO's temporary residence during the war) and before the war ended, the ILO had already drafted the main document that outlined its employment policy and its plans for restructuring the economy during the transition period from war to peace. This was a long document that dealt with a variety of issues, one of which was women's employment. The declaration was clear: "the redistribution of women workers in the economy should be organized on the principle of complete equality of opportunity for men and women on the basis of their individual merit, skill, and experience" (International Labour Conference 1944, 96).

It is interesting to note that this principle was presented to the conference as part of a long and consistent tradition of equality promoted by the ILO. In the present study, however, I portray a different picture, that of a long and consistent tradition of protective measures for working women as mothers and not of a "principle of complete equality." It is true that the original ILO constitution (adopted in 1919) included the principle of equal pay, yet this was of no assistance when women's organizations, during the 1930s and 1940s, lobbied the organization to enact it. The recommendation for equal pay only got its start in the postwar period; still, it was presented by the ILO as being consistent with the past.

Similar reconstructions of the past, to be consistent with the present "spirit of the time," were made when the ILO presented its first resolution to deal with women's work after the war. Among other issues this resolution was about "the right of individuals to work" not only "without regards to sex" but also without regard to "marital status." It was important for the conference to adopt such a resolution because, according to the American representative, "it seems desirable that the ILO, as the oldest of the international organizations in active operation today, and the one whose responsibility it is to speak on the question of labor . . . should state in a somber and clear form its existing recommendations on the status of working women, as a guide to the related work of the newer international agencies " (International Labour Conference 1947, 236).

Whereas before the ILO was the only official international organization set up to deal with economic and social issues, now others inhabited the same niche. Amid this state of affairs the ILO's officials felt that it should take the lead and show the "right way " to the newcomers to the international scene, and for now this meant promoting the status of women.

The justification for this policy, however, was not so new. One reason for the "establishment of wage rates based on job content, without regard to sex" echoed those brought up during the economic crisis of the 1930s. The fear was that such competition with women's wages might result in lower wages for male workers. In another speech the resolution was presented as one of "homage and at the same time an expression of our gratitude to millions of women" for their war effort, and, therefore, "in simple justice there should be a recognition of that service." In both cases women's rights to equality were recognized either for the sake of protecting men's wages or as gratitude for the help they offered by working in men's jobs during the war.

In the years to come major international documents that were adopted and organizational activities that took place within the context of the ILO and the United Nations incorporated and enacted the principle of economic rights for women and the demand to take action to ensure their equal pay. Already in 1946 a Committee of Experts met to propose measures that would "ensure to them [women] equitable conditions" and recommended "fixing of remuneration according to the job content, regardless of sex" (International Labour Office 1946, 424). The Universal Declaration of Human Rights adopted by the UN General Assembly in 1948 formally stipulated that "everyone, without any discrimination, has the right to equal pay for equal work" (Art. 23[2]). Similarly, the preamble to the revised constitution of the ILO, from 1948, proclaimed that "improvement (of conditions of labor) . . . is urgently recognized," and it will be achieved by "recognition of the principles of equal remuneration for work of equal value."

Other international organizations joined the campaign as well. In the prewar era women's organizations had been alone in the movement to promote their economic rights. Now major labor organizations joined in, and the newly created world organization, the United Nations, and its affiliated bodies were mobilized as well. The first step was initiated by the World Federation of Trade Unions. It proposed adding to the agenda of the UN Economic and Social Council an item on the "question of the principle of equal pay for equal work for men and women workers." The Commission on the Status of Women, early in 1948, adopted a series of resolutions regarding women's rights and notified the Economic and Social Council that certain issues required "urgent action." The demand for equal pay was one of them.

As a result, the council adopted a resolution that called for abolishing all types of discrimination in employment, invoking arguments of human rights and defining *discrimination* as a violation of the "dignity of woman": "recognizing that restrictions with regard to the equality of rights of men and women constitute an infringement of fundamental rights of the human person and are incompatible with the obligations assumed by the States members" (United Nations 1947–48, 604).

Economic rights and the right to equal pay have thus been framed within a larger context of fundamental rights, and not only as a way to protect men's wages. Nation-states were instructed to take all necessary measures so that all women "shall benefit by the same rights as men in regard to employment and remuneration." The council requested the ILO to proceed as rapidly as possible on that matter and to report to the council on any action taken. In the discussion of the resolution most members agreed on the principle of equal pay for equal work. The only objections were based on technical arguments, focusing on the difficulties involved in implementing the principle. This kind of response would be typical of future discussions around this issue. No world forum of the postwar era would reject the principle of equality or object to the notion of women's rights.

Differences in opinion did not follow the expected lines. First, the main division was between the employers' representatives, on the one hand, and the representatives of workers and governments, on the other. The employers' representatives consistently pointed to different kinds of negative consequences. Whereas the representatives from core countries were the ones who hesitated about its feasibility, the representatives from less-developed countries supported it much more enthusiastically. This points to the fact that, contrary to conventional wisdom, the principle of equal pay was not imposed by the more developed countries on the rest of the world. No group openly challenged the actual principle of rights in general and of right to equal pay in particular. In 1950 it was proposed that an international convention on the matter be adopted.

As preparation for drafting the convention, a Committee on Equal Remuneration was appointed. Its reports, presented to the conference, included information on the current measures being taken by the various countries, their positions on the issue, and a draft proposal for a convention. The introduction to these reports, in which the problem was presented and outlined, suggests the context in which the issue was framed and discussed. The problem of universal rights was seen through the lens of labor market theories. Contemporary ideas about economic dynamics and market processes valued efficiency and flexibility over notions of "women's proper place" and "family wages" (International Labour Conference 1950). As the 1950 report indicated, since paying lower wages to women threatened men's jobs, men workers fostered a distinction between men's jobs and women's jobs. The latter led to "freezing of the employment market to a substantial extent, restricting the free choice of the individual worker and hampering a rational utilization of the available labor supply. With the prevailing recognition that maximum production would be maintained or achieved by the most efficient utilization of the labor resources of the country, it becomes apparent that equal treatment of men and women workers as regards remuneration would facilitate the distribution of the labor supply according to the capacities and abilities of workers and would promote labor mobility in the interests of production" (International Labour Conference 1950, 2).

Scientific evidence (e.g., cross-national data) was brought in to support the claim that the share of women in the labor market was increasing substantially, making the problem of their equal employment acute and urgent. Equal wages were the right measure to be taken, since they promoted labor mobility and contributed to market efficiency.

After reviewing all references made and resolutions adopted on the need for measures to ensure equal pay and summarizing the attitudes of governments and representatives of employers and workers in the various countries, the report concluded that, "on the whole, the principle of equal remuneration for men and women workers for work of equal value is no longer challenged openly" (International Labour Conference 1950, 17) and that, in general, there was an agreement that "the time is ripe" for adoption of international regulation of some sort. And, as declared in the meeting of the following year, "the International Labour Organization owes it to itself to remain the promoter of social progress in the world" (International Labour Conference 1951, 341). In other words, social progress was now equated not only with the improvement of working conditions and protection of women's employment but with promoting the rights of women as well.

Still, it would be misleading to think that there was a full consensus. Certain elements were still debated and contested. The decision that the regulation should take the form of a convention (instead of a recommendation, e.g.) was rejected by many employers' representatives, who declared that they had always supported the basic principle, since it was "close to their heart," but preferred not to adopt a binding document in the form of a convention, at least not at the present. While accusing others (those who supported convention) of refusing "to face what appear to be the realities of the situation," they claimed to know, firsthand, the real difficulties and catastrophes that might arise if such a convention were to be adopted. It seemed that such a convention, if countries indeed were to implement it and incorporate it in their national legislation, would endanger the whole economic system that had "historically [been] built upon the basis of the family responsibilities of the bread winner." They predicted that it would lead to "a considerable disturbance in the economic life," would result in an "inflationary tendency," would create "more discrimination between men and women workers," would "completely upset the process of collective bargaining" and in general would have a "disastrous effect upon a national wage structure."

The U.S. employers' delegate, on the other hand, supported the idea of a convention and put his argument in a businesslike manner: "We need equality in the labor market," he said, "not as a gesture of gallantry, nor any excess of generosity, but simply the application of sound business principles and good management." The two economic reasons that he brought up were, first, that the need for high productivity requires "securing the person who is best qualified to do the work that has to be done, regardless of sex" (International Labour Conference 1951, 355) and, second, that women constitute an important sector in the domestic market and it is worthwhile making them viable consumers. Thus, ideas of rationality and efficiency started to erode the primordial and gendered conception of labor market processes. Almost all of the workers' representatives supported a convention "to make effective the reign of justice throughout the field of labor," and the proposed convention was thought of "as the only instrument that will give due consideration to human rights and human dignity."

The old argument from the turn of the century regarding the need for international legislation because of international competition was brought up again: "it would be extremely unjust to continue to penalize, in the economic sphere, the countries which have advanced socially, by placing and keeping them in a position of unjust competition on the international market" (International Labour Conference 1951, 340). This perception implied that the principle of equal pay, like limiting women's working hours in the pre-ILO period, would lead to disadvantages in the world economy. This position would later be challenged and wholly replaced by the idea that equality is a prerequisite, not a hindrance, to full economic development planned rationally and implemented bureaucratically. According to this logic, discrimination, and not egalitarian policy, was defined as the costlier strategy.

Eventually, an international convention—the Equal Remuneration Convention (no. 100)—was drafted and adopted in the 1950 and 1951 conferences, respectively. This was the first multilateral treaty to focus exclusively on women's rights and to express the notion of equality with the intention that nation-states would take action in that direction. The United Nations adopted the

Convention on the Political Rights of Women only one year later. Previous international documents that addressed the principle of equality as a principle to which all nation-states should adhere (e.g., the UN Charter) had specified "sex" among other criteria, but sexual equality was not its main focus. Other documents that focused on women's rights were in the form of resolutions or declarations (i.e., mainly expressive statements). The previous conventions about women's rights were adopted by regional organizations, such as the Organization of American States. Thus, the 1951 convention was the first women's rights treaty to be adopted by an international official body and to be endorsed by a large number of nation-states.

In the years to follow there was a proliferation of activities around women's employment, all framed in the context of the convention. Various resolutions were adopted regarding different aspects of women's work and referring to various categories of women workers. Expert committees on women's employment continued to convene, initiating and carrying out more studies and research on various aspects of women's employment, including part-time employment, employment of older women workers, and employment of women having dependent young children. It was in the name of "freedom and dignity" as well as "economic security" and "equal opportunities with men" that the new studies and the collection of more data were now initiated and carried out.

A proliferation of expert committees (e.g., Committee of Experts on Women's Employment) "produced" a multiplicity of groups of women workers (e.g., textile workers, nonmanual workers, domestic workers) whose problems were now deemed relevant to the work of such experts. The proposal to establish a permanent committee further emphasized the importance of the issue of women's employment. It was recommended that the committee have an official status and be composed of governments', workers', and employers' official representatives (International Labour Office 1957). These bureaucratic actions were perceived as necessary, in view of the influx of women into the labor market and the request to implement what "we most of all desire: equality," as explained at the fortieth International Labour Conference.

Six years after the Equal Remuneration Convention was adopted, a much more comprehensive convention, the 1958 Employment (Discrimination) Convention, was adopted. Whereas the former was concerned with eliminating sex distinction regarding pay only, the latter referred to all aspects of employment (promotion, vocational training, access to and conditions of employment), to particular occupations, and to discrimination based on other social criteria in addition to sex (e.g., race, color, religion, political opinion, national extraction, or social origin).

It is interesting to compare the draft proposal with the final text that was eventually adopted. The most telling difference concerned the obligation of the ratifying nation-states. Their commitment, as expressed in the proposal, was found to be too vague and not binding enough. Thus, promotion of "educational programs to secure the acceptance of the non-discrimination policy" (from the original proposal) was substituted in the final draft with "legislation to prohibit discrimination" (International Labour Conference 1958b). This change is highly informative regarding the legitimacy of both the principle of equality and the idea that this principle could be imposed on nation-states by an international agreement. There was no discussion at that point about the infringement upon the sovereignty of nation-states. Now international bodies were assigned the role of standardizing and monitoring domestic labor laws.

Since the convention intended to deal with the general issue of equality in employment, it was suggested that an article that specified the need to guarantee sexual equality be excluded. The argument was that there was already a convention on the matter. The fact that this suggestion was rejected outright once again reiterated the importance attached to the principle.

During that discussion discrimination was criticized on economic and moral grounds. Some brought up the issue of economic efficiency: "discrimination is not only morally unjust but also economically indefensible" (International Labour Conference 1958a, 404). In that way the economic consequences of equality were transformed in meaning: equality turned out to be efficient, rather than a costly policy. This argument would be elaborated much further during the 1970s with the introduction of "national development" as the major rationale for equality.

In addition, an evocative, morally motivated, frontal attack on discrimination was voiced. "Let us call a spade a spade and give discrimination its true name: a crime, to be included and punished in our penal codes! Discrimination is in very truth a crime that outrages human dignity and defies all canons of morality and decency, and unless we deal with it as we deal with murder, robbery or any other crime, that is by punishing it, all our high-flown pronouncements exalting equality of opportunity or treatment are but as sounding brass and tinkling cymbal" (International Labour Conference 1958a, 407).

As in the discussion of the previous convention, the main objections had to do with fears that the convention was too rigid and that it would not be ratified by many countries. In both cases the reverse held true. The two conventions, portrayed by the ILO as "more than a mere statement of legal obligations; they represent a further milestone on the road leading by educational processes to respect for human dignity" (International Labour Office 1960, 16), are among those ILO conventions to be ratified by the highest number of countries.

At the time that the principle of economic equality was proposed, debated, and finally codified in an international agreement, very few countries embodied it in their national codes. But during the 1960s a worldwide process began. Nation-states across the globe modified their labor codes, enacting the new prescribed notion of "working women," along the lines of "working men" and no longer associated with children.

## Worldwide Endorsement of Equality-in-Employment Laws

Why do countries ratify international conventions? Unless one considers the symbolic value of these ratifications, it remains incomprehensible why countries would get involved at all. After all, when ratifying a convention, the state submits itself to the scrutiny of various international bodies; it has to deliver periodic reports on the actions it has taken and to account for it when and if it has not done so. Moreover, internally, it gives social groups legitimate claims to press demands on the state to meet its international obligations. Note also that a country can simply go ahead and pass a given law without ratifying the relevant convention. Still, by 1991 the average number of ratifications of ILO conventions per country was approximately thirty-seven (International Labour Conference 1992).

A country's ratification of an international convention constitutes a symbolic enactment expressing an endorsement of shared ethical understandings within the world community. This endorsement further helps to constitute the universal claim put forward in international conventions and enhances the evaluation of the principles embodied in the convention. More directly, such an endorsement represents a commitment to act upon those principles. Signaling the affirmation of globally accepted principles implies and deepens membership in the world community that promotes these ideas.

As elaborated in the previous section, the ILO adopted two equality-in-employment conventions (in 1952 and 1958). By 1991 the two conventions were ratified by 112 and 110 countries, respectively. These figures are impressive in and of themselves but even more so if we consider the fact that, out of 157 ILO conventions, only 8 of them have been ratified by more than 100 countries (International Labour Conference 1992). Also, in some countries these were the only ILO conventions that have been ratified. In this way the majority of the countries have conveyed to the world community that they actively support equality-in-employment conventions and have expressed a commitment to take action. The novel idea that it is wrong to treat, reward, or promote women any differently than men has been endorsed worldwide.

Graph 2 shows how recent this global acceptance is; it shows the level of ratification over time of the various conventions. Ratifying the night work conventions (i.e., protective legislation) represents the legitimization of a differential treatment of women in employment, whereas ratifying the equality-in-employment conventions and the United Nations Convention of Elimination of All Forms of Discrimination against Women signals endorsement of the principle of equalizing the status of men and women. The gradual increase in the ratification of the protective legislation conventions was rapidly surpassed by the equality conventions. The steep slope of ratification of both the Elimination of Discrimination and the equality-in-employment conventions reflects the swift endorsement of those ideas, once codified in international conventions.

More important than ratifying equality-in-employment conventions is, of course, passing the appropriate legislation. Examining the current prevalence and trends of proliferation of equal-pay legislation across countries reveals a similar pattern. At present 129 countries have some form of this legislation. After excluding cases that incorporated the principle only in their constitution and those that did not include a specific reference to sex in their antidiscrimination laws, we find that 112 countries (66 percent of 169 existing countries) have adopted legislation that specifically refers to women's equality in wages (see app. 1).

In some cases the principle of equal pay was first incorporated into collective labor agreements and only later became part of a state's legislation extending the right to equal pay to workers in all sectors. Such was the case, for example, in Austria, Belgium, Denmark, Greece, Italy, and Norway. These cases underline the fact that, even though the principle of equal pay was already institutionalized in forms other than in state laws which were not necessarily less effective, these countries still found it imperative and suitable to pass statutes officially endorsing those international principles.

Graph 3 presents world patterns in the proliferation of economic equal rights for women. It shows the countries that passed the relevant legislation as a percentage of the existing countries in the world. It is clear that 1960 serves as a turning point. Until then only 10 percent of all countries adopted equal pay laws, but since then there has been a sharp and steady increase. During the 1970s there was a 30 percent rise in the number of countries granting these rights. By the mid-1970s more than half of the countries in the world had granted equal economic rights for women. This swift proliferation is quite remarkable considering the fact that before 1950 only a few countries had incorporated it into their national legislation.

World War II presented special circumstances for a few countries to adopt this principle, though "prematurely." In Great Britain it had been laid down in

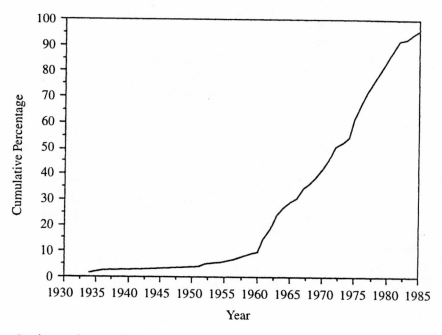

Graph 3.  Adoption of first equal pay legislation, by year, 1930–1985.

certain collective agreements as an essential condition for the employment of women in work hitherto reserved for men. In Australia a Women's Employment Board was set up during the war to authorize the substitution of women workers for men and the employment of women in new jobs. The board was required to fix women's wages at the rate set for males in cases in which permission had been granted to substitute women for men. The rule of equal pay in cases in which the work and output were the same has also been adopted by the national war labor boards in the United States and in Canada in settling disputes concerning women's wages (International Labour Conference 1944). These, however, were only temporary measures, aimed at attracting women to join the workforce during emergency times. After the war the arrangements were not institutionalized as part of national legislation. It took several decades and other events for these countries to legislate the measures.

When in the 1960s and 1970s countries started to enact equality-in-employment laws, they were initially limited to remuneration only and usually postulated strictly as "equal pay for equal work." In most cases, however, these laws were soon replaced by "equal pay for work of equal value" and later followed by "equality of opportunity" legislation. The scope was extended to most sectors of the workforce. More important, it seems that broadening the application and scope of these laws was, by no means, limited to one set of countries but, rather, was undertaken worldwide.

Most social scientific theories that investigate the adoption of policy and legislation provide country-level explanations, focusing on either economic, social, or political characteristics, or any combination of the three, of a given country. Yet the fact that an overwhelming majority of countries, and not a specific group, roughly around the same historical period, modified their national codes to incorporate women's employment rights points to the fact that it was a world phenomenon; that is, these states' actions were externally, not internally, generated. To provide more solid evidence of this assertion, elsewhere I conducted a multivariate analysis (event-history analysis) in which I showed that, when controlling for national-level variation, it is world-level events and countries' exposure to these events which account for the patterns and rate of adoption of equal pay laws (Berkovitch 1994). Here I will present, in very general terms, the various tested explanations and some of the findings.

In most general terms I compared internal and external effects on states' adoption of equal pay laws. The internal factors, or country-level explanations, included the level of modernization, degree of state power, extent of women's political power, and level of democracy which exist in a given country. Each of them was based in a different rationale. The rationale for the modernization argument is that rights to women would be granted once a country achieved a certain level of socioeconomic development, the main idea being that economic development is coexistent with the erosion of traditional modes of social organizations. This erosion parallels a modern normative set of rules based on rational ideologies. Gender is one such basic institution (it includes the gendered division of labor, culturally assigned gender roles, the gendered hierarchy of power, etc.) which is likely to be transformed when a country becomes more developed and wealthy. Modernization was measured by the most widely used indicator, gross domestic product (GDP) per capita.

Social political explanations focus on the structure and strength of the state and of the political groups in order to account for state actions. One such interpretation is that strong states, in terms of their extractive powers and control over economic activities, will also tend to expand their jurisdiction over more domains of society. In the present case strong states will intervene and regulate employment relations and pay scales for different groups of workers. States' power was measured by government share of GDP.

A voluntaristic bottom-up approach will see legislation as the result of the ability of relevant groups to exert pressure on the appropriate legislative bodies or of having direct access to it. Women's political power was measured by the proportion of seats women had in parliament, or equivalent bodies.

Granting women equal economic rights can also be the result of the degree to which democracy exists in a given country. Democracy was measured by an index that indicates the existence of institutions and procedures for citizen participation, a check on the exercise of executive authority, and a guarantee of civil liberties. Being aware of the obvious limitation of such a scale, this measure provides a possibility for systematically analyzing a large number of countries over time.

External factors, or world-level explanations, included the degree of economic dependence of a country, the extent to which the phenomenon under investigation is already prevalent in the world (diffusion), the historical period, and the degree of linkage to world polity. Dependency theory links state's action and state's structure to its location within the wider economic system, the global network of economic exchange and power relations. The argument is that being embedded and dependent on the flow of resources makes a country more open to other influences—that is, economic openness leads to cultural openness. It was measured by the export/import ratio's share of real GDP.

Another way to conceptualize world effects on state's activities is through a simple diffusion process. A diffusion process implies that, once a critical mass of countries adopts a certain feature, it becomes a legitimate model for other countries to emulate. It acts like an "epidemic" process of simple imitation. The "contagion" effect was measured by the proportion of nation-states that adopted equal-pay laws one year before a given country adopted it.

During the 1960s the ILO promoted the issue of women's rights. That was the time when the second, highly ratified ILO convention came into existence. And, indeed, as is clear from graph 3, 1960 was a turning point in the process of states' adoption of equal-pay laws. Therefore, a dummy variable of the period, before and after 1960, was included.

The diffusion effect and the historical time period are expected to affect all countries uniformly. All countries are expected to respond similarly. Yet not all countries are connected in the same way, and the degree to which they are related to the world cultural and political system varies. Though they are all members in the same system, not all are embedded in it to the same extent. One would expect that some countries are more sealed off from global events, while others are subject to greater international pressures. The extent to which a country is expected to be influenced by world models and norms depends on its linkages to the carriers of these norms.

One such linkage is membership in international organizations. In the first

TABLE 1
*Internal and External Effects on States' Adoption of Equal Economic Rights*

|  |  | Model 1 | Model 2 |
|---|---|---|---|
| Country-level explanations | Modernization | Effect | No effect |
|  | State's power | Effect | No effect |
|  | Women's power | No effect | No effect |
|  | Democracy | No effect | No effect |
| World-level explanations | Dependence |  | Effect |
|  | Diffusion |  | No effect |
|  | Historical period (1960) |  | Effect |
|  | State linkages to world polity |  | Effect |

part of this book I discussed the increasing coherence of the organizational infrastructure of world society and the increasing attention to women's issues, conceptualized as women's rights. A country's participation in world events and its organizational activities are likely to serve as a mechanism through which ideas and models that are being propagated on the global level can affect its own actions. Therefore, I tested the effect of a country's membership in women's international organizations on the adoption of equal-pay laws.

A second linkage is ratification of international conventions. Ratification is one of the ways in which a state affirms its membership in the global community. It does so by endorsing the winning ideas, principles, and models promulgated by various global actors and codified in international conventions. Instead of focusing on the two ILO conventions only, in my study I included also the eight UN women's rights conventions to get a measure (cumulative index for number of conventions a country ratified for each year) of a more diffuse commitment to the idea of women's equality and not specifically to the implementation of equal pay.

Table 1 summarizes the results and shows which explanations were found to hold. When looking only at country-level characteristics (model 1), the level of development and state power have an effect on the rate of adoption of equal-pay laws. Indeed, in numerous studies, as well as in folk wisdom, the level of modernization accounts for a series of events and characteristics inherent to the developmental process. Based on those conventional modernization assumptions, one could stipulate that women's rights, especially in the economic sphere, are a luxury that only rich and modern states can afford. Or it could be argued that women's rights is an idea that can be envisioned only by progressive enlightened states, that is, developed nation-states. Similarly, a rich body of literature that emerged as a reaction to both pluralist and Marxist theories of the state continued to use the nation-state as the decisive unit of analysis. This literature has focused on state capacity and state bureaucracy as the main determinants in policy formation and implementation (e.g., Skocpol 1985). Thus, based on model 1, when internal characteristics were considered without any consideration to the global context, the level of economic development and state power were found to have an effect.

These effects vanish, however, when we place the state in its wider economic and cultural context, as can be seen from the results of model 2. When global factors are considered, none of the country-level characteristics have an impact on a state's tendency to grant women economic rights. What was found to have an effect is a series of world-level characteristics: economic dependence, time period, membership in women's international organizations, and ratification. This body of evidence strongly indicates that it is the world-level characteristics and linkages to the world polity (to the political-cultural context) which affect the rate of adoption of equal-pay laws, rather than factors on the national level. Note that diffusion was not found to have an effect; this implies that the adoption of state laws regarding women does not operate as a simple process of imitation to which all countries are equally exposed. Instead, nation-states are more likely to adopt these policies in specific time periods and contingent on their degree of integration into the wider system.

## Protective Legislation Falls from Grace

The emerging postwar ideology of human rights and the new emphasis on equality started to shape much of global discourse on women and women's issues. It also modified the ways in which the century-old principle of states' regulation of women's employment was perceived and enacted. Old ways of incorporating women as gendered workers into the labor market—their rights for employment being affected by their primordial/cultural functions—were now denounced. According to the equality principle, differentiating between men and women in employment has a discriminatory effect on women. Now state action was declared to be required not to protect women but to eliminate all possible sources of unequal treatment. World organizations, headed by the ILO, once the big "protector" of working women, were mobilized in this campaign.

The first doubts to be raised in an official form were voiced in 1950 in the Asian Regional Conference of the ILO: "the strict enforcement of legislation for the protection of women and young persons might have the undesirable effect of reducing employment possibilities for women and young persons." A resolution to conduct a study into the matter did not result in any concrete action.

Aside from occasional reference to the issue in the years that followed, not much action was taken. Moreover, organizations such the World Health Organization continued to contribute to its legitimacy. So, for example, an article published in 1971 gives medical scientific reasons for the elaboration of protective laws. The article details the physical differences between men and women (blood circulation, muscles, oxygen uptake, heartbeats, menstrual cycle, etc.) and specifies the effects of these on their working capabilities. The conclusion was that restricting women's employment in certain cases certainly benefited the "working woman." Ideas that some of these restrictions "reduce her human rights" were dismissed as a luxury for "a small minority of fortunate women." In most parts of the world, it was declared, "the working woman needs encouragement, aid and protection" (Karvonen 1971, 7).

The intense activity that took place during the International Women's Year in 1975 gave a major boost to the topic and brought it back to the agenda but in a different context and in modified form. The ILO, the major advocate of protection of women (and children) since its inception in 1919, changed its position radically, and it has devoted a major effort since then to revising and modifying this policy.

Thus, in the mid-1970s all discussions relating to protective legislation began to be shaped by the discourse of equality between men and women. This discourse took away the ground for claims that women should be treated differently because of their roles that are external to the labor market. In that spirit the ILO, like most other international bodies in 1975, adopted a series of resolutions, drafted declarations, and initiated studies, all expressing the goal of equality and rights. In all these documents one can find many references to protective legislation, all of which cast doubt and expressed the need to rethink and modify its gender-based legislation. One such example is a study undertaken by the ILO on the various types of special protective measures for women and their "adequacy in the light of present circumstances and concepts regarding the need for protection and for equal treatment of workers of both sexes" (International Labour Conference 1977, 69).

The central document that was adopted during the IWY, the 1975 Declaration on Equality of Opportunity and Treatment for Women Workers, was very clear about the need for *general* protection and dismissed any notion of the unique needs that women, as women, might have. Covering a vast array of employment issues, it stated that "women shall be protected from risks inherent in their employment and occupation on the same basis and with the same standards of protection as men" (Art. 9[2]). The 1975 ILO resolution "Concerning a Plan of Action" expressed an explicit call to nation-states to take measures to "review all protective legislation applying to women in the light of up-to-date scientific knowledge and technological advances and to revise, supplement, extend to all workers . . . retain or repeal such legislation according to national circumstances" (para. 6). Other important documents, such as the 1979 UN Convention of Elimination of All Forms of Discrimination (Art. 11[3]) and the central document adopted in the 1985 World Conference, the Nairobi Forward-Looking Strategies for the Advancement of Women (para. 139), discussed protective legislation explicitly in relation to all workers and not women alone.

In 1987 the ILO published a very long study on the topic. Its title, *Women Workers: Protection or Equality?* reflects the new spirit: *protection* and *equality* are being posed in contradictory positions, implying that the latter should be preferred to the former. The study includes a compilation of existing protective measures in 148 countries and the positions and views of government agencies, employers, employees, and nongovernmental organizations. In 1989 a meeting of experts was convened to discuss the relevance of such measures and the need for their revision, repeal, or retention.

This process of rethinking and revising gender-based legislation was not confined to the United Nations and the ILO. Other international bodies went through the same process as well. The European Economic Community (EEC) Directive on Equal Treatment from 1976 called for a revision of laws "when the concern for protection which originally inspired them is no longer well founded." In 1981 an Action Program was adopted that called on governments to abolish "unjustified protective legislation . . . and to promote equal standards of protection of men and women" (Vallance and Davies 1986). In the late 1980s the EEC commission issued a report stating that many national measures have a negative influence on women's employment and have lost their original justification. Member states were asked to review the compatibility of all such provisions with the principle of equality. The commission took the position that protective legislation that does not relate to pregnancy or maternity should be applied equally to both sexes and recommended that certain protective measures should either be extended to both sexes or be repealed or reassessed in the context of further research (Docksey 1987).

Consequently, these revisionary activities, articulated on the global level by authoritative international organizations, led to the reconceptualization of how nation-states should deal with working women. Nation-states stopped ratifying protective legislation conventions, some had denounced previously ratified ones, and a clear trend of repealing some of the protective measures became apparent worldwide.

The extent of ratification of international conventions can serve as an indicator of the legitimacy a principle that has been codified internationally holds among nation-states. Following the same logic, denouncing a convention has a symbolic meaning as well. While the nonratification of a convention is a passive act that can result from a variety of reasons (e.g., not accepting the legitimacy of an international organization to act on the specific matter or noninvolvement in international affairs), the act of denunciation is an active one that implies a rejection of a previously endorsed policy. Thus, figures of ratification and of denunciation can be used as indicators of the legitimation and delegitimation, respectively, of any principle that has been codified in international conventions.

As a result of two revisions (1934 and 1948) to the first Night Work Convention from 1919, there are three such conventions that could have been ratified.[4] Altogether, eighty-six countries have ratified at least one of the three night work conventions. Looking at the process of ratification over time (see graph 2), one can see a gradual increase in the number of countries that ratified at least one of the three night work conventions. The trend changed, however, toward the end of the 1970s. It slowed down significantly, and in 1983 it stopped completely. Bahrain, Belize, Swaziland, and the United Arab Emirates were the only countries to ratify a night work convention in the early 1980s. Since then no other country has endorsed the principle that is embodied in these conventions, indicating a clear decline in the legitimacy of gender-specific protective measures.

Not only did the process of ratification stop, but a new process of denunciation emerged. Countries do not usually tend to denounce a convention that they have ratified. Very few conventions have ever been denounced, and, when it has happened, only a very small number of countries has done so. None has denounced either the Equal Remuneration or the Discrimination in Employment Convention. But the picture changes when we look at the protective conventions. Altogether, fourteen countries, out of the eighty-six that ratified at least one convention, have denounced previously ratified conventions (either one, two, or three) and have never ratified another one.[5] Similarly, eight out of eighty-eight countries that have ratified the Underground Work (Women) Convention have denounced it (International Labour Conference 1992). A typical reason for the denunciation was given by the government of Uruguay:

4. In many cases countries have ratified more than one convention. More than thirty countries have "replaced" the old conventions with more recent ones; that is, they denounced (revoked) a previous convention that they had ratified in the past and implemented the revised one. About the same number of countries ratified new ones without denouncing the older versions.

5. Since sometimes a country denounces a convention in order to ratify its revised version, I counted only those cases in which denouncing one convention was not followed by the ratification of a more recent one.

"Today, owing to various factors, including technological and scientific progress as well as the widespread expansion of education and vocational training, the former intention to protect women against dangerous work has become a discriminatory favor which restrict their access to employment" (International Labour Office 1987, 179).

The relatively high rate of denunciation marks a falling from grace of an idea that had once been embraced globally. The principle that women (and children) need to be protected from the forces of the market in a way that men do not has lost ground worldwide. Nation-states have responded to new ideas about gender equality which have been promoted globally by not ratifying or denouncing the relevant international conventions and, more important, also by modifying their respective laws and policies.

In order to estimate correctly the significance of the changes discussed here, a brief summary of the contemporary situation worldwide is needed. According to a comprehensive report published by the ILO, in about one hundred countries there are some restrictions on night work for women. In a similar number of countries there is at least one provision of the regulation on working time which applies to women only, either in the form of prohibition of overtime or prescribing a specific length of the workday. In a limited number of countries, about twenty-five in all, special requirements for facilities (e.g., seats, rest facilities, sanitary facilities, and nursing rooms) for women workers in the workplace or nearby exist. In one hundred countries there are provisions restricting or prohibiting the employment of women in certain types of occupations—those considered dangerous, arduous, or unhealthy. One category of prohibited work includes activities liable to be detrimental to women's morals. Some of the provisions apply specifically to pregnant and young mothers, and some are directed toward all women (International Labour Office 1987).

Thus, overall, in an overwhelming majority of countries, there are specific labor laws that regulate either the type of jobs or worktime for women. In many countries the restrictions apply to all women, regardless of family status or age, for example. Given that such a wide range of countries share similar conceptions of women in their role as workers and the widespread acceptance of the idea that their employment situation requires special action by the state, it is worthwhile to examine the changes that have taken place more recently.

In a substantial number of countries doubts have emerged about the advantages and usefulness of the various measures undertaken on behalf of women. They were seen as having discriminatory effects and to disrupt economic development. Many countries have expressed intentions to evaluate these measures and to introduce necessary changes, and many other states have already done so. This trend is shared worldwide and is not limited to a specific set of countries.

Conferences were held in which these ideas were expressed and publicly supported by official figures. For example, in Australia a national conference on legislative restrictions on women's employment was held in 1986 with the objective "to identify changes that should be made to restrictive provisions in legislation's regulations . . . in order to eliminate discrimination against women in employment." The conference concluded that "it has been recognized that restrictive provisions in legislation . . . run contrary to the anti-discrimination legislation and Australia's international obligations" (International Labour Office 1987, 132–33). Similarly, official reports were published, calling for a reformulation of existing legislation. The Swiss Federal Office of Industry, for example, in its report on the legislative program, "Equality of Rights between Men and Women," declared that: "All provisions which restrict the employment of women, such as those relating to night and Sunday work . . . should be re-examined. Provisions which call for employers to consider household responsibilities and the physical constitution of women workers should be reworded in neutral terms so that such considerations are given to workers in general, not just to women" (International Labour Office 1987, 147).

In various countries the call to "reevaluate" existing legislation came from official bodies that had been formed in the context of the Decade for Women. In Venezuela, for instance, a Congressional Committee on the Evaluation of the Decade for Women, in its draft bill to revise the labor code, declared that "restrictive provisions on women's employment should be eliminated. Today, with the technological and scientific progress, there is no reason for these provisions to continue to exist" (International Labour Office 1987, 153).

Indeed, many countries relaxed various protective measures, limiting their application or repealing them altogether. Protective laws adopted in the Scandinavian countries during the 1970s did not distinguish between men and women workers.[6] In the United States, with the adoption of the antidiscrimination act in 1963 and 1964, protective legislation was virtually eliminated, a trend that was backed and supported by a series of court decisions (Ratner 1980). A similar tendency can be observed in countries like Australia, Canada, Ireland, Italy, Greece, Japan, and New Zealand (International Labour Conference 1985).

---

6. Note, however, that the Scandinavian countries always supported protective measures that were based on the type of work and not the gender of the worker.

Several countries repealed some of the measures with gender-specific restrictions concerning night work.[7] Similarly, other countries abolished restrictions on overtime and different lengths of the workday for women.[8]

The case of Sri Lanka is highly informative with respect to the ways in which economic and political interests, interwoven with old and new gender images, play in the decision to abolish the restriction on women's employment. A letter of 28 January 1980, from the Ministry of Labour to the ILO, stated:

> The present government has set up an economic commission whose objectives is to attract to the country foreign firms interested in setting up industries. Some of these firms have pointed out that it was essential that the workers in their factories should be women and that it was also essential for the manufacturing process that there should be a third shift. However, the fact that Sri Lanka has ratified the Night Work convention prevents the employment of women at night on a third shift . . . In addition, several national women's organizations have pointed out that this legislation was discriminating against women and has acted as a constraint against equality of opportunity of employment for women . . . Since a third shift for women workers has to be introduced almost immediately if this country is to attract foreign investors for electronic and allied industries . . . this government intends repealing the national legislation relating to night work for women and allowing a third shift for women workers to operate. (173)

Potential investors in Sri Lanka, for efficiency reasons, insisted on having a night shift. But the clear preference for female workers (who were cheaper and perceived to be a more docile workforce) posed a problem—existing laws prohibit night work for women. The economic need to attract foreign investment pushed for the abolition of this prohibition. It was, however, the new ideology of equality, and seeing protective laws as discriminatory, which provided the legitimacy for its abolition. Complying with this globally prescribed meaning of protective laws also yields political gains. In another document that refers to the same issue state officials presented the repeal of the law as being linked to a survey taken by the women's bureau which found that more than 80 percent of the women interviewers agreed to night work for economic reasons.[9] The views of women's movements were quoted as well to signal that their position had been influential as well. It is highly likely that similar economic necessities would motivate similar state actions in other places. The cynical use of the equality argument is not the point. I make no argument regarding the motiva-

7. Barbados, Canada, Chile, Guyana, Ireland, Israel, New Zealand, Spain, and Surinam.
8. Bahamas, Great Britain, Guyana, Ireland, Surinam, and the United States.
9. United Nations, *Country Statements: National Policies for the Advancement of Women*, n.d.

tions of state officials. The point is that nowadays accommodating economic needs is being done in the name of equality. The two no longer seem in contradiction, as in previous periods, but, rather, enable each other.

The centrally planned economies of Eastern Europe, at least until the late 1980s, did not follow the global path and, as such, pose a clear counterexample to the worldwide trend presented here. A statement by state officials says that "women have clearly distinctive physiological and psychological characteristics," and "we do not believe that protective legislation has outlived its usefulness" (International Labour Conference 1985, 39). Indeed, these countries are characterized by the most comprehensive protective legislation in addition to a very elaborate system of maternity protection and provision.[10]

The development in China set yet another model: the establishment of market institutions was coupled with transition from equality to protection. The beginning of the late 1970s marked a period of pragmatic legal and economic reforms. Together with the reestablishment of institutions that had previously been abolished, the decentralization and autonomy of industries, and the appearance of private enterprise, China turned to protective legislation. This focus on the biological differences between women and men constitutes a marked departure from the prior policies of the Cultural Revolution, which emphasized the belief that "women are the same as men" (Woo 1994, 279).

The Chinese regime and the 1982 constitution have provided limited antidiscriminatory legislation to ensure similar treatment of men and women in the workplace. Still, recent legislation, by and large, has taken the approach of emphasizing the differences between men and women. For example, the Women's Rights Protection Law states clearly that there are "certain work categories or positions that are unfit for women." And, in addition to pregnancy and childbirth, menstruation and menopause are also recognized as periods in the life of a woman worker in which she must be accorded special treatment. For each of these periods the regulations impose limits on the types and conditions of work women can perform.

Woo (1994) suggests that these changes ought to be understood as a response to fluctuations in the labor market and to internal institutional arrangements. During times of labor shortages women have been called on to participate in the workforce, whereas in times of oversupply, as has been the case recently, their "patriotic duty" is to be "socialist housewives." The timing of these trends does not correspond to the global trends that I have been discussing. Still, the

---

10. Unfortunately, I do not have systematic data on changes in legislation that took place after the political and economic reforms of the late 1980s and early 1990s.

same factors can account for both situations—the global trend and China's exception to it. China's special model results from an explicit attempt to resist external pressures to conform to normative models of citizenship and rights. This is apparent not only in regard to women's rights but human rights in general. China's participation in the world polity has indeed been very limited. It ratified only 2 out of the 8 women's rights conventions and 17 out of 159 ILO conventions. Chinese women are members in a relatively small number of WINGOs. Not all countries are subject to the same pressures of homogenization. It is the level of connection and degree of integration of nation-states into the world polity which account for effects of the latter on the former and for the degree of compliance with world models.

## From "Working Mothers" to "Workers with Family Responsibilities"

The decline in the legitimacy of protective measures was not accompanied by a parallel decline in maternity provisions. On the contrary, there was an expansion of maternity provisions in all international documents as well as in national legislation. This expansion was accompanied, and actually enabled, by a transformation of its definition and purpose. "Maternity protection" was broadened through its conceptualization as a necessary prerequisite for the implementation of the principle of equal treatment. The previous aim of maternity measures—caring for the well-being of newborns or for the protection of motherhood—disappeared and was replaced with the rationale of equality of workers. Thus, the decline of protective measures and the expansion of maternity provisions are not incongruent but, rather, complement each other, embodying the new conception of the role of the state in respect to working women.

In the early 1950s two international conventions and a recommendation concerning maternity protection were adopted by the International Labour Conference. The Maternity Convention from 1919 was revised, expanded, and broadened in scope and resulted in the 1952 Maternity Protection Convention no. 103 (revised). The new convention was extended to apply also to women wage earners who work at home and to all nonindustrial undertakings. It fixes the rate of cash payments at not less than two-thirds of previous earnings. The revision also specified that there would be no distinction based on age, nationality, race, or creed. The benefits provided for were higher and more precise. It was accompanied by a recommendation (no. 95) that provided for even wider benefits and protection. In addition, the 1952 *Social Security (Minimum*

*Standards)*, which dealt with similar matters as part of a wider range of issues, was adopted.

The discussion around the 1952 Maternity Convention shows a broad consensus regarding the need to revise and expand the old provisions. At that point, in addition to the aim of safeguarding "the future by protecting the physical health of the future citizen and worker, which is essential of the continuance of the economic life of a country" (International Labour Conference 1952, 340), the chair of the maternity committee added the "basic and scientific principles of social justice" as the main motivation for the new convention. The former argument would in time lose out to the latter, when accompanied by pro-development rhetoric.

The provisions proposed by the convention were intended to facilitate the reentry of mothers into paid employment. Thus, they guaranteed their ability to exercise what was defined as a basic right, the right to work. This was evident also in the way the representative of Poland put it: "protection of maternity is a logical consequence and a prerequisite of woman's right to work and to receive equal pay" (International Labour Conference 1952, 342).

It would be misleading to ignore the objections that nevertheless existed. In the same conference meeting of 1952 the government representative of the Netherlands evoked "scientific studies" done by the World Health Organization to support his argument that mothers of little children should stay at home, basically until the children are grown. It was found, he claimed, that separating the mother from the child, in the early years, "has proven to have disastrous consequences on the health of the child and on his psychological and physical development." He did not argue, however, with the right of women to work but, rather, in the interests of the national economy: "We need to weigh the needs of the child against those of national production . . . This is the heartbreaking problem of working mothers" (International Labour Conference 1952, 341). Note that, by presenting the problematic involved in the reentry of mothers into the labor market, the economic value of women's work was actually emphasized and defined as essential to the national economy.

The Dutch representative was, however, alone in his position. Most representatives objected on the grounds of feasibility. Representatives of developing countries claimed that his proposal would be "unworkable" in their countries, since there was no social security scheme available to provide for benefits. A few found it incompatible with the principle of equality and therefore were afraid that it might result in discrimination against women. In general, the main arguments against the 1952 convention were technical and concerned whether it provided for the best means to protect working mothers against discrimination. The context that framed the debate—social justice and national growth—replaced the framework of protection of mothers and children which had dominated the scene in previous years.

The UN Commission on the Status of Women, usually focusing on the demand for equal pay, began to concern itself with issues of motherhood and employment. It engaged the ILO in conducting surveys, studies, and reports on its own activities and on measures taken by nation-states on actual and desired measures regarding the employment of "working women with family responsibilities" (e.g., United Nations 1966b).

In the 1960s the changes that had begun to show a decade earlier became evident, now accompanied and reinforced by the emerging discourse of development. These changes were expressed clearly in a series of resolutions and recommendations that were proposed in 1964 by the Committee on Women Workers. These texts mark a clear departure from previous conceptions of the needs of women workers and the former emphasis on the states' obligation to protect women's maternal functions.

First, it was suggested that the conference adopt a recommendation on "Women with Family Responsibilities" so that women "who wish or have to work away from their homes" would be able "to do so without being exposed to any discrimination" (International Labour Conference 1964, 457). The recommendation was supplemented by four resolutions[11] in which the emphasis was not only on "providing the services and facilities for the care of children" but also on meeting "the needs and preferences of the women concerned" so that their possibilities of employment and promotion would not be hampered and to "facilitate entry and re-entry into employment after an absence due to family responsibilities."

Indeed, this tone was so loud and clear that it alarmed some of the delegates. The Italian delegate was concerned, for example, that, "when we recommend the adoption of measures necessary to facilitate the integration of women in economic and social life and to enable them to discharge their family responsibilities, we are concerned more with the emancipation of women than with the moral and material integrity of the family" (International Labour Conference 1964, 465).

Another opposition was voiced by delegates from some of the developing countries. They argued that, since these measures came out of a context in which there was a labor shortage, they were not compatible with the conditions

11. The resolutions were: Women Workers in a Changing World; Economic and Social Advancement of Women in Developing Countries; Part-Time Employment; and Maternity Protection.

in the developing countries which were in a constant state of unemployment. They objected to adopt measures that encouraged women to enter the market, when there are not enough jobs for men. On the one hand, this opposition resembled the voices of the 1930s when there was an outcry against employing women, since they "take away men's jobs." The old notion of men as the "breadwinners" and woman being only supplementary workers was reiterated once again. On the other hand, this objection was based on the new notion that maternity protection was indeed designed and capable of facilitating women's reentry into the labor market and, as such, of turning women into workers capable of competing with men in the labor market. The objection did not derive from concern for the welfare of the neglected child but, rather, that of the threatened male worker.

The following year, in 1965, when the Recommendation on Women Workers with Family Responsibilities was eventually adopted, it was seen primarily as an antidiscriminatory measure to assist "the woman worker effectively to become integrated in the working population on an equal footing" (International Labour Conference 1965).

Thus, the main emphasis was to enable women to exercise their right as citizens to employment and to contribute to the "well-being of society" and for "greater national income." Note the change from the notion of having provisions that allow women to work without threatening their maternal functioning; now it is not their work that should not threaten their familial roles but, rather, their familial roles should not hamper their equal access to employment and its benefits. Their opportunities in the public sphere should not depend on their roles in the private one.

The mid-1960s was also the time in which a further step in the direction of transforming gender relations and the gender paradigm was taken. For the first time it was recognized that men have, in addition to their public roles, certain family (noneconomic) responsibilities. The home was not the exclusive domain of women. And it was put very clearly during the discussion: "We must get rid of the traditional view that women only are responsible for the personal care of the family, whereas men only are responsible for the economy of the family" (International Labour Conference 1965, 386).

From then on we see that *working mothers* disappeared almost completely from discussions; instead, the labor market is populated with "working parents." Moreover, in 1970, in the context of economic rights, the Commission on the Status of Women began to discuss "the need for an educational campaign to provide guidance on the sharing of responsibilities within the family" (United Nations 1970). Campaigns for new international standards usually aim at nation-states to modify policies and codes. Now, for the first time, an international body deemed it appropriate to shape the actual caretaking of the household chores. The domestic division of labor was usually perceived to be negotiated privately between the wife and the husband. Now, however, when it was connected to higher ends such as national well-being and equality of the sexes, it became a domain for a global campaign as well.

In 1981 this principle was codified into a convention—The Convention on Workers with Family Responsibilities (no. 156), whose most striking characteristic is its gender-neutral language. It talks about the need to introduce measures in response to the specific needs of those workers who had family responsibilities, to equalize their position with those who do not have such responsibilities. In other words, domestic roles could be assigned to either partner, and, as such, they lose their gendered nature. The most significant step in that direction was taken with the introduction of parental leave, according to which either parent can obtain leave of absence or paid leave for the purpose of taking care of children or other member(s) of the immediate family.

Thus, the inseparable link that had been established between women and children was replaced by the new construction of parental responsibility. Working men were "brought in" to the family, and working women were released from being the exclusive caretakers of children. Linking men to childcare—that is, incorporating men into the domestic sphere, alongside women—was recognized as an essential step for equal incorporation of women into the public sphere. This degendering process was reinforced by the development argument that emerged in the 1970s.

The same idea was expressed over and over again in other major documents produced by international bodies other than the ILO. For example, the 1979 Convention on the Elimination of All Forms of Discrimination against Women and the 1985 Nairobi Forward-Looking Strategies (paras. 71 and 140) encouraged the introduction of parental leave and advocated the principle of shared domestic responsibilities. The European Commission proposed a Directive on Parental Leave and Leave for Family Reasons. The commission characterized the sharing of family and occupational responsibilities as a sine qua non for attaining an effective equality of economic opportunities (Docksey 1987). The proposed directive was vetoed over many years by the United Kingdom but reappeared in the Social Charter of 1989 as a nonbinding recommendation on childcare policy (Meehan 1992).

This global campaign resulted in a dramatic cross-national expansion of the maternity provision, a process that took place in two ways. First, more and more countries, all over the world, have adopted maternity provisions that look

TABLE 2
*Proportion of Countries with Maternity Provision*
*Policy, by Time Period (cumulative)*

| Time Period | |
|---|---|
| Until 1900 | 0.12 |
| By eve of World War I | 0.34 |
| By the end of World War II | 0.62 |
| By mid-1980s | 0.86 |

very much alike. Second, in the last two decades countries have expanded various aspects of maternal leave and provisions. This expansion, though more pronounced among European countries (socialist and nonsocialist), to a lesser degree has also taken place in other parts of the world.

Currently, the majority of the countries of the world—145 altogether—have passed statutes specifically providing for at least some maternity protection. Only 9 countries have not done so, among them South Africa, Switzerland, and the United States.[12]

Even though countries started to institute maternity provisions as early as the late nineteenth century, it became a world phenomenon only after World War II. By 1900 only Belgium, Germany, and parts of Austria-Hungary instituted such provisions. And, as table 2 shows, by the eve of World War I one-third of the states (that existed then) had passed such laws. At that point it was only a European phenomenon. Only later, during the interwar period, maternity provisions spread to Latin America and Japan, and by 1944 more than half of the countries in the world (62 percent) had adopted maternity provisions. After World War II and even more so in the 1960s, these provisions lost their regional character and spread to the new countries of Asia and Africa. By 1985, 86 percent of all independent nation-states had granted their respective women workers maternity provisions.

Moreover, new countries that have recently gained their independence are likely to adopt maternity protection legislation, which has already become a legitimate model. Consider the figures presented in table 3, which shows how long it took the various countries, classified by the historical period of their independence, to adopt maternity provisions. The oldest countries took the longest to do so (about a hundred years), while the newly independent nation-states were the quickest (an average of four years). The first row in the table includes all the countries that were considered independent nation-states by the eve of World War I, that is, mainly European states that were formed during the

12. Data for maternity measures are taken from Berkovitch 1994.

TABLE 3
*Length of Time until Adoption of Maternity Protection,*
*by Time Period of Independence*

| Period of Gaining Independence | Average No. of Years to Adopt Maternity Protection |
|---|---|
| Before World War I | 100 (approx.) |
| Interwar period | 14 |
| 1945–59 | 6 |
| 1960–present | 4 |

eighteenth and nineteenth centuries and the Latin American countries that gained independence during the nineteenth century. The former adopted maternity polices at the turn of the century and the latter only in the interwar period. Latin American countries gained independence at a time in which maternity measures were already a known phenomenon. Still, the European countries did not serve as a model to be emulated by the Latin American countries. Clearly, these two categories of nation-states had to cope with different conditions, and hence they adopted policies at different times. No external pressure was put on new states to adopt such measures, so that countries were responding more to internal forces than to external ones. At that time, when international negotiations took place at various international expert conferences and congresses of state officials regarding various forms of labor legislation, Latin American countries did not participate.

In the interwar period, however, with the formation of the League of Nations and the ILO, other parts of the world joined the emerging world polity. These organizations, especially the ILO, played a major role in promoting and disseminating models of "progress," which, at the time, was equated with the improvement of working conditions for women workers. These models were translated into specific guidelines that states should follow. States started to comply. In addition, the new states that arose as a result of the breakup of the Austria-Hungarian Empire inherited the empire's maternity policies and maintained them. The result was that by then about half of the countries already had this policy; the average number of years it took a country to adopt a maternity policy was fourteen.

With the consolidation of a world polity after World War II the pressures to conform to world conventions and the modular availability of legislative blueprints for women's labor conditions increased. The first wave of decolonization that took place then led to the formation of independent states mainly in Asia. At that point, and following independence, many countries adopted maternity policies, reducing the average length of time it took to adopt new maternity provisions after independence was gained to a mere six years. A significant number of countries implemented those legislative measures right after independence. This tendency increased with the formation of the new African states in the 1960s and 1970s, when the average number of years from independence to legislation was no more than four. In several cases maternity protection was even provided before independence. In these cases it was taken over by the new governments either from the colonial ruler directly or from the quasi-autonomous regime that sometimes existed before full independence.

This phenomenon was not confined to the adoption of maternity policy. Ramirez, Soysal, and Shanahan (1997) report on similar findings regarding the extension of suffrage to women. The more recent a state has gained independence, the shorter the lag between granting men and women suffrage. No country gaining independence after 1945 extended suffrage rights to men solely. Two factors explain this rapid implementation. One relates to certain realities of a time period. That is, nation-states gaining independence at this particular time period were subject to strong pressures to adopt certain kinds of policies. These policies were made available and were channeled through the growing globalization of international conventions. The second aspect relates to the specific state structures and requirements, which made young and peripheral states more susceptible to the adoption of world models, in this case those of women's incorporation into paid employment.

The pressure to adopt a certain model and conformity by nation-states worldwide become even more evident when we examine the content of the maternity policies. The policies tend to include the same components and to grant the same rights and provisions, all following the specific guidelines prescribed in the relevant international documents. The three conventions (the two Maternity Protection Conventions from 1919 and 1952 and the 1952 Social Security Convention) specify exactly the minimum mandatory length of leave, kind of protection from dismissal, rate of cash benefits to be paid, and a demand that nursing breaks should be permitted. Examining an ILO report from 1984 which gives a detailed account of the different policies in 115 countries, one finds a striking similarity (International Labour Office 1984). Almost all countries provide for at least six weeks of postnatal mandatory leave, and only 5 of them do not stipulate that it should be paid leave. In 92 countries there is a protection against dismissal from work at least during the leave (and in many countries also during pregnancy). Seventy-two countries provide for nursing breaks during work, usually fully paid. To be sure, countries differ in regard to the length of leave and the rate of cash benefits. Still, it seems that, in light of differences among countries in terms of economic systems, structure of labor markets, number of births, and the share of women in the workforce, the similarities are striking.

Moreover, in the last two decades this policy has begun to change, and in all countries the changes look alike. Countries have expanded the provisions and applied them to more categories of working women. There is a growing emphasis on medical care before, after, and during childbirth. With only a few exceptions there has been a lengthening of the leave with a loosening up of qualifying conditions and an increase in the sums paid out in maternity benefits. In most countries it exceeds 50 percent of the salary, and in many countries, both developing and developed, it amounts to 100 percent (Brocas, Cailloux, and Oget 1990).

Another notable change has taken place together with the broadening of maternity provisions. When "workers with family responsibilities" replaced the concept of "working mothers" in the global discourse, the notion of parenthood, family, and homemaking which used to be associated exclusively with women's domains had begun to lose its distinctive gendered character. This degendering process found its expression in another novelty. In the 1970s and 1980s several European countries introduced parental care policy. By the late 1980s there were seventeen countries altogether which had adopted this measure: Belgium, Bulgaria, Canada, Denmark, Finland, France, Germany, Greece, Ireland, Italy, Luxembourg, Norway, Poland, Portugal, Spain, Sweden, and Yugoslavia. In Bulgaria and Germany this measure is actually a "care leave," since it is not only parents who can take advantage of it. In Bulgaria it includes the grandparents and in Germany any member of the family who normally looks after the child. In Greece parents can take a paid leave also to visit the child's school and get informed about the child's progress (four days a year). But still, in some countries, parental care is not granted on the same terms as maternity care. In Poland, for example, the father can take the leave only if the mother cannot. In France the father is not entitled to pay for prenatal leave. In Italy it is accompanied with an allowance at a lower rate than maternity leave, and in Belgium this measure applies to the public sector only. Still, one has to bear in mind that this phenomenon did not even exist prior to the 1970s. Following the logic of the argument presented so far, one has seen its diffusion to other parts of the world during the 1990s, especially with the tightening of the linkage between "introducing men into the family" and the campaign "to integrate women on an equal footing with men" into paid employment and to development.

# CHAPTER FIVE

# From *"Mothers of the Race"* to *"Human Resources"*

After World War II a fundamental shift took place in the global discourse regarding the incorporation of women into the public sphere. With the rise of human rights as an international concern and with the triumph of the liberal model of nation-states, in which individual members are granted equal status (formally defined) as citizens, women "lost" their distinctive gendered character. Women's traditionally close association with the domestic sphere began to erode and was no longer a salient issue in debates over participation in the public sphere. The new world model conceives of women as being entitled to rights and access to public institutions as individuals, not as women. In the 1960s and 1970s the emergence of "development" as a global concern added another layer to the global discourse on women. Development became a world project and came to shape much global activity, including that relating to women. It helped further blur the gendered nature of women, who were now constructed as "valuable resources" essential for national development; it augmented and expanded the entire international campaign for women's rights; it incorporated the "women component" into a range of global activities; it led to a bureaucratic expansion of governmental bodies and units designated to deal with women's issues; and it triggered the proliferation of women's movements of all kinds. This fusion of "women" with development, culminating in three United Nations–initiated world conferences—in 1975, 1980, and 1985—also helped put women's issues on the agenda of nation-states to an extent not known before.

In the mid-1960s the discourse of development emerged and became institutionalized, gradually coming to dominate all discussions and activities in the international arena (Chabbott 1999). This shift in the world's agenda was, in a large part, the result of the decolonization process that accelerated during the 1960s. This process had two major consequences that are relevant in the present context. First, it led to the proliferation of nation-states. All new independent territories became organized politically in the same way and, regardless of internal differences, were all defined as nation-states with the desire, and capability, to join world bodies. Becoming officially equal members, they changed the composition of the United Nations and other international bodies and, consequently, world agenda.

Second, many of the new nation-states suffered permanent economic crises, which, for various reasons, became of interest to wealthier countries. Thus, a new issue was defined as a world problem: the growing disparity and economic inequality among countries. The world was now conceived as being composed of "developed" high-income countries and "underdeveloped" low-income countries. The gap between the two became a major concern for the world community to act upon and to remedy. Though the meaning of the term *development* has gone through several changes (Chabbott 1999), in each stage it was conceptualized and defined as being the result of an "unjust" system and thus requiring intervention. The wealthier countries embarked on an ambitious project: to develop the poorer countries. This new "global regime" (e.g., Coate 1982) began to color most activities taking place on the international level. Most world campaigns of the 1960s and 1970s were reshaped by and incorporated into the development discourse. For example, "population control," a highly controversial issue, became a legitimate concern for the United Nations only when framed within the context of development: the argument of "population control for development" increased immensely the number of countries that joined the campaign (Barrett 1995).

A wide range of new bureaucratic agencies, ad hoc bodies, task forces, permanent units, and programs were founded to assist, monitor, and coordinate the various development efforts. A distinct community of transnational organizations was emerging. Chabbott (1999) indicates that from 1900 until 1985 more than two thousand international nongovernmental organizations were founded in addition to thirty UN agencies designated for the sole purpose of investigating and managing development. An overwhelming influx of research and wide-ranging data collection efforts were initiated to assist and inform the decision-making and implementation processes, adding to, modifying, and intensifying links between the various international bodies. The world polity, which had begun to gain coherence in the years following World War II, became increasingly rationalized and consolidated.

Based on the premises of modernization theory (Luke 1991; Manzo 1991), development has become a "central organizing principle" that is fundamental to much of our thinking about the world. It serves as a conceptual grid for interpreting and defining possible solutions to a wide variety of social, economic, and political issues. It also drives and standardizes various national projects for economic and social transformation so that they fit the standard institutional frames for purposes of funding and administration by international agencies (Escobar 1984–85; Ferguson 1993). Understanding the problematic of development and the process of rationalization is thus central to our understanding of both contemporary world culture and nation-states' polities in general and those that pertain to women's issues in particular.

## Woman Power as "Untapped Brains and Skills"

It was a socialist women's nongovernmental organization that was the first to address the issue of "women in developing countries." The International Council of Social Democratic Women (the predecessor of Socialist Women's Organization) discussed it in its annual conference already in 1955. Five years later the United Nations put it on its agenda. The General Assembly adopted a resolution stating that a long-term program or fund be established to meet the special needs of women in developing countries. Before establishing such a program, a study had to be taken to examine the existing conditions and to assess the needs of the target population. In the years to come such research became a standard initial stage in development projects. Indeed, research activities devoted to women's development issues became elaborate projects in and of themselves. But in the 1960s they were still carried out on a relatively small scale. A study done then was titled "Appropriate Measures and Special Assistance" (United Nations 1960). A second study, larger in scale, was carried out to prepare the ground for "a long-term program for the advancement of women, particularly in the developing countries," which surveyed the various technical cooperation programs the UN bodies have undertaken, "with special emphasis on those which may be of interest from the point of view of women" (United Nations 1967). In 1965 the council recommended that countries using technical cooperation programs should give greater priority to projects and programs directed toward the advancement of women. Specialized agencies and international NGOs were asked to cooperate in the effort to "ensure that all technical co-operation experts should be alert to the potential of *woman-power* for national development" (United Nations 1965; emph. added).

Through these technical cooperation programs and various other projects, other UN bodies were brought in and incorporated into the "women's project."

Previously, most of the activities around women, viewed mainly in a human rights context, were dealt with by the UN Commission on the Status of Women (CSW) and the UN Economic and Social Council. The new generation of women-related activities proliferated to numerous other organizations, both in and outside of the United Nations.

Increasingly, the concepts of "woman power" and women's integration into the public sphere (especially into wage labor) took on a new meaning; they came to be seen as a necessary conditions for the economic well-being of society as a whole. This argument reversed the causal order of the idea, previously widely shared, that economic and social development would bring about the desired changes in the status of women. The new theory stated that active steps have to be taken to raise the status of women in order for economic and social development to take place.

This new argument was expressed fully for the first time in a series of resolutions on women workers adopted in 1964 by the International Labour Conference.[1] At that time the ILO, in the name of social progress, justice, and economic efficiency, had already changed its employment policy from one of protection to antidiscrimination. In the 1960s it adopted the development rhetoric as well. The main message of these resolutions was that, since women's employment is vital for the well-being of society and in order to produce greater national income, it is essential that women workers "become integrated in the working population on an equal footing." "It became urgent to take all possible steps to raise the economic and social status of women and to integrate them more closely and effectively into the whole process of developing human resources which is characteristic of our era" (International Labour Conference 1964, 753, 374).

The 1968 Conference on Human Rights in Teheran gave the issue a major boost when it inserted an explicit reference to the "women component" in the International Development Strategy for the Second Development Decade. It was then that the Commission on the Status of Women mobilized as well, abandoning its fears that too much emphasis on economic development might divert attention from its primary goal of achieving equal rights (Tinker 1990).

From that period on "the general need to utilize fully all human resources" became the dominant framework, the rationale for equality, the means for its achievement as well as its indicator. In that context another layer of meaning

---

1. Resolution Concerning Women Workers in a Changing World; Resolution Concerning the Economic and Social Advancement of Women in Developing Countries; Resolution Concerning Part-Time Employment; Resolution Concerning Maternity Protection.

was added to the notion of discrimination. The exclusion of and restrictions on women's participation in the public sphere, especially in the sphere of paid employment, became seen as an "underutilization of human resources" and a source of economic waste. Typical in this respect is the 1967 Declaration on the Elimination of Discrimination against Women, which stated that discrimination against women is not only "incompatible with human dignity" but also "is an obstacle to the full development of the potentialities of women in the service of their countries and humanity" (United Nations 1967). Preventing women from fully contributing to development thus came to be seen as "inadequate recognition and utilization of the potential contribution of women toward national development," resulting in "a considerable waste of human resources" (United Nations 1968, 573).

The Second UN Development Decade contributed significantly to this process, especially when it coincided with the UN Decade for Women (1976–85). While in the first decade "women" were almost completely absent, in the second decade their agenda became highly visible. And, as the development decade colored all other international campaigns, so it reshaped the women's rights one. Also, the timing of the Women's Decade paralleled a shift in the development discourse. In the 1970s a new element was added: nation-states must ensure that development does not exacerbate existing inequalities among various social groups (Chabbott 1999). This new imperative was compatible with the growing concern over women's position. The United Nations adopted a new set of resolutions, based on the 1970 widely publicized survey "The Role of Women in Development," which provided for the creation of "a unified long-term program." The program included the establishment and maintenance of a list of experts and the setting forth of objectives and targets to be achieved during the second development decade. International and national agencies were encouraged to allocate more resources to planning and implementation of development programs for women (United Nations 1972).

In the middle of the Development Decade the United Nations proclaimed 1975 as International Women's Year (IWY). Preparations for IWY began with a massive data collection effort. An ILO committee collected statistical data on women in different economic sectors in all countries and then prepared a special report (*Women Workers in a Changing World*) as part of the discussion of "Equality of Opportunity and Treatment for Women Workers" at the 1975 International Labour Conference. Two major resolutions and a declaration were adopted in that session, all of them dealing with the promotion of equality of opportunities between men and women (International Labour Conference 1975). It is interesting to note that there was no debate about the main themes of these documents. A heated controversy arose regarding one paragraph stating that the establishment of a new international economic and social order would improve work and living conditions for women. It reached a point that intervention by a legal advisor was required. One side of the debate was argued by "first-world" countries, which saw the text as "counterproductive" and motivated by "political and meaningless considerations." They were opposed by "third-world" countries and blamed by them for "being afraid of reality" and for resisting changes to the older, "exploitative order."

For our purposes the debate is crucial not for what was said but, rather, for what was not said. No one disputed the content of the documents that pertains to women. Nobody claimed, as before, that too much attention was being devoted to the "emancipation of women," that equality for women contradicted the well-being of the family or of any other collective. The reverse was true. Women's equality was viewed as compatible with and contributive to the well-being of the family, the community, and the national economy. After these basic axioms were established, other types of disagreements could emerge.

During the years that followed, especially during the Decade for Women, central documents adopted by international bodies expressed a clear causal link between development and women's rights. Note the statement in the document adopted by the 1975 World Conference in Mexico: "The full and complete development of any country requires the maximum participation of women as well as of men in all fields: the under-utilization of the potential of approximately half of the world's population is a serious obstacle to social and economic development."[2] Arguments stating that women's contribution is necessary for the full development of their respective countries and for the world as a whole were reiterated in various documents. One such clear example is provided by the preamble to the most comprehensive convention on women's rights, the 1979 Convention on the Elimination of All Forms of Discrimination: "Recalling that discrimination against women violates the principles of equality of rights and respect for human dignity, is an obstacle to the participation of women, on equal terms with men, in the political, social, economic and cultural life of their countries, hampers the growth of the prosperity of society and the family and makes more difficult the development of the potentiality of women in the service of their countries and of humanity . . . Convinced that the full and complete development of a country, the welfare of the world and the cause of peace require the maximum participation of women on equal terms with men in all fields."

2. Declaration of Mexico on the Equality of Women and Their Contribution to Development and Peace, para. 15.

One of the factors that accounts for the poor economic situation of some countries, so the argument goes, is the low status of their respective women. Women's low status is the result of their restricted access to the labor market. In the contemporary highly interdependent global system the implications of this situation are not confined to the national borders of one country or to the poor countries alone but, rather, affect the whole world. It keeps poor countries in their weak position in the international economy and thus recreates, once again, the uneven distribution of wealth in the world. Thus, raising the status of women will lead to the betterment of their own countries and of the world as a whole.

This argument in some ways resembles the campaign for women's suffrage that took place at the turn of the century. Both movements define women's full participation in the public sphere as essential for the well-being of the whole society. They both emphasized the instrumental argument over the justice argument, seeing equality as a means for higher ends: that of the betterment of society and the world.

But at the turn of the century the granting of political rights to women was justified on the ground that women would make a *distinct* contribution to the welfare of their respective societies. The campaign for suffrage was predicated on the construction of women as being essentially different from men and as having higher ethical standards and superior characteristics. This would make women's contributions, once they were politically equal with men, essential for making a morally better society. Women's suffrage would purify politics, help pass prohibition laws, help abolish state regulation of prostitution, help eliminate wars, and secure peace. These were only a few of the potential implications of women's suffrage envisaged by its proponents. In all cases women's participation in public activities, mainly political, was expected to change and improve the nature of society substantially.

The modern campaign, by contrast, argued for women's participation for its quantitative addition to the pool of resources that are required for full national development. Women, as "half the world's population," are constructed as "workers" and "resources" who differ from men only in their level of training. Resources are either utilized or not; resources have no family responsibilities nor maternal functions to be guarded and protected. In the new rhetoric the wealth of the nation calls for women's working hands and not for their virtue.

Moreover, in the earlier period women's distinct contributions stemmed from their higher moral worth and nurturing capacities cultivated in the domestic sphere. In the modern period the necessary skills for women's contribution are to be acquired through public institutions such as "vocational training" and will be implemented with the help of "technical assistance" (two main themes in all modern global projects). These methods of "women's enhancement" would transform women into beings as capable of yielding production as their male counterparts. This would be possible, in turn, only when women are fully "incorporated into the development process on equal footing with men."

Thus, the "mothers of the race" and the "custodians of the ages" became "human resources." The incorporation of the cause of women into the development discourse, in the context of employment, transformed women as gendered workers who were typically discussed in the context of "family responsibilities" into valuable workers and nongendered resources.

## Development and Bureaucratic Expansion of Women's Issues

Whereas the discourse of the postwar era was expressed mainly in activities such as drafting declarations, publishing resolutions, and holding conventions, most development efforts of the 1970s are expressed in the expansion of bureaucratic activities and proliferation of new bureaucratic bodies. Then, most of the work, shaped within the context of human rights, focused on setting international standards in the form of international conventions. In the 1970s a whole new process was set in motion. "World plans of action" were created, specifying developmental objectives, establishing mechanisms to monitor plan implementation, and initiating development-related research projects of all types. This process eventually led to the establishment of new organizational units to coordinate existing projects and development bodies. This coordination, in turn, required further cooperation among the different international bodies and subsequently resulted in a far more consolidated world polity.

New bureaucratic bodies, projects, mid-term and long-term programs, and multiplicity of research activities have replaced the conventions and declarations. No convention that concerned women has been adopted by the United Nations since 1966 (when the International Covenant on Civil and Political Rights was adopted) other than the 1979 *Convention on the Elimination of All Forms of Discrimination against Women* (CEDAW). All international conventions were adopted during the 1950s and 1960s. Also much of the global activity surrounding women's issues up until the 1970s was confined to a few designated bodies and ad hoc committees of experts initially created to draft the declarations and conventions and coordinated mostly by the Commission on the Status of Women. With the shift in emphasis the commission lost its central role and declined in importance. Its involvement in the work of women and development was only peripheral (Reanda 1992). Very telling in that respect is the fact that it was not charged with the preparation of the first two UN world conferences and played a relatively minor role in the UN Decade for Women, all of them major events with far-reaching implications.

The first event was the proclamation of the IWY. The idea came from outside the UN system. Pietila and Vickers (1990) refers to "an oral tradition in the U.N. family" that identifies the Women's International Democratic Federation (WIDF) as the source of the proposal for an International Women's Year. Initially, there was skepticism. The doubts echoed those that had accompanied the establishment of the Commission on the Status of Women: should women's issues be singled out and treated as a separate issue? Yet, despite initial resistance, the assembly eventually endorsed the idea and proclaimed 1975 as International Women's Year. At first no conference was guaranteed. Only with the repeated efforts of relatively powerful women, like Helvi Sipila, the first woman assistant secretary-general to the United Nations, the General Assembly conceded. Still, no regular UN funds were allocated for this effort (Tinker 1990).

The first world conference on women took place in Mexico City with the themes of equality, development, and peace.[3] Equality was the theme promoted mainly by the First World, peace was included after pressure by the Second World, and development was very much the concern of the Third World. One hundred and thirty-three states participated in the conference, designating the 1976–85 period as the UN Decade for Women and endorsing two major documents: *The Mexico Declaration* and the 1975 *World Plan of Action*. The *World Plan of Action* was the first major document to rationalize and bureaucratize world activity for women in a substantive way. It specified minimum goals to be achieved by the end of the first five-year period and designated specific domains for national, regional, and international action. It also emphasized the need to establish specific targets and to set up procedures for monitoring the progress made in meeting those targets.

Representatives from 145 countries attended the 1980 Mid-Decade Conference held in Copenhagen, convened as a "mid-point review of progress and obstacles in achieving the goals of the Decade," and adopted a "Programme of Action." The end of the decade was marked by the 1985 Nairobi World Conference, the second largest world conference ever, attended by representatives from 157 countries. The conference adopted a document entitled *Nairobi Forward-Looking Strategies for the Advancement of Women* (FLS).

The FLS document differs from previous such documents in several respects. Stienstra (1994) points out that, while the Mexico Plan of Action was a

---

3. The following overview is based on *Yearbook of the United Nations* from relevant years. For more detailed accounts of the meetings, see Stienstra 1994.

"shopping list of women's issues," the FLS offers an analytical approach, much broader in scope and much more feminist in orientation. But the differences are even larger when we consider the image of the total mobilization of global society which emerges from this document. Every sector, domain, and area is to be covered by rationalized plans that will include goals, subgoals, means and procedures, and a timetable, with special bodies to consult, implement, and monitor programs, all of which are to be supported by appropriate data and statistics based on new concepts and methods. According to the document, this activity must be carried out at all levels, from the national level down to the most remote village, family, and neighborhood. The activity was envisioned as being supported by a major public relations campaign to be carried out through the mass media, educational programs, and new curricula, with the express intent of changing the attitudes and perceptions of individuals and policy makers. According to the spirit of the Nairobi document, each and every existing policy and program employed by international, regional, and national bodies must be evaluated and changed to fit the new goals and guidelines.

These events, including the nonofficial conferences that were held in conjunction with the official ones, were highly consequential with respect to the quantity and quality of global attention to women. From the 1970s on, the women's component was incorporated into World Plans of Action and a diverse array of projects covering a wide range of domains. It was typically accompanied by the establishment of a new organizational unit and a new rhetoric that elaborated upon different aspects of the relation between women and development. Topics such as women's presence and potential contribution to development (usually claimed to be underestimated and/or mismeasured) and the implication of development for women's situation are an integral part of the rhetoric that legitimizes the entire project.

Note, for example, how the environment became a gender issue. The UN Environment Program (UNEP) stated that since "a major burden of the environmental crisis in most developing countries [has fallen] . . . on women . . . an improvement in their status would bring added emphasis to the environmental cause" (United Nations 1985, 944). In that way the environment turned out to be relevant to women's life, and global attention to women's life came to affect the environmental campaign. Similar statements and projects were also initiated in other domains. The 1974 World Food Conference recognized that the world food situation could not be improved without full integration of women into development policies (Pietila and Vickers 1990, 75). In the same year the "Women's Amendment" was included in the *World Population Plan of*

*Action* (Barrett 1995). Other such areas were science and technology, old age, racial discrimination, refugees, energy, and international trade. In each area the women's component started to feature in the documents, plans, and programs produced by respective organizations.

This was the first time that any reference had been made to women in most of these areas. In others the previously existing treatment of women's issues has changed as a result, reflecting the transformation in conceptions regarding gender relations and the family. In the field of women's health, for example, the World Health Organization (WHO) used to take into consideration only women's role as mothers when creating projects and studies targeted for women. In the 1980s the link between women's health and development started to color most of the WHO's women-related activities, and maternal health issues became only one topic among many affecting women.

As in other organizations, this focus on development led to greater attention being paid to women's issues, including the establishment of a designated unit for women's affairs—a Multidisciplinary Working Group. Also, more space was devoted to women's health issues in WHO's publications. A review of *World Health*, WHO's official (monthly) magazine, reveals a substantial increase in the amount of space devoted to women. In the period between the early 1950s and 1975 *World Health* published only two issues focusing on women.[4] Between 1975 and 1985, however, five issues were dedicated to the health situation of women in the world.[5]

A nonsystematic review of these issues hints at a change also in the topics that were considered relevant to women's health. A new element introduced into the debate was a comparison between health services and resources directed to men and to women and between the "health status" of men and women. Women's health and health services, no longer considered only in reference to their maternal functions, were now seen as measurable and were expected to improve until they matched those of men. This new focus is similar to the shift that took place in labor legislation for women. As I have shown with respect to employment laws, the transition from protective legislation (typically, laws providing similar protection to women and children) to equal pay (for men and women) indicated that the notion "women and children" has been replaced by that of

4. "Women in White," Sept.–Oct. 1969; "Women and Work," Jan. 1971.
5. "International Women's Year," Jan. 1975; "Mexico: International Women's Year," June 1975; "Decade for Women, 1976–85," Aug. 1976; "Women, Health, and Development," June 1976; "Women: The Next Ten Years," Apr. 1985.

"women and men." In both areas a shift took place from legislation and services that put women and children in the same frame of reference to one that equates the situation of adult women with that of adult men.

The ILO, in addition to the shift in emphasis, also set up for the first time, in 1976, an official permanent body—the ILO's Office for Women Workers' Questions—which replaced the previous ad hoc expert bodies. In 1977 the International Bank for Reconstruction and Development appointed an advisor on Women and Development. The UN Industrial Development Organization announced in 1986 the creation of a Unit for the Integration of Women in Industrial Development (UNIDO). In the same year it issued a set of detailed guidelines that "would help increase the ability of staff to consider, as a matter of routine, women specific concerns in all phases of projects and promotional activities" (UNIDO 1989, 2).

In addition to designated units within existing bodies, two major autonomous organizations were established within the UN system: the International Research and Training Institute for the Advancement of Women (INSTRAW) and the UN Development Fund for Women (UNIFEM), originally under the name the Voluntary Fund for Women. UNIFEM was initially intended to operate during the Decade for Women only, but, as in the case of many other ad hoc organizations founded in the context of the decade, it became a permanent body. It has an autonomous status and works in conjunction with the UN Development Program (UNDP).

The establishment of INSTRAW signified a major step in the process of rationalization and scientization accompanying the 1970s international campaign for women. It augmented, and carried much further, the already existing emphasis on data collection. The Commission on the Status of Women repeatedly stressed in its meetings that there was an urgent need to enhance research and data collection. Over and over again in the various documents adopted in the three world conferences the need for improved methods and better data was emphasized. Such improvement can be gained by obtaining breakdowns by sex for a number of indicators that were already in use and through formulating new indicators to measure women's actual contributions inside and outside of official national data collection systems. A link was established between elimination of discrimination and the existence of reliable data banks and the usage of appropriate measures. Early on, the data collection project was supposed to be implemented in cooperation with existing research agencies (the Statistical Commission, the Research Institute for Social Development, and regional commissions), national statistical officers, and INGOs (United Nations 1976). In

1979, however, it was decided that a new organization whose sole purpose would be to focus on research, information, documentation, and communication—the International Research and Training Institute for the Advancement of Women—would be created.

The new organization was expected to improve measurement methods, promote "standardized terms of reference, and "develop harmonized data collection" (United Nations 1981). Its projects included repeated modification of the reporting system by nations-states to the CSW. This modification resulted each time in a more rational and more standard method. In 1985 alone INSTRAW held five workshops and seminars with the UN regional economic commissions, the statistical office, and the UN University (United Nations 1985). All of its publication focus on formulating appropriate measurements of women's activity and ways for analyzing women's participation in development. The titles of these publications are extremely telling—for example, *Methods for Measuring Women's Participation and Production in the Informal Sector, Selected Guidelines and Checklists for Women in Development, Classifying Women's Activities,* and *Improving Concepts and Methods for Statistics and Indicators on the Situation of Women.*

The motivation behind the formation of INSTRAW, its activities, and the texts it produced constitute a clear representation of the assumptions underlying the conceptual and organizational link between development and women, especially in the ways in which it produces and organizes knowledge about women, using the conceptual grid of development as its organizing principle (see also Mueller 1986).

Each international document that was adopted during the 1970s and 1980s contributed to the process of broadening and rationalizing the production of women-related data. There was a need for further data collection to monitor and appraise their implementation. The most notable example is the Committee on the Elimination of Discrimination against Women, which was created to monitor the implementation of the 1979 convention. This committee gained a central position in regard to women's rights within the UN system (Jacobson 1992).

Another example of how rationalized this project can get is the forty-four-page detailed guide for *Assessing the Status of Women,* published in 1988 by the International Women's Rights Action Watch. And the 1985 FLS resulted in numerous studies that used its objectives as a reference point. The General Assembly and the Economic and Social Council often initiated studies on women. The new genre of studies can be characterized as "multisectoral" and "interdisciplinary." It replaced the more focused, one-domain studies of the past (e.g., on the economic situation or nationality rights).

Women's international nongovernmental organizations dedicated time, energy, and resources for the purpose of data collection as well. Out of a total of about two hundred women's INGOs, approximately forty organizations are engaged in some form of information-gathering and/or research activities. Many of them maintain data banks of various sorts and provide information services for other, governmental and nongovernmental bodies. The overwhelming majority of them were founded during the Decade for Women. Thus, information and data gathering, among other research activities, have themselves turned into an enormous project, not as a means but, rather, as an essential part of the solution itself. Producing more standardized knowledge in a rationally planned and monitored way has been one of the main contributions of the modern campaign on women's issues—women in development—to the world.

Note that the processes described here are mutually constituting. Women's status is defined as a problem at the global level, giving rise to an elaborate series of documents and organizational mechanisms set up to collect data to verify the existence of the problem and to measure the progress of nation-states in rectifying the problem (Berkovitch and Bradley 1994).

Prior to the 1970s the notion of "women's rights" did not gain much currency within the regional organizational system. The contemporary campaign, framed as "women in development," infiltrated the existing regional infrastructure and reached areas and mobilized countries that perhaps would not have responded otherwise. In the 1970s and 1980s we witness an expansion of *women* across the board to include most of the various official (governmental) regional organizations.[6] UN- and non–UN-affiliated organizations adopted new documents, reformulated existing ones, founded new organizations, and added new units, offices, and functions to already established ones. Yet the process of reaching out and the ways in which the different regional organizations responded to and participated in the women's campaign differed in terms of degree as well in organizational and discursive framework.

The first special program for women was established in Africa in 1971 by the UN Economic Commission for Africa. Four years later the African Training and Research Center for Women (ATRCW) and the African Women's Development Task Force were established. ATRCW is an autonomous unit that func-

6. The data for this review were collected mainly from Taubenfeld Falk and Taubenfeld (1983) and Union of International Associations, various years.

tions as the regional Women-in-Development (WID) structure of the UN system in Africa. It was designed to mediate between governments and women in the framework of development, to assist African countries in developing machinery, and to meet the needs of women in national and project plans. Also in 1975, the fifth ILO African Regional Conference adopted a report calling for the integration of women into development by abolishing all forms of discrimination. In 1979 another bureaucratic layer was added with the formation of a subsidiary to the Economic Commission for Africa, the African Regional Coordinating Committee for the Integration of Women in Development. Its aim was to coordinate and integrate all the subregional programs on women.

Non-UN-affiliated bodies joined as well. The Organization of African Unity, established in 1963, did not concern itself with women's issues until 1975, when it declared that it was endorsing the International Women's Year and urged all member states to intensify women's involvement in the development of their countries. Today it cooperates on various projects with UNIFEM and the UN Commission on the Status of Women. Other African governmental organizations include women's issues in their policies (e.g., the African Development Bank) and/or have established permanent contacts or official links with the UN Commission on the Status of Women (e.g., the African National Congress and the Southern African Management Institute).

In contrast to Africa, Asia did not develop an elaborate network of regional organizations. Also, its central organization—the Association of South East Asian Nations (ASEAN)—founded in 1967, was hardly involved in the Decade for Women activities. Still, the 1976 ASEAN Concord Declaration, though concerned mainly with political and economic matters, devoted one section to its support for the "active involvement of women in all sectors and levels of the ASEAN community."

The United Nations established several economic commissions in Asia, all of which "discovered" women during the decade. The Commission for Asia and the Far East expanded its Action Programs at the regional and country levels by incorporating plans and procedures for the "advancement of women." The Commission for Asia and the Pacific (ESCAP) adopted in 1975 several resolutions on the integration of women in national development, and the basic principles were formulated in the Regional Plan of Action for the Enhancement of the Role of Women in Development. In 1977 it founded the Asian and Pacific Centre for Women and Development for the purpose of encouraging member governments of ESCAP to undertake further research on women's development issues and to establish training programs. In 1986 the Women's International

Network for Asia and the Pacific was founded, also with an emphasis on research and data collection to supply information required by government policy makers and donor agencies as well as by researchers and the general public.

The activities of the Arab regional organizations present an interesting illustration of the combination of values such as the family, motherhood, and Islam with global notions of equality and women's rights. The balance between these sets of concerns shifted over time. In the 1960s there was only minor attention paid to women's issues. The Charter of the Arab Cultural Unity of 1964 contained only one reference to women. It stated that women's education should be promoted in accordance with religious principles while taking into consideration the woman's "message to be a mother and a good citizen . . . with the rights and duties which go alongside with her responsibilities in the society."

In 1971 the League of Arab States (founded in 1945) established the Commission on the Status of Arab Women under its Department of Social Affairs. It is interesting to note that there are several accounts for the origin of the commission. One version says that it was the initiative of the 1968 Conference of Arab Ministers of Labour which called upon the Arab League to set up a permanent committee on the status of women (United Nations 1973). Another document refers to the Inter-American Commission on the Status of Women as a source of inspiration (CIM 1974). A third account attributes the decision to form such a commission to the efforts of women's associations in Egypt, which were reported to have first introduced the notion into the league (Elwan 1974).

The mandate and activities of the commission indicate a shift toward "citizenship" and gaining rights, though still in the name of motherhood. The primary objective of the commission was "the realization of the equality of men and women in all spheres of life." The preamble to the basic statutes adopted in its first session, reaffirmed the principles of the UN Charter and the Universal Declaration of Human Rights and those embodied in the 1979 Convention on Elimination of Discrimination against Women. At the same time, it also expressed a more functional view of complementary gender relations than one might find in other documents: "men and women are partners in life and destiny and . . . they must share together in the creation of life on the basis of co-operation and equality" (United Nations 1973, 3). In 1972, in cooperation with UNICEF, it held a conference entitled "Arab Women and National Development" which called upon Arab governments to set up consultative committees on the status of women, to follow up on agreements concerning women's rights, and to act as a link between their respective governments and the Commission on the Status of Arab Women (Elwan 1974).

In 1975 the Arab Labour Organization (ALO)[7] adopted Arab Convention no. 5, Concerning Women at Work, which advocated strong protective measures. Alongside provisions such as that factories employing women must provide seating facilities, it also advanced the "principle of equality of male and female workers in placement, remuneration and working conditions, [and] the right to professional training and promotion." Only Iraq and occupied Palestine ratified the convention (Taubenfeld Falk 1983).

In 1979, for the first time, the non-aligned countries devoted a conference to the role of women in development. The conference adopted a wide-ranging plan—the Baghdad Program of Action—to be submitted to the World Conference in Copenhagen in 1980. The program recommended that member states adopt all measures necessary to remove obstacles obstructing women's involvement in all aspects of development. Also, the Conference of the Heads of States of Non-aligned Countries devoted a chapter to the role of women in development in an economic declaration that was adopted in 1983 (International Labour Office 1983[1]).

In contrast to Africa, and like the Arab countries, most of the work related to women in the European context is not linked, organizationally, to the UN system. Still, action in Europe for the promotion of women started to be taken in the mid-1970s and spread throughout the European system during the 1980s.

The 1957 Treaty of Rome—the document that established the European Community—endorsed the principle of equal wages (art. 119). This part of the treaty was never implemented by member states, however, and remained dead for years. In the early 1970s it was reactivated by three court cases that resulted in rulings by the European Court of Justice stating, for the first time, that the article was binding on member states (Hoskyns 1992). A further step was made in 1974, when the EEC announced its Social Action Program, in which three Equality Directives were adopted and a direct reference to women's rights was made explicit. These directives extended the notion of equal pay to include equality in regard to other aspects of employment. They have been complemented in the 1980s by two additional directives—referring to equal treatment in regard to social security plans and to self-employed pregnant workers—further extending the notion of equality in employment (Byre 1988; Douchen 1992). The importance of these directives stems from the fact that the European

7. The Arab Labour Organization (ALO) was founded in 1965 and was confirmed in 1970 as a specialized agency on labor and work. It is interesting to note that, although the ALO does not report cooperation or links with the International Labour Organization, its publications significantly resemble those of the ILO.

Community law is just as binding on member states as are their individual national laws, and in any case of a conflict between national and EEC law the latter takes precedence over the former. In order to promote, coordinate, and monitor the implementation of these directives, the EEC established a Women's Employment Bureau in 1976 and set up a Woman's Information Bureau (Docksey 1987; Vallance and Davies 1986).

The European Parliament (founded in 1958) got involved as well. In 1979 it established an ad hoc committee to prepare a debate on the situation of women in Europe. Following the debate, two permanent bodies were established. In addition, a network of independent experts, lawyers, trade unionists, and academics drawn from all member states was formed to monitor the implementation of the directives. A New Community Action Program on the Promotion of Equal Opportunity for Women, for 1982–85, was adopted. Whereas the 1974 Social Action Program had made only minor references to women, the new one specifically targeted women. Consequently, other bodies such as the Organization for Economic Cooperation and Development (OECD) and the European Trade Union Confederation established committees, held conferences, and developed programs that followed the guidelines laid down in the social action programs (Vallance and Davies 1986).

This overview of the regional activities on women's issues is not intended to suggest that all regions have joined the international campaign for women's rights with the same degree of enthusiasm. Clearly, there has been regional variation with respect to the extent and patterns of participation in world events as well as in the implementation of their principles. Yet, while recognizing the variations, it is important to realize the similarities: most of the main regional organizations did join the campaign, they did so around the same time, and all initiated similar bureaucratic steps.

## The Emergence of Global Sisterhood

During the Decade for Women international women's groups' membership, agenda, and ways of organizing have changed dramatically. With the intensification, proliferation, and expanding agenda of official world bodies, nongovernmental organizations have responded by increasing their numbers dramatically, developing new structures, dealing with new issues, and changing their geographical representation. The UN conferences were a main arena for, and key trigger of, these changes.

Much larger and richer nonofficial meetings were held in conjunction with the official UN conferences. These conferences were organized and attended by individual women and women's groups from all over the world: four thousand participants at the 1975 IWY Tribune in Mexico City, seven thousand at the 1980 NGO Forum in Copenhagen, and a remarkable fourteen thousand at the 1985 Non-Governmental World Conference of Women, Forum '85, in Nairobi.[8] Also, in 1976, in response, and in clear opposition to the UN meetings in Mexico City, an International Tribunal on Crimes against Women was held in Brussels, attended by two thousand women.

Overall these events were highly consequential with respect to women's movements in individual countries and with respect to international organizing. The conferences conducted workshops, discussion groups, lectures, and informal gatherings, bringing national and international women's groups together to make connections, initiate joint projects, exchange ideas, and form new organizations. They enabled women from all over the world to meet and realize the dividing lines that exist between them as well as to create shared understanding, which encouraged cooperation for present and future activities. They helped develop a sense of solidarity while also providing an arena in which different groups (re)discovered the wide gaps separating them. In that sense these world gatherings helped shape and reshape the women's movement, mapping its internal conflicts and setting the parameters for divergence and controversy within a framework of universal similarity and shared value commitments (Berkovitch 1999).

Whereas the first two conferences in Mexico City and in Copenhagen were dominated by women from North America and Europe, the scene had changed in 1985. In Nairobi the presence of women of color from the North and women from the South was highly visible and influential (*South* and *North* have replaced *developing* and *developed countries*). Their growing numbers and active participation clearly helped shape the agenda. The 1975 and, even more so, the 1980 conferences were highly conflictual to a point that some raised doubts about the possible benefits to be gained from these world gatherings (see the lively debate in *Signs* 1980–81, 6[3], 6[4], 7[4]; and 1982, 8[2]). The controversy revolved around the question of what constitutes women's issues. Women from the South insisted that economic exploitation and political oppression of their peoples and regions should be part of the agenda. Women from the North argued, however, that these are "men's issues" and, as such, are irrelevant to the

---

8. These conferences were documented extensively elsewhere. See Ashworth 1982; Barnard 1987; Bunch 1987; Bunch and Carrillo 1990; Eisler and Loye 1985; Hendessi 1986; Papanek 1975; Whitaker 1975; also *Signs* 1, no. 1 (1975); 6, no. 3 (1980–81); 6, no. 4 (1980–81); 7, no. 4 (1981–82); 8, no. 2 (1982); 11, no. 3 (1986).

feminist cause. The former argued that the oppression that resulted from apartheid and Zionism were an integral part of oppressive sexism, while the latter denounced this argument as an unnecessary and damaging "politicization" of women's issues, as succumbing to men's politics instead of maintaining a distinct feminist agenda. In the 1980 conference in Copenhagen another issue divided the movement. A highly charged conflict around the issue of female genital mutilation arose when feminists from countries where this practice is common objected to the ways it was characterized and used by Western feminists: "Third World women felt that as First World women promoted the issue, it seemed to establish a hierarchical relationship to their Third World sisters through intellectual neocolonialism" (Gilliam 1991, 218).

"How do you take one tune and encourage variation while at the same time eliciting orchestral support?" (Tinker 1980–81, 532). This question crystallized the burning issue of the movement: the relations between commonality, difference, and appropriate strategy. It was raised in 1981 after the Copenhagen conference and was echoed in much of the literature that followed the meeting. One possible answer was given in the 1985 conference in Nairobi. This conference exhibited a different spirit, one that was more consistent with a rephrasing of the earlier question: "Once we have the orchestra, how can we arrange the variations to play not one tune but a symphony?" (Arizpe 1981–82, 715). There was a growing sense of mutual understanding, recognition of both commonality and difference, and willingness to maintain a dialogue. The agenda broadened to include issues such as survival, provision of basic needs, and racism, alongside more traditional Western feminist issues (see various articles in *Signs* 1986; and Eisler and Loye 1985). This is not to say that all conflicts have been resolved and disappeared. The reverse is true. In addition to old controversies such as those regarding imperialism and national liberation struggles, new ones have emerged. Such was the conflict between black American women and African women, between those who advocated the need for an autonomous women's movement and those who saw their cause tied to other struggles. There were also heated debates on the positions of lesbianism and prostitution (Hendessi 1986). Also, many have challenged the notion of "global sisterhood" as expressing century-old imperialist tendencies of white, patronizing feminism (Amos and Parmer 1984; Bulbeck 1988). Still, it seems that the new understanding that has emerged is capable of surviving these new divisions.

With the growing diversification of the international movement's agenda came a similar change in its organizational form. Throughout the first half of the nineteenth century most of the women's groups had a permanent formal structure, hierarchical in character, with headquarters and a main constituency located mainly in the North. Since the establishment of the United Nations, and particularly during the Decade for Women, these organizations focused their activities on the United Nations and its affiliated bodies, working as lobbying groups. In the 1970s, as Steinstra (1994) points out, a new type of organization emerged. These new organizations were more feminist in orientation and more innovative in structure and activity. Many of them did not maintain a standard bureaucratic infrastructure but, rather, employed a network form, nor did they have members in the conventional sense. Their headquarters and the majority of their constituencies were located in the South.

These organizations put on the agenda new issues such as environmental concerns (e.g., World Women in the Environment), genital mutilation (e.g., Inter-African Committee of Traditional Practices affecting the Health of Women and Children in Africa), and reproductive rights (Women's Global Network for Reproductive Rights); they reshaped and radicalized old issues such as the sexual exploitation of women (International Feminist Network against Prostitution and Other Forms of Forced Slavery) and peace (International Resistance of Women against War), and they pointed at the gendered implications of old issues such as health (e.g., International Council on Women's Health Issues) and communication (Fempress), all framed and enacted within a conscious feminist orientation.

The main framework within which most of the new organizations operated was development. But, unlike the UN bodies, aid agencies, and established women's organizations, the new bodies offer criticism of existing theories and provide alternative approaches (e.g., Development Alternative with Women for a New Era [DAWN]). Their approach is that of "empowerment of women," emphasizing the need for fundamental social transformation (Marchand and Parpart 1995; Moser 1993).

This transformation in the type and content of activities was accompanied by an immense increase in the number of new women's organizations established during the Decade for Women. Throughout a period of 110 years, from 1875 to 1985, more than two hundred women's international nongovernmental organizations have been founded. It is striking that 40 percent of them were created during the UN Decade for Women (1975–85). The rest (60 percent) were founded during the one hundred years that preceded the decade.

Table 4 shows the number of new women's organizations by time period.[9] During the first period (1875–1914) 22 such organizations were created (an average of 0.6 organization per year). After a sharp decline during the years of

9. For a full list of organizations, founding dates, and data sources, see Berkovitch 1994, app. 1.

TABLE 4
*Number of New Women's INGOs Formed, by Time Period*

| Time Period | | No. of New Women's INGOs |
|---|---|---|
| Until World War I | 1875–1914 | 22 |
| Interwar era | 1915–39 | 38 |
| Post–World War II until UN Decade for Women | 1940–74 | 59 |
| UN Decade for Women | 1975–85 | 80 |

the war, a swift recovery brought the number of new women's organization in the second period (1915–39) to 38 (an average of 1.6 per year). Immediately after World War II ended, there was a big jump, soon to be offset during the late 1950s and 1960s, when the number of new organizations declined (not shown here). In some years only one new organization was created, while in others none were formed. Altogether, in the years 1940 to 1974, 59 new women's international organizations were founded (an average of 1.7 per year). Note that these were the years in which much of the effort was devoted to setting international standards for nation-states in the form of conventions and declarations, a kind of global activity that did not involve significant organizational expansion. The biggest surge for founding of women's INGOs took place in the 1970s. The rate started to accelerate in 1975 and was sustained until 1985, the end of the period under investigation. In some years 13 organizations per year were created. Altogether, more than 80 new organizations were founded during these ten years, bringing the average figure to more than 8.[10]

The pattern of founding of women's organizations cannot be seen as merely a part of expansion of general world organizational activities, following the pattern of proliferation of INGOs in general. Until the 1950s the two exhibit a similar trend. Yet the peak for general INGOs took place after World War II, and the high rate has held steady and not declined since (Boli and Thomas 1997). The founding of women's organizations declined during the 1950s and 1960s and rose sharply in the 1970s. These changes reflect events that are unique to the women's rights campaign and its changing forms. More specifically, the United Nations–initiated activities that incorporated development into the discourse on women's rights and the three world conferences are the major sources for the proliferation of women's organizations.

Looking closer at some of the women's organizations founded in the 1970s

10. The figures for this period are less accurate than for earlier ones, since many of the new organizations did not follow the conventional mode of organizing.

can tell us more about the circumstances leading to their creation. Many of them were formed as a result and in response to the UN conferences. One such example is the African Women Task Force, formed in 1985, which was charged with establishing an institutional means for collective African NGO efforts to pursue the implementation of the 1985 Nairobi plan. In 1988 the task force fulfilled its mandate by establishing the African Women Development and Communication Network (FEMNET). Other examples are the International Women Tribune Center, which was created in Mexico in 1975, and the International Women's Rights Watch, which was founded in Nairobi in 1985 as a result of workshops on the Convention on the Elimination of All Forms of Discrimination. Other organizations that were formed with the specific aim of promoting the IWY and/or the UN Decade for Women are the Women's International Network (1975), the Asian Women Institute (1975), the Caribbean Women and Development Unit (1978), and the International Committee of African Women for Development (1985). In some cases the UN agencies themselves founded nongovernmental bodies, indicating the blurring of boundaries between official and nonofficial organizations. For example, during the 1975 Mexico conference UNESCO and UNFPA founded an information network on women and population, the Women's' Feature Service. Within this framework in 1980 UNESCO created the Arab Women's Feature Service.[11]

During this period many existing women's organizations were integrated into the "women in development" campaign. Many became involved in activities such as awarding fellowships to women from developing countries, organizing seminars, initiating regional projects, and contributing funds to UN bodies for technical assistance programs.[12] These activities led to the reinforcement of linkages and cooperation with the various UN special agencies involved in development activities, adding more layers and coherence to the overall global effort for the sake of women, rights, and development.

Overall, this massive mobilization of a wide range of global bodies—international and regional, governmental and nongovernmental—have produced a long list of resolutions, plans of action, projects, organizational units, and agencies, all of which have reflected and enacted the new model of women—a category of productive persons now free of much of their previous gendered charac-

11. Data for this review were drawn from *Union of International Associations* (various years). See also Steinstra 1994. Elsewhere I report a lower number, because I include mostly the conventional organizations (Berkovitch 1999).

12. See United Nations 1966, for a comprehensive review of various development projects that were incorporated into the regular activities of women's organizations.

terization. This campaign, promoting the rhetoric of women in development and producing a new notion of womanhood, was highly consequential in terms of its effect on national action and state's structure.

## Women as a State Concern

In the earlier period, during the 1950s and 1960s, when world action regarding women was involved mainly in standard setting and was expressed in the adoption of international conventions dealing with women's rights in various areas of public life, world actors called on nation-states to ratify these conventions and to modify their national legislation and labor codes accordingly. And indeed, as I have shown in chapter 4, as far as economic rights are concerned, the majority of countries have responded and modified their labor laws to take account of the new model of working women.

During the 1970s and 1980s, when the discourse on development intersected with that on women, transnational organizations started to articulate and promote a new specific model of state action regarding women. This model was based on the notion that women's status ought to be the concern of national policy and included a detailed "how to" set of instructions specifying the appropriate ways to make women a national concern; these instructions pointed at the character that this new "social problem" should have as well as the ways it should be rectified. These instructions specified the formation of designated state bureaucracies (dubbed "national machinery for the advancement of women") as an essential step in the overall project which were sometimes followed by material help from aid agencies aimed at creating and/or strengthening such machineries. And nation-states responded en masse.

The idea was first brought up by the Commission on the Status of Women in 1963 within the context of establishing a long-term program for the advancement of women. Since then, and more so in the late 1960s and during the Decade for Women, the issue was on the agenda of the Commission and the Economic and Social Council almost every year. Nation-states that had not yet established such machinery were encouraged to do so, and it was suggested that existing machinery be strengthened, that national machineries be given enough authority and resources, that such machinery be given an appropriate central location within the state structure, and that effective links to national planning units and other government departments be established (see, e.g., United Nations 1980).

All documents that were adopted during the three world conferences, as well as the plans of action, devoted much space to this issue. They specified the requisite action to be taken on the international, regional, and national levels for the creation of a unified, all-encompassing organizational apparatus in which state bureaucracies are assigned a pivotal role. All sectors of society are expected to go through a major transformation in order to enable the "full incorporation of women," and the machineries serve as "focal points" for the initiation and coordination of all related activities and "to ensure the effective implementation and evaluation of the World Plan of Action."

Establishing such state bodies was supposed to indicate whether or not "governments have in fact translated into action their willingness and commitment to integrate women in national life through the modalities of national machineries" (INSTRAW 1980, 5). At the same time, reports submitted to the UN Committee on Elimination of Discrimination against Women and various case studies include this piece of information as an indicator of the status of women. Thus, these machineries were viewed as an essential means for improving the status of women, and, at the same time, their existence became in and of itself an indicator for women's status. Either way, establishing such bureaucracy has gained a globally evaluated symbolic meaning.

The rapid response of nations-states is striking. The 1970s and 1980s witnessed a massive, global proliferation of different state agencies expressly created to deal with "advancing the status of women" and "incorporating women into development" to a degree that such agencies became a standard feature of almost all nation-states.[13] By 1992 almost all countries (a total of 153) reported the creation of at least one, and in most cases several, women-oriented agencies. Only 15 countries had failed to create such an agency.[14] Thus, having an official unit for women's affairs seems to be a standard feature of most contemporary governments.

There are two types of state offices designated to deal with women's issues. The first one was aimed at protecting women (usually with children). It was usually located within the labor department and dealt mainly with protective labor legislation. The United States was the first to do so, in 1920. This type gained some currency during the 1940s and 1950s, but it did not proliferate worldwide. It was a practice associated with a specific type of country—the

13. Finnemore (1993) describes a similar dynamic in her research on the proliferation of science policy bureaucracies.

14. For a full list of machineries in the different countries, see Berkovitch 1994, app. 6. The countries with no machineries are: Albania, Bahrain, Burma, Cayman Islands, Comoros, Monaco, Namibia, Nauru, Saudi Arabia, Singapore, South Africa, Tonga, Tuvalu, and Yemen.

Latin American and the European Socialist—both of which had an elaborate set of protective measures in place. By now less than thirty countries have established such protective state offices.

In the 1960s a new type of state designated unit has emerged—a unit that was charged with the "advancement/promotion" of the status of women. We can learn more about how it proliferated from the fact that by 1992—that is, in a period of thirty years—it existed in 123 countries. The overwhelming majority of countries around the world have established bodies—a commission, advisory boards, councils—whose explicit mission is to ensure women's rights, and almost all of them did so during the UN Decade for Women.

A common state method for establishing a special unit for the promotion of women has been the creation of an ad hoc committee, typically for the purpose of conducting research and publishing a report on the status of women in the context of the IWY or the UN Decade. Over time many of the ad hoc commissions became permanent agencies. Once such a unit has been put in place, it is likely both to expand and to lead to the formation of new "equality" machinery. Despite a few exceptions (see United Nations 1987), it seems that the overall process is one of rapid expansion and institutionalization within the state apparatus.

This is not to say that everywhere these state bureaucracies assume the same form or that they operate in the same way and affect state policy to the same extent. An abundance of studies proves otherwise (INSTRAW 1980; Ooko-Ombaka 1980; Stetson and Mazur 1995; United Nations 1991). Also, the context in which these organizations were established varies significantly, depending on internal processes and specific conditions in the individual countries. My argument is that internal differences account for the variation in content and actual action taken by these state bureaucracies, whereas external pressures trigger the very formation of these bodies. The following examples show how existing global models provide useful tools for different political purposes. The women's commissions in Poland and in Greece were formed as part of larger democratization processes (Kaplan 1992). In Pakistan, on the other hand, the 1979 establishment of a Women's Division within the Cabinet Secretariat coincided with strong Islamization processes (Jalal 1991). In Bangladesh a coup d'état that brought Zia ur-Rahman to power coincided with the 1975 declaration of the UN Decade for Women. Ur-Rahman built up considerable political capital by championing the causes of women, and in 1978 the Bangladesh Ministry of Women was created. Democratization, Islamization, and co-optation are all very different processes. They can account for differences in the authority, mandate, and resources available to the different state agencies. Yet, unless global processes are considered, the very action of establishing such a state agency cannot be accounted for. Contemporary global models on women supply policy makers with specific guidelines on how to deal with the "woman question."[15]

Establishing full-fledged ministries for women's affairs seems to involve more than just adding one more unit to the existing government. It has a higher symbolic meaning than the founding of an ad hoc committee or even a permanent bureau. By 1992 thirty-six countries had established a special ministry for women's affairs. The first two women's ministries were formed in 1971 by Trinidad and Canada, while the remainder were created between 1975 and 1992. Although countries are still more likely to form a commission than a full-fledged ministry, the fact that as many as thirty-six countries have taken such a step is surprising, given its high political and financial costs.

This is not to say that the governments that have created ministries are more committed to the idea of sexual equality and are willing to do more than those who have established machinery on a smaller scale. While this might be true in some cases, it is clearly not in others. Note also that the ministries vary in terms of budget, political clout, and mandate. The point is that those countries that have set up special resources for women's ministries with ministries have sent ⌐ signal to the international community that they endorse the notion that the expansion of state structure is required to deal with such problems as gender inequality.

Creating this kind of ministry is not a matter unique to old, established, and developed countries, as conventional wisdom might hold. A quick look at table 5 indicates otherwise. The table shows the countries that have founded a ministry for women's affairs by date of founding and date of independence. Many of these countries have one feature in common: most are new states that gained their independence during or after the 1960s wave of decolonization. Only nine of the countries with women's ministries are older countries that became nation-states in the nineteenth or early twentieth centuries.

It is clear that the formation of ministries is not an action first taken by core countries and then later emulated by the new countries. Thomas, Meyer, Ramirez, and Boli (1987) present various studies that report on similar results regarding the establishment of mass education, women's suffrage, and welfare programs. New, peripheral countries are more attuned to global normative pressures that define the appropriate steps for a state to take.

15. Similarly, it has been shown that, in the case of welfare programs, international standards have been purposefully appropriated to shape policy innovation (Strang and Chang 1993).

TABLE 5

*Founding of Ministry of Women's Affairs, by Country, Year of Founding, and Year of Independence*[a]

| Country | Year Ministry | Year Independence | Country | Year Ministry | Year Independence |
|---|---|---|---|---|---|
| Canada | 1971 | 1867 | Cameroon | 1983 | 1960 |
| Trinidad | 1971 | 1962 | Indonesia | 1983 | 1949 |
| France | 1974 | pre-1800 | Sri Lanka | 1983 | 1972 |
| Gabon | 1974 | 1960 | Tunisia | 1983 | 1956 |
| Ivory Coast | 1976 | 1960 | New Zealand | 1985 | 1907 |
| Jamaica | 1977 | 1962 | Zaire | 1985 | 1960 |
| Bangladesh | 1978 | 1971 | Austria | 1987 | 1918 |
| Dominica | 1978 | 1978 | Chad | 1988[b] | 1960 |
| Togo | 1978 | 1960 | Fiji | 1988 | 1970 |
| Germany (FDR) | 1979 | pre-1800 | Sweden | 1988[b] | pre-1800 |
| Antigua | 1980 | 1980 | Guinea-Bissau | 1991[b] | 1974 |
| Mauritania | 1980[b] | 1960 | Niger | 1989 | 1960 |
| Mauritius | 1980 | 1968 | Senegal | 1991[b] | 1960 |
| Paraguay | 1980[b] | 1811 | St. Kitts-Nevis | 1991 | 1983 |
| Venezuela | 1980[b] | 1830 | St. Vincent | 1991 | 1979 |
| Zimbabwe | 1980 | 1965 | Belgium | 1992 | 1830 |
| Grenada | 1982 | 1974 | Tanzania | 1992 | 1964 |
| Burundi | 1983 | 1962 | Uganda | 1992 | 1962 |

NOTES: [a] Total number of ministries = 36.
[b] Date is not of founding; the ministry is known to exist at that time.

In general, the formation of this machinery cannot be adequately explained by reference to internal processes or idiosyncratic historical or political events. The standardization, prevalence, and timing of the founding of "national machinery for the advancement of women" attest to the nation-states' affirmation of the notion that such official bureaucratic units are essential components of all states endorsing modern, globally articulated visions of women and their position in society.

Thus, the fusion of women's issues with the discourse on development has facilitated the institutionalization of the discourse on women and has turned it into an integral part of the global agenda through its embodiment in a massive organizational infrastructure. The international women's movement has grown in scope, number, and geographical distribution. By the end of the UN Decade for Women it had become truly international. It transformed previous notions of women, rights, and the public sphere. Women were not merely individuals with rights but also persons with skills and the "brains" necessary for the pursuit of national development. Equality and rights were discussed and justified within the context of the need to incorporate all human resources into the development process. Discrimination came to be seen as an economic waste and not simply a violation of human dignity. Thus, whereas in the early period the granting of rights to women was seen as an economic drawback expected to hurt national performance in terms of global economic competition, in the current period we can anticipate the exact opposite. Discrimination is now defined as a wasteful, damaging strategy that hinders the drive for national economic prosperity.

CHAPTER SIX

. . . . . . . . . .

# Setting a New Research Agenda

In this book I have examined the emerging world cultural and political system from the turn of the century until the present by investigating a key issue in the global discourse: women's position in the public sphere. Because women's issues have been part of the global agenda since early in the century, it is possible to follow the transformation in the world society and to look at the effects of these changes on the ways in which women's issues have been discussed and acted upon at the nation-state level. I focused on three main areas: First, I used the history of "women's issues" as a lens for researching the evolving world polity and expanding states' jurisdiction. Second, I explored the changing nature of global discourse and ways of organizing to understand the transformation of the notion of "womanhood" and the emergence and institutionalization of "women's rights." Third, I examined the relations between nation-states and the global system. I argued that the impact of global action is not confined to the international arena but also affects nation-states. The wider cultural and political contexts in which modern nation-states operate have influenced the pattern in which women's public status has been defined and regulated. These three theoretical/analytical foci, woven together, provide the axis and direction for this historical narrative of women's issues and women's rights.

My study begins at the end of the nineteenth century, when women and women's issues were first being discussed and acted upon in the emerging world society. Also during this period the international community began to concern itself with social and humanitarian issues. Much of the resulting activity was carried out by transnational social reform movements, both individuals and groups, driven by a progressive effort to remedy the era's social evils.

A combination of instrumental and moral motives also drew governments, however reluctantly, to make tentative arrangements for establishing international rules and for cooperating in various campaigns, such as fighting international trafficking in narcotics and in women and children; promoting public health and hygiene; and improving conditions in modern work settings.

Nation-states were hesitant, however, to set international standards regarding the status and rights of their own respective members. Such policies were seen as an infringement on the principle of sovereignty. Thus, international rules and proposals were loosely formulated with respect to nation-states' commitments to take specific actions, and no official global bodies were invested with the authority to deal with issues that were defined as a country's "internal affairs."

Within this expanding global setting women's issues played a prominent role. Ideas were put forward mainly as part of an effort to rectify past wrongs done to women: women's specialized roles (e.g., motherhood) and distinctive character (e.g., fragile physical constitution and moral fabric) required protection and rescue. In other cases women's distinctiveness was elevated, and their moral standards and nurturing capacities were claimed to be needed for the regeneration of society as a whole. Organized cooperation was initiated to rescue women from "falling" into prostitution, to protect women from exploitation and from hazardous conditions in the workplace, and to let women make their special contribution to politics (i.e., to grant women the suffrage).

The women's suffrage movement presented a new element into world culture: women's rights and women's equality. The rhetoric of justice and individual rights, however, was in tension with the rhetoric of collective social regeneration and moral purification. Thus, in the spirit of its time women's rights were conceptualized mainly as means for a wider moral and social reform that would benefit society and the world. Once granted access to the arena of official politics, women would bring in their higher moral standards and nurturing capacities, much needed qualities for the various reforms that were then on the agenda (e.g., prohibition, abolition, elimination of wars), and thus would contribute to an overall social regeneration. The suffrage movements demanded the incorporation of women into politics qua women. Consequently, their integration would result in the "feminization" of the public sphere—that is, an emphasis on caring, higher moral standards, and pacifism.

The tension was not resolved but, rather, continued throughout the period, reappearing even more forcefully in the interwar era. It was dramatized by the efforts of the different camps of the women's movement that lobbied the new international world bodies—the League of Nations and the International Labour Organization—to take action on behalf of women. Their activity illustrated the conflict between the idea of women's equality and women's protection.

The creation of the ILO and the League of Nations had two main consequences: both organizations expanded and elaborated much of the previous international activity on women's behalf, and, at the same time, their creation changed the ways in which women's organizations operated. It consolidated their activity and provided an arena for women's groups to voice their claims and to urge that world action be taken on their behalf. It was only toward the end of the 1930s that these activities started to have an impact, and the two official world bodies began to formulate women's issues in terms of women's rights and to take some action, though very cautiously.

In the second half of the twentieth century global society changed dramatically. The global arena was inhabited by thousands of international associations of all kinds and organized for all conceivable purposes. Official linkages were formed among governments to promote cooperation in such areas as apportioning outer space, controlling reproduction, recovering the ozone layer, and inventing methods to measure women's informal economic activity. This proliferation of activities was embodied in a number of international documents that made nation-states responsible for regulating various domains of life and involving specific categories of people.

The increasing coherence and consolidation of the international society were accompanied by two related novelties. Supranational organizations, established with broad mandates and aided by groups of experts, were vested with the authority to set rules for all countries to follow, regulating relations among nation-states and their members. Such relations were based on concepts of equal rights and citizenship. Thus, for the first time, by the second half of the twentieth century, rights of individuals became a main concern to be promoted and articulated in the global arena. At the same time, many areas of people's life became regulated by and acted upon global bodies. In this new setting states were instructed, for example, to ensure that all children would enjoy happy childhoods, to encourage married men to share household chores, and to guarantee the rights of women to participate in recreational activities (both appear in the 1979 UN Convention on the Elimination of All Forms of Discrimination against Women).

With the transformation of the world system, the ways in which women's issues were to be dealt with changed too. After World War II, with the emerging notions of rights and equality as an expanded world ideology, women were defined as a category of individuals that needs to be integrated into all domains of public life. A major international campaign for women's rights launched by the United Nations in the mid-1970s set a new agenda to be acted upon at both the international and the national levels. In this period the global interactions among nation-states increased dramatically, and linkages between nation-states and world organizations proliferated and intensified. Thus, the period in which transnational factors became critical in determining state actions and structures was also the period in which women's citizenship and rights as individuals, rather than as women, became an international focus.

Authoritative models that prescribed for nation-states what actions should be taken regarding women's status were articulated and promoted in global forums. These models were embedded in international documents and endorsed by an overwhelming majority of nation-states and in world plans of action that mobilized national and international organizations of many kinds into a highly coordinated and bureaucratized world campaign for the sake of women. The logic of national development, fused with the rhetoric of individual human rights, intensified and rationalized this project even further. Within this context discrimination was understood to result in the "underutilization of human resources" and, as such, to require eradication.

Moreover, as a result of the increasing cohesiveness and expanding authority of the global cultural and political system, more areas of nation-states' activities and more features of their structures came to reflect and enact principles and models that originated from and were endorsed by the world polity. Hence, nation-state actions regarding women came to depict, to a great extent, world ideas about women's proper roles and positions in national society.

This mode of conceptualizing the relations between nation-states and the wider system accounts for a world process in which most countries incorporated women into the public sphere during the same historical periods and in similar patterns. Almost all countries define their female members as citizens and as persons (in the legal and bureaucratic sense) and grant them a series of public rights (i.e., rights that give them access to various public institutions).

Women, however, were not just a marginalized group that "entered" citizenship at a later stage than most men. The patterns in which women claimed and were granted the right to participate in public institutions were fashioned by the gender system, one of whose main organizing principles is the public/domestic split that relegates the two genders to two domains and privileges the former (men and their association with the public) over the latter (women and their association with the private). All international campaigns, well into the twentieth century, "smuggled" women into the public sphere by way of the domestic sphere. Thus, in earlier periods states' policies regarding women's economic activities were aimed primarily at protecting their maternal functions; laws and regulation were passed to guarantee that their participation in public life would not hamper their assigned responsibilities in the domestic sphere. Only with the emergence of the new global models of women, anchored in the discourse of "rights" and "equality," were new laws adopted to keep women's public participation from being hampered because of their association with the domestic sphere. As a result, nation-states' policies that incorporated women as individuals and not as women have proliferated worldwide. Countries have moved from setting a particular path for women to follow in order to participate in the public sphere to emphasizing the need to make women's patterns of participation as close as possible to those of men. The decline in the significance of gender as a marker for states' official policies regarding their women members has been generated, to a great degree, by global events and processes.

## Incorporating the Domestic Realm of Public Rights and Citizenship into Rights Discourse

The new model of the modern nation-states that proliferated especially after World War II is predicated on the principle that citizenship organizes the relations between the state and its members. In addition to membership in a political community being defined by a set of formal rights, citizenship now is being used in a much wider sense. It implies, alongside the notion of "personhood," participation and involvement in the various public institutions of the community. Accepting this premise, much research effort has been devoted to unmasking departures from this ideology. Those who do not have equal access to public institutions and enjoy fewer goods and resources are defined as "second-class citizens." What are the mechanisms and practices that create various classes of people whose very existence violates the official criteria of universal entitlement?

Women can be conceptualized as one such group of second-class citizens who were late to be granted access to rights that, in addition, were never complete and full. Yet it is not only a matter of timing. As far as economic rights were concerned, women had to travel a different path: it was by disassociating themselves from the domestic sphere that they could become integrated into the public sphere; only through their constitution as nongendered persons (in the same way that men are portrayed to be) were they granted equality.

Moreover, as with the franchise, formal rights do not guarantee equal participation. Indeed, much research is being devoted to reveal the mechanisms that keep the majority of women in lower strata and prevent them from reaching top positions in most economic and political institutions. Explanations vary from accusing employers of having sexist attitudes, the idea that there is a male conspiracy to "keep women in their place," to claiming that capitalism requires a work force that is being taken care of for free (through women's unpaid domestic services) to blaming women's position on their own lack of motivation, assertiveness, or necessary skills. All these explanations point to the fact that the domestic sphere is still the women's sphere. Thus, whereas women have been "permitted into" the public sphere—that is, they have been granted official rights of participation in public institutions of society, they did not "leave" the private sphere, nor did men truly enter it. In other words, whereas the public is no longer exclusively a men's domain, the domestic is still women's. This "stalled revolution," or the discrepancy between the changing gendered nature of the public and the private, is responsible, to a large degree, for the gender inequality that characterizes all areas of public life.

Within this framework of research the conventional formulation of citizenship is being expanded to include accounts of women's "deficient" citizenship by considering the significance of the domestic realm.[1] Still, even within this conceptualization the focus is on public citizenship, and the frame of reference is men's patterns of participation. Citizenship is being defined as (rights to and patterns of) participation in public institutions alone. Patterns of participation in (assigned responsibility and association with) the domestic sphere are being examined only in terms of their effects on patterns of participation in the public sphere. Thus, the public domain remains at the center and is still defined as the sole arena in which to grant and practice citizenship.

Thus, I suggest a new research (and action) agenda that, in contrast to what exists, grants the domestic sphere and domestic rights equal status with public rights. It would include analyses of the ways in which domestic rights affect wives' citizenship and personhood vis-à-vis their husbands along with the ways that public rights affect women's citizenship and personhood vis-à-vis men.

One such possible direction is to constitute members of the family as persons with individual rights requires applying the logic of the public to the private and thus replacing the notion of a communal group based on responsibility, duty, and hierarchy with one based on rights and individual interests. In that way wives and husbands are granted equal legal capacity, and married

---

1. This consideration is relevant for understanding men's citizenship as well. It is exactly the assignment of women to the "private" realm that enables men's full dedication to the public. This fact escapes most researchers when studying citizenship "in general," that is, men's citizenship.

women are constituted as citizens and persons in the same way that nonmarried women are, thus blurring the relevance women's marital status has for determining their citizenship status and legal personhood.

One can explore a wide array of domestic rights. I suggest focusing on what Pateman calls "the paradigm of all that is private" (1989, 3), sexual relations between husband and wife. More specifically, I am referring to marital rape legislation. This legislation recognizes the concept of rape within the context of marriage and does not consider the relationship between the victim and the perpetrator as relevant to how rape is defined. Thus, it defines the rape of a wife by her husband in the same way as rape between nonmarried persons. It grants the wife's consent to having sexual relations with her husband the same status as consent to a man that is not her husband. In both cases the woman's consent defines the meaning of the act—that is, whether it is rape or not. The alternative, as exists in many examples of national legislation, is to grant the husband "immunity" to charges of rape, or what is usually referred to as a "marital exemption." Immunity is given when the law defines rape as "sexual intercourse by a male with a female not his wife without her consent."

Changing the law—that is, eliminating the marital exemption—has far-reaching consequences for the notions of gender, citizenship, the private/public split, and patriarchy, which organizes them all. It applies the logic of the public to what constitutes the "heart" of the private—the sexual relations between husband and wife—and to what constitutes the wife as a "person" vis-à-vis her husband, granting her the right to sexual autonomy, physical integrity, and choice. All of these are denied from her under a marriage contract (Pateman 1988). We need to look at the ways in which state regulation transforms or maintains the existing relations between men and women as well as between husbands and wives—that is, at the changing territoriality of the private and public—for understanding women's citizenship and personhood (Berkovitch 1996).

## The Construction of Gender, the Measurement of Equality, and Social Action

In this book I discuss the notions of equality and discrimination as cultural elements that frame our thinking about gender in society. I have not chosen the more traditional strategy that treats equality as a point of departure and then moves on to show how state action (or other social actors, for that matter) deviates from this desired goal and brings about opposite results. Neither do I "reveal" the discrepancy between ideology and practice that can be found when looking at either state action or international organization's activity. Instead, I see the very notion of equal rights as a cultural product with its own history that needs to be accounted for. I argue that this notion shapes much current social scientific research; it affects social action and underlies the ways in which we define social problems and act upon them. Thus, in the present context I can use the concept of "gender equality" to provide some illustrations of the ways in which ideology, social research, and political action are interwoven and feed one another.

First, the definition of the public as a domain open equally to both men and women enables policy makers, social researchers, social reformers, and people in general to worry about the ongoing differential patterns of women's participation. Thus, for example, a phenomenon such as occupational segregation by sex, prevalent in all countries, is being defined as a problem and, as such, draws much attention for research and policy making. The existence of an elaborate equality-in-employment legislation alongside a gender-patterned labor market augments the problem and makes it into a state concern and a worthy cause around which to mobilize social action.

Second, paradoxically, the more pronounced and elaborated the principle of equality, the larger the gap that is "discovered" between men's and women's positions and, hence, the larger the perception of discrimination and the sense of inequity that is produced. Also, since men and women are now defined as similar individuals, having the same ontological status, with similar entitlements to public resources and opportunities, more dimensions of their relative status and aspects of life are subject to comparisons using standardized measures. At least in the short run, the more "accurate" and comprehensive the measurement, the larger the degrees of discrimination and the greater the number of areas of discrimination that are found to exist.

In addition, conventional standardized measures were designed to measure official economic activities—that is, those that are paid for and which occur in the public sphere—the result being that much of women's activity, which has traditionally taken place within the informal economy and especially in the domestic sphere, was not counted. Women's domestic labor—housework—was defined as "labor of love" and classified as unproductive work, and housewives were defined as outside of the workforce. Yet since the 1970s there has been a new research and policy trend. An immense amount of research effort, on the national and international levels, has been dedicated to finding new methods for quantifying women's economic activity, including housework and work within the informal sector. Several resolutions have been adopted by the United

Nations women's conferences calling on nation-states to acknowledge the economic value of housework, and the ILO requested a change in the classification of housework to "productive work."

This trend clearly indicates how the "logic of the public" has expanded to incorporate women, now perhaps more symbolically, into its realm. Note that this process has two consequences. First, women who were formerly outside the wage economy are now considered to be workers in the same way that conventional workers (e.g., wage-earning employees) are. Whereas before they were outside the reach of state regulation, now all kinds of state policies—such as insurance, compensation, and protection from sexual harassment—apply to them as well. Thus, counting women's work is bound up with the expansion of the state, which now has a new, and broad-ranging set of activities under its jurisdiction. Second, if this kind of informal economic activity is given an official measure, and the "updated" figures for women's economic contribution can be compared to their rewards (and to men's ratios of contribution and rewards), a larger degree of discrimination and inequity between the sexes is likely to be found.

Concomitantly, social research in areas such as the sociology of work and stratification has undergone changes that reflect this trend as well. New scholarly work has emerged that has broadened the conventional definition of work to include housework so that it can be studied as any other job or occupation within the labor market. Stratification researchers have inquired into ways to conceptualize the class/occupational position of housewives.

This type of research obviously grows out of and further blurs the lines that divide private and public. The assumption is that it assists in "taking women out of the 'private,' " out of the periphery and into the mainstream, and that this leads to an improvement in their position. In fact, this action reproduces, once again, the privileged position of the public. It is another means by which women's activity is reconsidered symbolically and made more like that of men. It inevitably subsumes what used to be women's exclusive domain under mainstream public activity and makes the world of men and women converge in one logic of action—that of men.

These cognitive frames have far-reaching implications regarding collective action and state activities. Since women are constituted, via the extension of public rights, as legitimate actors in the public sphere, they are empowered, as a group, to be mobilized and to mobilize others for action on their behalf. The ideology of equality works to mobilize social action into two channels. As the principle of equality becomes more prominent, the more discrimination can be found, and the more the situation is defined as unjust. Usually, this more unjust situation is coupled with an empowered category of women vested with the authority to act publicly on their own behalf. At the same time, more state action is required to remedy the situation. States can more easily be lobbied by groups, in both developed and developing countries, to take action to rectify the newly defined injustices against women. This can involve modifying legislation, establishing committees to review the content of textbooks, launching campaigns to change public attitudes, raising levels of literacy among women, or ensuring equal access to vocational training, among many other possible ventures.

This is not to understate the problems and inequalities in women's positions all over the world. In the same vein the process of granting women public rights does not imply that women have indeed gained equality anywhere. Women have suffered injustices and oppression to various degrees everywhere. I am simply pointing at the assumptions that we need to make in order fully to discuss gender relations in terms of discrimination. The way in which the women's question is currently conceptualized is not the only possible way. "Equality" and "discrimination" are historical concepts that emerged and were institutionalized and embedded in elaborate structures and activities—for example, in research and in states' and grassroots groups' activities—at a certain point in time and as a result of particular historical circumstances.

. . . . . . . . . .

# Countries by Date of Adoption
## of Equal Pay Law

| Country | Year | Country | Year | Country | Year |
| --- | --- | --- | --- | --- | --- |
| USSR | 1918 | São Tomé | 1962 | Sudan | 1970 |
| Cuba | 1934 | Luxembourg | 1963 | Ecuador | 1971 |
| Colombia | 1934 | Turkey | 1963 | Panama | 1971 |
| Venezuela | 1936 | El Salvador | 1963 | Malta | 1971 |
| Costa Rica | 1943 | US | 1963 | Canada | 1971 |
| Korea N. | 1945 | Italy | 1964 | Romania | 1972 |
| India | 1950 | Congo | 1964 | France | 1972 |
| Hungary | 1951 | Ivory Coast | 1964 | Japan | 1972 |
| Dominica | 1951 | Israel | 1964 | New Zealand | 1972 |
| Korea S. | 1953 | Kuwait | 1964 | Somalia | 1972 |
| Philippines | 1954 | Lebanon | 1965 | Thailand | 1972 |
| Vietnam S. | 1956 | Chad | 1966 | Argentina | 1973 |
| Iran | 1959 | Burundi | 1966 | Vanuatu | 1973 |
| Honduras | 1959 | Djibouti | 1966 | Ireland | 1974 |
| Syria | 1959 | Benin | 1967 | Togo | 1974 |
| Egypt | 1959 | Cameroon | 1967 | Burma | 1974 |
| Guinea | 1960 | Vietnam N. | 1967 | Czechoslovakia | 1975 |
| Madagascar | 1960 | Rwanda | 1967 | Belgium | 1975 |
| Mongolia | 1960 | Zaire | 1967 | Netherlands | 1975 |
| Germany E. | 1961 | Brazil | 1968 | Iraq | 1975 |
| Iceland | 1961 | Germany W. | 1969 | Ethiopia | 1975 |
| Paraguay | 1961 | Australia | 1969 | Antigua | 1975 |
| Guatemala | 1961 | Ghana | 1969 | Jamaica | 1975 |
| Central Africa | 1961 | Indonesia | 1969 | Denmark | 1976 |
| Burkina Faso | 1962 | UK | 1970 | Algeria | 1976 |
| Gabon | 1962 | Spain | 1970 | Bolivia | 1976* |
| Mali | 1962 | Mexico | 1970 | Jordan | 1976 |
| Niger | 1962 | Libya | 1970 | Nepal | 1976 |
| Senegal | 1962 | Finland | 1970 | Bahrain | 1976* |

| Country | Year | Country | | Country | |
|---|---|---|---|---|---|
| Austria | 1977 | Naura | no data | Guyana | no law |
| Norway | 1978 | Solomon I. | no data | Bahamas | no law |
| Papua New Guinea | 1978 | Cayman I. | no data | Oman | no law |
| N. Yemen | 1978 | Liechtens | no data | Uganda | no law |
| Sweden | 1979 | Monaco | no data | Liberia | no law |
| Portugal | 1979 | Namibia | no data | Fiji | no law |
| Grenada | 1979 | Tonga | no data | St. Lucia | no law |
| UAE | 1980 | Tuvalu | no data | Belize | no law |
| Swaziland | 1980 | Taiwan | no data | Seychelles | no law |
| Angola | 1981 | Mauritani | no data | St. Vincent | no law |
| Equat. Guinea | 1982 | Tanzania | no data | Poland | 1 |
| Zimbabwe | 1982 | Singapore | no data | Yugoslavia | 1 |
| Greece | 1983 | St. Kitts-Nevis | no data | Peru | 1 |
| Tunisia | 1983 | Trinidad | no data | Nicaragua | 1 |
| Haiti | 1984 | Laos | no data | China | 1 |
| Comoros | 1984 | Mauritius | no data | Morocco | 1 |
| Sri Lanka | 1985 | Gambia | no law | Qatar | 1 |
| Cape Verde | 1985 | Kiribati | no law | Afghanistan | 1 |
| Mozambique | 1985 | S. Africa | no law | Suriname | 1 |
| Bulgaria | 1986 | Bhutan | no law | Chile | 2 |
| Guinea-Bissau | 1986 | Brunei | no law | Botswana | 2 |
| Albania | 1989 | Dominican R. | no law | Kenya | 2 |
| Uruguay | 1989 | Pakistan | no law | Lesotho | 2 |
| Western Samoa | 1991* | Cyprus | no law | S. Arabia | 2 |
| | | Cambodia | no law | Malawi | 2 |
| | | Malaysia | no law | Zambia | 2 |
| | | Nigeria | no law | Sierra L. | 2 |
| | | Banglades | no law | | |
| | | Barbados | no law | | |

SOURCES: International Labour Office, *Women at Work*, an ILO Newsbulletin, various years; Blanpain 1977–90; Morgan 1984; United States Department of Health 1984 and various case studies.

KEY: 1. Equal pay in constitution only.

    2. No specific reference to sexual equality.

NOTE: *Date is of current legislation, not necessarily of first law.

# REFERENCES

. . . . . . . . .

Adams, Carolyn Teich, and Kathryn T. Winston. 1980. *Mothers at Work: Public Policies in the United States, Sweden, and China*. New York: Longman.

Addams, Jane, Emily G. Balch, and Alice Hamilton. 1915. *Women at the Hague: The International Congress of Women and Its Results*. New York: Macmillan.

Adler, Nancy J., and Dafna N. Izraeli, eds. 1988. *Women in Management Worldwide*. Armonk, N.Y.: M. E. Sharpe.

Amos, Valerie, and Pratibha Parmer. 1984. "Challenging Imperial Feminism." *Feminist Review* 17:3–19.

Anderson, Bonnie, and Judith P. Zinsser. 1988. *History of Their Own*. New York: Harper and Row.

Archer, Clive S. 1992. *International Organization*. London and New York: Routledge.

Arizpe, Lourdes. 1981–82. "Comments on Tinker's 'A Feminist View of Copenhagen.'" *Signs* 7:714–16.

Armstrong, David. 1982. *The Rise of the International Organization: A Short History*. New York: St. Martin's Press.

Arnaud, Andre-Jean, and Elizabeth Kingdom, eds. 1990. *Women's Rights and the Rights of Man*. Aberdeen: Aberdeen University Press.

Ashworth, Georgina. 1982. "The UN 'Women's Conference' and International Linkages in the Women's Movement." In *Pressure Groups in the Global System: The Transnational Relations of Issue Oriented Non-Governmental Organizations*, ed. P. Willetts, 125–47. London: Frances Pinter.

Barnard, Jessie. 1987. *A Female World from a Global Perspective*. Bloomington: Indiana University Press.

Barrett, Anne Deborah. 1995. "Reproducing Persons as a Global Concern: The Making of an Institution." Ph.D. diss., Department of Sociology, Stanford University.

Barrett, Anne Deborah, and David Frank. 1999. "Population Control for National Development: From World Discourse to National Policies." In *Constructing World Culture: International Non-Governmental Organizations since 1875*, ed. J. Boli and G. M. Thomas. Stanford: Stanford University Press.

Becker, Susan D. 1981. *The Origins of the Equal Rights Amendment: American Feminism between the Wars*. Westport, Conn.: Greenwood Press.

———. 1983. "International Feminism between the Wars: The National Woman's Party versus the League of Women Voters." In *Decades of Discontent: The Women's Movement, 1920–1940*, ed. L. Scharf and J. M. Jensen, 223–42. Westport, Conn.: Greenwood Press.

Bell, Susan Groag, and Karen Offen, eds. 1983. *Women, the Family, and Freedom: The Debate in Document*. Stanford: Stanford University Press.

Benavot, Aharon. 1989. "Education, Gender, and Economic Development: A Cross-National Study." *Sociology of Education* 62:14–32.

Bendix, Reinhard. 1974. *Nation-Building and Citizenship*. Berkeley: University of California Press.

Berger, Peter, and Thomas Luckman. 1967. *The Social Construction of Reality*. New York: Doubleday.

Bergesen, Albert. 1990. "Turning World-System Theory on Its Head." In *Global Culture: Nationalism, Globalization and Modernity*, ed. M. Featherstone, 6–81. London: Sage.

Berkman, Joyce. 1993. "Feminism, War and Peace Politics: The Case of World War I." In *Women, Militarism and War*, ed. B. J. Elshtain and S. Tobias, 141–60. Lanham, Md.: Rowman and Littlefield.

Berkovitch, Nitza. 1994. "From Motherhood to Citizenship: The Worldwide Incorporation of Women into the Public Sphere in the Twentieth Century." Ph.D. diss., Department of Sociology, Stanford University.

——. 1996. "Women's Rights and Wives' Rights: Gendering Citizenship Talk." Paper presented at the American Sociological Association meeting, New York.

——. 1999. "The Emergence and Transformation of the International Women's Movement." In *Constructing World Culture: International Non-Governmental Organizations since 1875*, ed. J. Boli and G. M. Thomas. Stanford: Stanford University Press.

Berkovitch, Nitza, and Karen Bradley. 1994. "Women as a Global Project." Paper presented at the American Sociological Association meeting, Los Angeles.

Blanpain, Roger, ed. 1977–90. *International Encyclopedia of Labour Law and Industrial Relations*. Deventer: Klumer.

Bock, Gisela, and Pat Thane, eds. 1991. *Maternity and Gender Policies: Women and the Rise of the European Welfare States, 1880s–1950s*. London: Routledge.

Boli, John. 1987. "World Polity Sources of Expanding State Authority and Organizations, 1870–1970." In *National Development and the World System*, ed. G. M. Thomas, J. W. Meyer., F. O. Ramirez., and J. Boli, 77–91. Newbury, N.Y.: Sage.

Boli, John, and George M. Thomas. 1997. "World Culture in the World Polity: A Century of International Non-Governmental Organizations." *American Sociological Review* 62:171–90.

Boris, Eileen. 1989. "The Power of Motherhood: Black and White Activist Women Redefine the Political." *Yale Journal of Law and Feminism* 34:25–49.

Boulding, Elise. 1977. *Women in the Twentieth Century World*. Beverly Hills, Calif.: Sage.

——. 1988. *Building a Global Civic Culture: Education for an Interdependent World*. New York: Teachers College, Columbia University.

Boxer, Marilyn, and Jean H. Quataert. 1978. "The Class and Sex Connection: An Introduction." In *Socialist Women: European Socialist Feminism in the Nineteenth and Early Twentieth Century*, 1–18. New York: Elsevier.

Boxer, Marilyn J., and Jean H. Quataert, eds. 1987. *Connecting Spheres: Women in the Western World: 1500 to the Present*. New York: Oxford University Press.

Bradley, Karen, and Francisco O. Ramirez. 1996. "World Polity Promotion of Gender Parity: Women's Share of Higher Education, 1965–1985." *Research in Sociology of Education and Socialization* 11:63–91.

Bristow, Edward J. 1977. *Vice and Vigilance: Purity Movement in Britain since 1700.* Dublin: Gill and Macmillan.

———. 1982. *Prostitution and Prejudice: The Jewish Fight against White Slavery, 1870–1939.* Oxford: Clarendon Press.

British, Continental, and General Federation for the Abolition of Government Regulation of Prostitution. 1876. *The New Abolitionist: A Narrative of a Year's Work.* London: Dyer Brothers.

Brocas, Anne-Marie, Anne-Marie Cailloux, and Virginie Oget. 1990. *Women and Social Security: Progress towards Equality of Treatment.* Geneva: International Labour Office.

Bryan, Turner. 1994. "Postmodern Culture/Modern Citizen." In *The Condition of Citizenship,* ed. B. V. Steenbergen, 153–68. London: Sage.

Bulbeck, Chilla. 1988. *One World's Women's Movement.* London: Pluto Press.

Bunch, Charlotte, ed. 1987. *Passionate Politics.* New York: St. Martin's Press.

Bunch, Charlotte, and Roxana Carrillo. 1990. "Feminist Perspective in Development." In *Persistent Inequality,* ed. I. Tinker, 70–82. New York: Oxford University Press.

Bussey, Gerthrud, and Margaret Tims. 1980. *Pioneers for Peace: Women's International League for Peace and Freedom: 1915–1965.* WILPF, British section.

Buttafuoco, Annarita. 1991. "Motherhood as a Political Strategy: The Role of the Italian Women's Movement in the Creation of the Cassa Nazionale di Maternita." In *Maternity and Gender Policies: Women and the Rise of the European Welfare States, 1880s-1950,* ed. G. Bock and P. Thane, 178–96. London: Routledge.

Byre, Angela. 1988. "Applying Community Standards on Equality." In *Women, Equality and Europe,* ed. M. Buckley and M. Anderson, 20–32. London: Macmillan.

Cammack, Paul, David Pool, and William Tardoff. 1989. *Third World Politics: A Comparative Introduction.* Baltimore: Johns Hopkins University Press.

Carsten, Francis, Ludwig. 1982. *War against War: British and German Radical Movements in the First World War.* Berkeley: University of California Press.

Chabbott, Colette. 1999. "Defining Development: The Making of the International Development Field, 1945–1990." In *Constructing World Culture: International Non-Governmental Organizations since 1875,* ed. J. Boli and G. M. Thomas. Stanford: Stanford University Press.

Charles, Maria. 1992. "Cross-National Variation in Occupational Sex Segregation." *American Sociological Review* 57:483–502.

Coate, Roger A. 1982. *Global Issue Regimes.* New York: Praeger.

Coliver, Sandra. 1989. "United Nations Machineries on Women's Rights: How Might They Better Help Women Whose Rights Are Being Violated?" In *New Directions in Human Rights,* ed. E. Lutz, H. Hurst, and B. Kathryn, 25–49. Philadelphia: University of Pennsylvania Press.

Comisión de Interamericano Mujeres CIM; (Inter-American Commission of Women).

1974. *Inter-American Commission of Women, 1928–1973.* Washington, D.C.: General Secretariat, Organization of American States.

Connell, B. H. 1980. "Special Protective Legislation and Equality of Opportunity for Women in Australia." *International Labour Review* 119:199–216.

Connelly, Mark T. 1980. *The Response to Prostitution in the Progressive Era.* Chapell Hill: University of North Carolina Press.

Costin, Lela B. 1982. "Feminism, Pacifism, Internationalism and the 1915 International Congress of Women." *Women's Studies International Forum* 5:301–15.

Cova, Anne. 1991. "French Feminism and Maternity: Theories and Policies, 1890–1918." In *Maternity and Gender Policies: Women and the Rise of the European Welfare States, 1880s–1950s,* ed. G. Bock and P. Thane, 119–37. London: Routledge.

Creighton, William B. 1979. *Working Women and the Law.* London: Mansel.

Degen, Marie Louise. 1972. *The History of the Woman's Peace Party.* New York and London: Garland.

Dietz, Mary. 1992. "Context Is All: Feminism and Theories of Citizenship." *Daedalus* 116:1–24.

Dimaggio, Paul J., and Walter W. Powell. 1991. "Introduction." In *The New Institutionalism in Organizational Analysis,* ed. W. Powell and P. Dimaggio, 1–40. Chicago: University of Chicago Press.

Docksey, Christopher. 1987. "The European Community and the Promotion of Equality." In *Women, Employment and European Equality Law,* ed. C. McCrudden, 1–23. Oxford: Eclipse.

Donnelly, Jack. 1986. "International Human Rights: A Regime Analysis." *International Organization* 40:599–642.

Douchen, Claire. 1992. "Europe: A Community for Women? Understanding the European Community—A Glossary of Terms." *Women's Studies International Forum* 15:17–19.

Douglas, Mary. 1986. *How Institutions Think.* Syracuse, N.Y.: Syracuse University Press.

Dubois, Ellen Carol. 1991. "Woman Suffrage and the Left: An International Socialist Feminist Perspective." *New Left Review* 186:20–45.

Eisler, Riane, and David Loye. 1985. "Will Women Change the World?" *Futures* 17:550–55.

Elwan, Shwikar. 1974. *The Status of Women in the Arab World.* New York: League of Arab States, Arab Information Center.

Epstein, Barbara L. 1981. *The Politics of Domesticity: Women, Evangelism, and Temperance in Nineteenth-Century America.* Middletown, Conn.: Wesleyan University Press.

Escobar, Arturo. 1984–85. "Discourse and Power in Development: Michel Foucault and the Relevance of His Work to the Third World." *Alternatives* 10:377–400.

Evans, Richard. 1977. *The Feminists: Women's Emancipation Movements in Europe, America and Australia, 1840–1920.* London: Croom Helm.

Farnsworth, Beatrice. 1980. *Aleksandra Kollontai: Socialism, Feminism and the Bolshevik Revolution.* Stanford: Stanford University Press.

Fawcett, Millicent G. , and E. M. Turner. 1927. *Josephine Butler: Her Work and Principles, and Their Meaning for the Twentieth Century.* London: Association for Moral and Social Hygiene.

Ferguson, James. 1990. *The Anti-Politics Machine: "Development," Depolitization, and Bureaucratic Power in Lesotho.* Cambridge: Cambridge University Press.

———. 1993. "Concluding Comments." Paper presented at "Historicizing Development" conference, Emory University, Atlanta.

Finnemore, Martha. 1993. "International Organizations as Teachers of Norms: UNESCO and Science Policy." *International Organization* 47:565–98.

———. 1996. "Norms, Culture, and World Politics: Insights from Sociology's Institutionalism." *International Organization* 50:325–47.

Foggon, George. 1988. "The Origin and Development of the ILO." In *International Institutions at Work,* ed. P. Taylor and A. J. R. Groom, 96–113. London: Frances Pinter.

Follows, John, W. 1951. *Antecedents of the International Labour Organization.* Oxford: Clarendon Press.

Foner, Philip, S. 1980. *Women and the American Labor Movement.* New York: Free Press.

Foster, Catherine. 1989. *Women for All Seasons: The Story of the Women's International League for Peace and Freedom.* Athens: University of Georgia Press.

Friedland, Roger, and Robert Alford. 1991. "Bringing Society Back In: Symbols, Practices, and Institutional Contradictions." In *The New Institutionalism in Organizational Analysis,* ed. W. W. Powell and P. Dimaggio, 232–63. Chicago: University of Chicago Press.

Galey, Margaret E. 1979. "Promoting Nondiscrimination against Women." *International Studies Quarterly* 23:273–302.

Geertz, Clifford. 1973. *The Interpretation of Cultures.* New York: Basic Books.

George, W., and Lucy Johnson. 1909. *Josephine Butler: An Autobiographical Memoir.* London: J. W. Arrowsmith.

Gibson, John. 1991. *International Organizations, Constitutional Law, and Human Rights.* New York: Praeger.

Giele, Janet Zollinger. 1995. *Two Paths to Women's Equality: Temperance, Suffrage, and the Origins of Women's Feminism.* New York: Twayne.

Gilliam, Angela. 1991. "Women's Equality and National Liberation." In *Third World Women and the Politics of Feminism,* ed. C. T. Mohanti, A. Russo, and L. Torres, 215–36. Bloomington: Indiana University Press.

Gluck, Sherna. 1983. "Socialist Feminism between the Two World Wars: Insights from Oral History." In *Decades of Discontent: The Women's Movement, 1920–1940,* ed. L. Scharf and J. M. Jensen, 279–97. Westport, Conn.: Greenwood Press.

Gordon, Elizabeth P. 1924. *Women Torch Bearers: The Story of the Woman's Christian Temperance Union.* Evanston: National Woman's Christian Temperance Union.

Grieco, Joseph. 1990. *Cooperation among Nations.* Ithaca: Cornell University Press.

Gross, Leo. 1948. "The Peace of Westfalia." *American Journal of International Law* 42(1): 20–42.

Haas, Ernst B. 1964. *Beyond the Nation State.* Stanford: Stanford University Press.

Halliday, Fred. 1988. "Hidden from International Relations: Women and the International Arena." *Millennium: Journal of International Studies* 17:419–28.

Hendessi, Mandana. 1986. "Fourteen Thousand Women Meet: Report from Nairobi, July 1985." *Feminist Review* 23:147–56.

Hevener, Natalie Kaufman. 1983. *International Law and the Status of Women.* Boulder, Colo.: Westview.

Hobsbaum, Eric. 1988. "Working Class Internationalism." In *Internationalism in the Labour Movement, 1830–1940,* ed. F. Van Holthoon and M. Van Der Linden, 1–18. Leiden: E. J. Brill.

Honeycutt, Karen. 1979. "Socialism and Feminism in Imperial Germany." *Signs* 5:30–41.

——. 1981. "Clara Zetkin: a Socialist Approach to the Problem of Women's Oppression." In *European Women in the Left,* ed. J. Slaughter and R. Ker, 29–49. Westport, Conn.: Greenwood Press.

Hoskyns, Catherine. 1992. "The European Community Policy on Women in the Context of 1992." *Women's Studies International Forum* 15:21–28.

Inis, Claude. 1988. *States and the Global System: Politics, Law and Organization.* London: Macmillan.

International Bureau for the Suppression of Traffic in Women and Children. 1949. *Traffic in Women and Children: Past Achievements, Present Tasks.* London: International Bureau for the Suppression of Traffic in Women and Children.

International Council of Women. 1912. *Women's Position in the Laws of the Nations: A Compilation of the Laws of Different Countries. Prepared by the ICW standing Committee on Laws concerning the Legal Position of Women.* Published by the Authority of the International Council of Women. N.p.

——. 1966. *Women in a Changing World: The Dynamic Story of the International Council of Women since 1988.* London: Routledge and Kegan Paul.

International Labour Conference. 1919. *First Session, Record of Proceedings.* Geneva: International Labour Office.

——. 1928. *Eleventh Session, Record of Proceedings.* Report of the Director. Geneva: International Labour Office.

——. 1935. *Nineteenth Session, Record of Proceedings.* Geneva: International Labour Office

——. 1937. *Twenty-third Session, Record of Proceedings.* Geneva: International Labour Office

——. 1944. *The Organization of Employment in the Transition from War to Peace.* Report 3, 26th Session. Montreal: International Labour Office.

——. 1947. *Thirtieth Session, Record of Proceedings.* Geneva: International Labour Office.

——. 1950. *Equal Remuneration for Men and Women Workers for Work of Equal Value,* report 5(1), 33d session. Geneva: International Labour Office.

——. 1951. *Thirty-fourth Session, Record of Proceedings.* Geneva: International Labour Office.

——. 1952. *Thirty-fifth Session, Record of Proceedings.* Geneva: International Labour Office.

——. 1958a. *Forty-second Session, Record of Proceedings.* Geneva: International Labour Office.

——. 1958b. *Discrimination in the Field of Employment and Occupation. Report 4(1).* Geneva: International Labour Office.

——. 1964. *Forty-eighth Session, Record of Proceedings.* Geneva: International Labour Office.

——. 1965. *Forty-ninth Session, Record of Proceedings.* Geneva: International Labour Office.

——. 1975. *Sixtieth Session, Record of Proceedings.* Geneva: International Labour Office.

——. 1977. *Report of the Director-General to the International Labour Conference,* pt. 2: *Equality between the Sexes in the Field of Employment and Special Regulation on Women's Work.* Geneva: International Labour Office.

——. 1984. *Seventieth Session, Report of the Director General.* Geneva: International Labour Office.

——. 1985. *Equal Opportunities and Equal Treatment for Men and Women in Employment. Report VII, 71st session.* Geneva: International Labour Office.

——. 1992. *List of Ratification by Convention and by Country (as of 31 Dec. 1991), 79th session, 1992, report 3(5).* Geneva: International Labour Office.

International Labour Office. 1926. *Official Bulletin* 6(2). Geneva.

——. 1931. *Year-Book.* Geneva: International Labour Office.

——. 1933. *Year-Book.* Geneva: International Labour Office.

——. 1934–35. *Year-Book.* Geneva: International Labour Office.

——. 1935–36. *Year-Book.* Geneva: International Labour Office.

——. 1936. *Official Bulletin* 26(1). Geneva.

——. 1936–37. *Year-Book.* Geneva: International Labour Office.

——. 1946. *Official Bulletin* 29(7). Geneva.

——. 1957. *Official Bulletin* 40(8). Geneva.

——. 1960. "Appraisal of the ILO Programme, 1959–1964." *Official Bulletin* 43. Geneva.

——. 1983. *Women at Work.* ILO Newsbulletin, no. 1. Office for Women's Workers Questions. Geneva.

——. 1984. "Protection of Working Mothers: An ILO Global Survey (1964–1984)." *Women at Work.* ILO Newsbulletin, Office for Women's Workers Questions, Geneva.

——. 1987. "Women Workers: Protection or Equality?" *Conditions of Work Digest* 6(2).

International Research and Training Institute for the Advancement Women (INSTRAW). 1980. *National Machineries for the Advancement of Women: Selected Case Studies.* New York: United Nations.

International Woman Suffrage Alliance (IWSA). 1909. *The Presidential Address.* Report of the Fourth Conference of the International Woman Suffrage Alliance. London: IWSA.

——. 1913. *Woman Suffrage in Practice.* London: National Union of Women's Suffrage Societies.

Jacobson, Roberta. 1992. "The Committee on the Elimination of Discrimination against Women." In *The United Nations and Human Rights*, ed. P. Alston, 444–72. Oxford: Clarendon Press.

Jalal, Ayesha. 1991. "The Convenience of Subservience: Women and the State of Pakistan." In *Women, Islam and the State*, ed. D. Kandiyoti, 77–114. Philadelphia: Temple University Press.

Jenson, Jane. 1988. "Paradigms and Political Discourse: Protective Legislation in France and the United States before 1914." *Canadian Journal of Political Science* 22:235–58.

Jewish Association for the Protection of Girls and Women. 1910. *Official Report of the Jewish International Conference on the Suppression of the Traffic in Girls and Women*. London: Werthimer, Lea.

Joekes, Susan. 1987. *Women in the World Economy*. Oxford: Oxford University Press.

Johnston, G. A. 1924. *International Social Progress: The Work of the International Labour Organization of the League of Nations*. London: George Allen and Unwin.

Kabeer, Naila. 1991. "The Quest for National Identity: Women, Islam and the State of Bangladesh." In *Women, Islam and the State*, ed. D. Kandiyoti, 115–43. Philadelphia: Temple University Press.

Kaplan, Gisela. 1992. *Contemporary Western European Feminism*. New York: New York University Press.

Kaplan, Temma. 1988. "The Socialist Origins of International Women's Day." In *Internationalism in the Labour Movement, 1830–1940*, ed. F. Van Holthoon and M. Van Der Linden, 188–94. Leiden: E. J. Brill.

Karvonen, M. J. 1971. "Women and Men at Work." *World Health* (January): 3–9.

Kedouri, Elie. 1984. "A New International Disorder." In *The Expansion of International Society*, ed. H. Bull and A. Watson, 347–56. Oxford: Clarendon Press.

Kessler-Harris, Alice. 1982. *Out to Work: A History of Wage-Earning Women in the United States*. New York: Oxford University Press.

Klaus, Alisa. 1993. "Depopulation and Race Suicide: Maternalism and Pronatalist Ideologies in France and in the United States." In *Mothers of a New World: Maternalist Politics and the Origins of Welfare States*, ed. S. Koven and S. Michel, 188–212. New York: Routledge.

Koven, Seth, and Sonya Michel. 1993a. "Introduction: 'Mother Worlds.'" *Mothers of a New World: Maternalist Politics and the Origins of Welfare States*, 1–43. New York: Routledge.

———, eds. 1993b. *Mothers of a New World: Maternalist Politics and the Origins of Welfare States*. New York: Routledge.

Kraditor, Aileen S. 1981. *The Ideas of the Woman Suffrage Movement, 1890–1920*. New York: Columbia University Press.

Krasner, Stephen D., ed. 1983. *International Regimes*. Ithaca: Cornell University Press.

Lake, Marylin. 1993. "A Revolution in the Family: The Challenge and Contradiction of Maternal Citizenship in Australia." In *Mothers of a New World: Maternalist Politics and the Origins of Welfare States*, ed. S. Koven and S. Michel, 378–95. New York: Routledge.

Latter, Christine. 1988. "The Beginning of Socialist Internationalism in the 1840s: The 'Democratic Friends of All Nations' in London." In *Internationalism in the Labour Movement, 1830–1940*, ed. F. Van Holthoon and M. Van Der Linden, 259–82. Leiden: E. J. Brill.

League of Nations. 1921. *Work of the League*, 18 August. Geneva.

———. 1922. *Official Journal*, 3 July. Geneva.

———. 1923. *Official Journal*, 28 June. Geneva.

———. 1925. *Official Journal*, 6 June. Geneva.

———. 1929. *Official Journal*, 1 June. Geneva.

———. 1929. *Official Journal*, 1 September. Geneva.

———. 1931. *Official Journal*, February. Geneva.

———. 1933. *Bulletin of Information of the Work of International Organizations*. Geneva.

———. 1934. *Official Journal*, 8 September. Geneva.

———. 1935. *Statements Presented by International Women's Organizations*. Secretary-General, A.19.1935. V. Geneva.

———. 1936. *Quarterly Bulletin of Information on the Work of International Organizations*. Geneva.

———. 1936. *Work of the League*, 20 July. Geneva.

———. 1937. *Status of Women*. Geneva. A.54.1937.V.

———. 1938. *Official Journal*, 18 July. Geneva.

———. 1939. *Official Journal*, 12 August. Geneva.

———. 1945. *Report on the Work of the League during the War*, October. Geneva.

Lehrer, Susan. 1987. *Origins of Protective Labor Legislation for Women, 1905–1925*. New York: SUNY.

Lipschultz, Sybil. 1991. "Social Feminism and Legal Discourse, 1908–1923." In *At the Boundaries of Law: Feminism and Legal Theory*, ed. M. Albertson Fineman and N. S. Thomadsen, 209–25. New York: Routledge.

Lloyed, Genevieve. 1984. *The Man of Reason: "Male" and "Female" in Western Philosophy*. London: Methuen.

Luard, Evan. 1977. *International Agencies: The Emerging Frameworks of Interdependence*. Oceana: Dobbs Ferry.

Lubin, Carol Riegelman, and Anne Winslow. 1990. *Social Justice for Women: The International Labor Organization and Women*. Durham: Duke University Press.

Luke, Thimoty W. 1991. "The Discourse of Development: A Genealogy of 'Developing Nations' and the Discipline of Modernity." *Current Perspectives in Social Theory* 11:271–93.

Mann, Michael. 1987. "Ruling Class Strategies and Citizenship." *Sociology* 21:339–54.

Manzo, Kate. 1991. "Modernist Discourse and the Crisis of Development Theory." *Studies in Comparative International Development* 26:3–36.

Marchand, Marianne H., and Jane L. Parpart, eds. 1995. *Feminism/ Postmodernism/ Development*. London: Routledge.

Marshall, L. Barbara. 1991. "Re-Producing the Gendered Subject." *Current Perspectives in Social Theory* 11:169–95.

Marshall, T. H. 1965. *Class, Citizenship, and Social Development.* New York: Doubleday.

McNeely, Connie. 1995. *Constructing the Nation-State: International Organization and Prescriptive Action.* Westport, Conn.: Greenwood.

Meehan, Elizabeth. 1992. "European Community Policies on Sex Equality: A Bibliographic Essay." *Women's Studies International Forum* 15:57–64.

Meyer, Alfred. 1977. "Marxism and the Women's Movement." In *Women in Russia,* ed. D. Atkinson, D. Alexander, and G. W. Lapidus, 85–112. Stanford: Stanford University Press.

Meyer, John W. 1987. "World Polity and the Authority of the Nation-State." In *Institutional Structure: Constituting State, Society, and the Individual,* ed. G. M. Thomas, J. W. Meyer, F. O. Ramirez, and J. Boli, 41–70. Newbury, N.Y.: Sage.

Meyer, John W., and Michael Hannan, eds. 1979. *National Development and the World System, 1950–1970.* Chicago: University of Chicago Press.

Meyer, John W., and Brian Rowan. 1977. "Institutionalized Organizations: Formal Structure as Myth and Ceremony." *American Journal of Sociology* 83:340–63.

Meyer, John W., John Boli, and George M. Thomas. 1994. "Ontology and Rationalization in the Western Cultural Account." In *Institutional Environments and Organizations,* ed. W. R. Scott and J. W. Meyer, 9–28. Thousands Oaks, Calif.: Sage.

Meyer, John W., John Boli, George M. Thomas, and Francisco O. Ramirez. 1997. "World Society and the Nation-State." *American Journal of Sociology* 103:144–81.

Miller, Carol. 1991. "Women in International Relations? The Debate in Inter-war Britain." In *Gender and International Relations,* ed. R. Grant and K. Newland, 64–83. Bloomington: Indiana University Press.

——. 1994. " 'Geneva the Key to Equality.' " *Women's History Review* 3:219–45.

Mogami, Toshiki. 1990. "The United Nations System as an Unfinished Revolution." *Alternatives* 15:177–97.

Morgan, Rubin, ed. 1984. *Sisterhood Is Global: the International Women's Movement Anthology.* New York: Anchor Press, Doubleday.

Morse, David. 1969. *The Origin and Evolution of the ILO and Its Role in the World Community.* Ithaca: New York School of Industrial and Labor Relations, Cornell University.

Moser, Caroline. 1993. *Gender Planning and Development.* London: Routledge.

Mueller, Addle. 1986. "The Bureaucratization of Feminist Knowledge: The Case of Women in Development." *Resources for Feminist Research* 15:36–38.

Mullaney, Marie Marmo. 1990. "Women and European Socialist Protests, 1871–1921." In *Women and Social Protest,* ed. G. West and R. Blumberg, 103–19. New York: Oxford University Press.

Myres, Denys. 1935. *Handbook of the League of Nations.* Boston: World Peace Foundation.

Nadelman, Ethan. 1990. "Global Prohibitions Regimes: The Evolution of Norms in International Society." *International Organization* 44:479–526.

National American Woman Suffrage Association (NAWSA). 1902. *Report: First Interna-*

*tional Woman Suffrage Conference, Washington, 1902.* N.p.: International Woman Suffrage Headquarters.

Nicholson, Linda. 1984. "Feminist Theory: The Private and the Public." In *Beyond Domination: New Perspectives on Women and Philosophy,* ed. C. Gould, 221–30. Totowa, N.J.: Rowman and Allanheld.

———. 1986. *Gender and History.* New York: Columbia University Press.

Northedge, Frederick. S. 1988. *The League of Nations: Its Life and Times—1920–1946.* Leicester: Leicester University Press.

Offen, Karen. 1987. "Liberty, Equality, and Justice for Women: The Theory and Practice of Feminism in Nineteenth-Century Europe." In *Becoming Visible: Women in European History,* ed. R. Bridenthal, C. Koonz, and S. Stuard, 335–73. Boston: Houghton Mifflin.

Ohlander, Ann-Sofie. 1991. "The Invisible Child? The Struggle for a Social Democratic Family Policy in Sweden, 1900–1960s." In *Maternity and Gender Policies: Women and the Rise of the European Welfare States, 1880s-1950s,* ed. G. Bock and P. Thane, 60–72. London: Routledge.

Okin, Susan M. 1979. *Women in Western Political Thought.* Princeton: Princeton University Press.

———. 1989. *Justice, Gender and the Family.* New York: Basic Books.

Oldfield, Sybil. 1995. "Jane Addams: The Chance the World Missed." In *Women in World Politics: An Introduction,* ed. Francine D'amico and Peter Beckman, 156–67. Westport, Conn.: Bergin and Garvey.

Ooko-Ombaka, Oki. 1980. "An Assessment of National Machineries for Women." *Assignment Children* 49–50:45–61.

Open Door International. 1929. *Report of the Conference Called by the Open Door Council.* Berlin: ODI.

———. 1931. *Proceedings of the Second Conference.* Stockholm: ODI.

———. 1933. *Proceedings of the Third Conference.* Prague: ODI.

———. 1935. *Proceedings of the Fourth Conference.* Copenhagen: ODI.

———. 1937. *The Modern Line of Attack on Women's Civil Rights.* London: ODI.

Papanek, Hanna. 1975. "The Work of Women: Postscript from Mexico City." *Signs* 1:215–26.

Paroli, Augusto. 1953. "Maternity Protection in Italy." *International Labour Review* 67:156–72.

Parpart, Jane L., and Kathleen A. Staudt. 1989. "Women and the State in Africa." In *Women and the State in Africa,* ed. J. L. Parpart and K. A. Staudt, 1–44. Boulder: Lynne Rienner.

Pateman, Carol. 1988. *The Sexual Contract.* Cambridge: Polity Press.

———. 1989. *The Disorder of Women.* Stanford: Stanford University Press.

Pedersen, Susan. 1993. "Catholicism, Feminism, and the Politics of the Family during the Late Third Republic." In *Mothers of a New World: Maternalist Politics and the Origins of Welfare States,* ed. S. Koven and S. Michel, 246–76. New York: Routledge.

Pfeffer, Paula. 1985. "'A Whisper in the Assembly of Nations': United State's Participation in the International Movement for Women's Rights from the League of Nations to the United Nations." *Women's Studies International Forum* 8:459–71.

Pietila, Hilkka, and Jeanne Vickers. 1990. *Making Women Matter: The Role of the United Nations.* London: Zed Books.

Pivar, David. 1973. *Purity Crusade, Sexual Morality and Social Control, 1868–1900.* Westport, Conn.: Greenwood.

Polani, Karl. 1944. *The Great Transformation.* Boston: Beacon.

Price, John. 1945. *The International Labour Movement.* London: Oxford University Press.

Quataert, Jean H. 1993. "Woman's Work and the Early Welfare State in Germany: Legislators, Bureaucrats, and Clients before the First World War." In *Mothers of a New World: Maternalist Politics and the Origins of Welfare States,* ed. S. Koven and S. Michel, 159–87. New York: Routledge.

Ramirez, Francisco O. 1981. "Statism, Equality and Housewifery." *Pacific Sociological Review* 24:179–95.

Ramirez, Francisco O., and John Boli. 1987. "Global Patterns of Educational Institutionalization." In *Institutional Structure: Constituting State, Society, and the Individual,* ed. G. M. Thomas, J. W. Meyer, F. O. Ramirez, and John Boli, 150–72. Beverly Hills, Calif.: Sage.

Ramirez, Francisco O., Yasemin Soysal, and Suzanne Shanahan. 1997. "The Changing Logic of Political Citizenship: Cross-National Acquisition of Women's Suffrage Rights, 1890–1990." *American Sociological Review* 62:735–45.

Ramirez, Francisco O., and Jane Weiss. 1979. "The Political Incorporation of Women." In *National Development and the World System,* ed. J. W. Meyer and M. T. Hannan, 238–49. Chicago: University of Chicago Press.

Ratner, Steinberg Ronnie. 1980. "The Paradox of Protection: Maximum Hours Legislation in the United States." *International Labor Review* 119:185–98.

Reanda, Laura. 1992. "The Commission on the Status of Women." In *The United Nations and Human Rights: Critical Appraisal,* ed. P. Alston, 265–303. Oxford: Clarendon Press.

Rendall, Jane. 1985. *The Origins of Modern Feminism: Women in Britain, France, and the United States, 1780–1860.* London: Macmillan.

Riegelman, Carol. 1934. "War-time Trade-Union and Socialist Proposals." In *The Origin of the International Labor Organization,* ed. J. Shotwell, 55–79. New York: Columbia University Press.

Riley, Denis. 1988. *"Am I That Name?" Feminism and the Category of "Women" in History.* Minneapolis: University of Minnesota Press.

Robertson, Roland. 1992. *Globalization: Social Theory and Global Culture.* London: Sage.

Rosaldo, Michelle Zimbalist. 1974. "Woman, Culture, and Society: A Theoretical Overview." In *Woman, Culture, and Society,* ed. M. Zimbalist Rosaldo and L. Lamphere, 17–42. Stanford: Stanford University Press.

———. 1980. "The Use and Abuse of Anthropology: Reflections on Feminism and Cross-Cultural Understanding." *Signs* 5:389–417.

Ruggie, Mary. 1984. *The State and Working Women: A Comparative Study of Britain and Sweden.* Princeton: Princeton University Press.

Sachs, Albie, and Joan H. Wilson. 1986. *Sexism and the Law: A Study of Male Beliefs and Legal Bias in Britain and the United States.* New York: Free Press.

Schneiderman, Rose, and Lucy Goldthwaite. 1967. *All for One.* New York: Paul. S. Erikson.

Schreiber, Adele, and Margaret Mathieson. 1955. *Journey towards Freedom. Written for the Golden Jubilee of the International Alliance of Women.* Copenhagen: International Alliance of Women.

Scott, W. Richard. 1987. "The Adolescence of Institutional Theory." *Administrative Science Quarterly* 32:493–511.

———. 1991. "Unpacking Institutional Arguments." In *The New Institutionalism in Organizational Analysis,* ed. W. W. Powell and P. J. Dimaggio, 164–82. Chicago: University of Chicago Press.

Sewall, May Wright. 1914. *Genesis of the International Council of Women and the Story of Its Growth, 1888–1893.* Indianapolis: n.p.

Shotwell, James. 1934. *The Origins of the International Labour Organization.* New York: Columbia University Press.

Siotis, Jean. 1983. "The Institutions of the League of Nations." In *The League of Nations in Retrospect,* ed. United Nations Library, 19–30. Berlin: Walter de Gruyter.

Sklar, Kathryn K. 1993. "The Historical Foundations of Women's Power in the Creation of the American Welfare State, 1830–1930." In *Mothers of a New World: Maternalist Politics and the Origins of Welfare States,* ed. S. Koven and S. Michel, 43–93. New York: Routledge.

Skocpol, Theda. 1985. "Bringing the State Back in: Strategies of Analysis in Current Research." In *Bringing the State Back,* ed. P. Evans, D. Rueschemeyer, and T. Skocpol, 3–37. New York: Cambridge University Press.

Smith, Jackie, Charles Chatfield, and Ron Pagnucco, eds. 1997. *Transnational Social Movements and World Politics: Solidarity beyond the State.* Syracuse, N.Y.: Syracuse University Press.

Snowden, Mrs. Philip (Ethell). 1921. *A Political Pilgrim in Europe.* London: Cassell and Co.

Sowerwine, Charles. 1982. *Sisters or Citizens? Women and Socialism in France since 1876.* Cambridge: Cambridge University Press.

———. 1987. "The Socialist Women's Movement from 1850–1940." In *Becoming Visible: Women in European History,* ed. R. Bridenthal, C. Koonz, and S. Stuard, 399–426. Boston: Houghton Mifflin.

Spencer, Anna Garlin. 1930. *The Council Idea: A Chronicle of Its Prophets and a Tribute to May Wright Sewall.* New Brunswick: J. Heidingsfeld.

Standing, Guy. 1989. "Global Feminization through Flexible Labor." *World Development* 17:1077–95.

Stanley, Edit Kirkendall. 1983. *Ten Decades of White Ribbon Service, 1883–1983.* Cincinnati: Revivalist Press.

Staunton, Dorothy. 1956. *Our Goodly Heritage: A Historical Review of the World's Woman's Christian Temperance Union, 1883–1956*. London: Walthamstow.

Steenbergen, Bart van, ed. 1994. *The Condition of Citizenship*. London: Sage.

Stetson, Dorothy McBride, and Amy G. Mazur, eds. 1995. *Comparative State Feminism*. Thousand Oaks, Calif.: Sage.

Stienstra, Deborah. 1994. *Women's Movements and International Organizations*. New York: St. Martin's Press.

Strang, David. 1990. "From Dependency to Sovereignty: An Event-History Analysis of Decolonization, 1870–1987." *American Sociological Review* 55:847–60.

Strang, David, and Patricia M. Y. Chang. 1993. "The International Labour Organization and the Welfare State: Institutional Effects on National Welfare Spending, 1960–1980." *International Organization* 47:235–63.

Strange, Carolyn. 1990. "Mothers on the March: Maternalism in Women's Protest for Peace in North America and Western Europe." In *Women and Social Protest*, ed. G. West and R. L. Blumberg, 209–24. New York: Oxford University Press.

Szego-Bokor, Hanna. 1978. *The Role of the United Nations in International Legislation*. Amsterdam: North-Holland.

Taubenfeld Falk, Rita, and Howard J. Taubenfeld. 1983. *Sex Based Discrimination: International Law and Organizations*. Dobbs Ferry, N.Y.: Oceana.

Tax, Meredith. 1980. *The Rising of the Woman: Feminist Solidarity and Class Conflict, 1880–1917*. New York: Monthly Review Press.

Taylor, Arnold H. 1969. *American Diplomacy and the Narcotic Traffic, 1900–1939: A Study in International Humanitarian Reform*. Durham: Duke University Press.

"Ten-Hour Maximum Working-Day for Women and Young Persons." 1913. *Bulletin of the U.S. Bureau of Labor Statistics*, no.118, Washington, D.C.

*The White Slave Trade: Transactions of the International Congress on the White Trade Slave*. 1899. London: Office of the National Vigilance Society.

Thomas, George M., and Pat Lauderdale. 1987. "World Polity Sources of National Welfare and Land Reform." In *Institutional Structure: Constituting State, Society, and the Individual*, ed. G. M. Thomas, J. W. Meyer, F. O. Ramirez, and J. Boli, 198–214. Beverly Hills, Calif.: Sage.

Thomas, George M., John W. Meyer, Francisco O. Ramirez, and John Boli, eds. 1987. *Institutional Structure: Constituting State, Society, and the Individual*. Beverly Hills, Calif.: Sage.

Thoolen, Hans, and Beth Verstappen. 1986. *Human Rights Mission: A Study of Fact Finding Practice of Non-Governmental Organizations*. Boston: Martinus Nijhoff.

Thornton, Margaret. 1991. "The Public/Private Dichotomy: Gendered and Discriminatory." *Journal of Law and Society* 18:448–63.

Tinker, Irene. 1980–81. "A Feminist View of Copenhagen." *Signs* 6:531–35.

———. 1990. "The Making of a Field: Advocates, Practitioners, and Scholars." In *Persistent Inequalities: Women and World Development*, ed. I. Tinker, 27–53. New York: Oxford University Press.

Turner, Bryan S. 1986. *Citizenship and Capitalism: The Debate over Reformism.* London: Allen and Unwin.

Tyrrell, Ian. 1991. *Woman's World/Woman's Empire: The Woman's Christian Temperance Movement in International Perspective, 1880–1930.* Chapel Hill: University of North Carolina Press.

Union of International Associations. Various years. *Yearbook of International Organizations.* Munich: K. G. Saur.

United Nations. 1947–48. *Yearbook of the United Nations.* New York: Office of Public Information.

———. 1960. *Yearbook of the United Nations.* New York: Office of Public Information.

———. 1965. *Yearbook of the United Nations.* New York: Office of Public Information.

———. 1966a. *Resources Available to Member States for the Advancement of Women.* E/CN 6/463. New York: United Nations.

———. 1966b. *Yearbook of the United Nations.* New York: Office of Public Information.

———. 1967. *Yearbook of the United Nations.* New York: Office of Public Information.

———. 1968. *Yearbook of the United Nations.* New York: Office of Public Information.

———. 1970. *Yearbook of the United Nations.* New York: Office of Public Information.

———. 1972. *Yearbook of the United Nations.* New York: Office of Public Information.

———. Economic and Social Council. 1973. *A Report of the League of Arab States to the Commission on the Status of Women.* E/CN.6/578.

———. 1976. *Yearbook of the United Nations.* New York: Office of Public Information.

———. 1980. *Yearbook of the United Nations.* New York: Office of Public Information.

———. 1981. *Yearbook of the United Nations.* New York: Office of Public Information.

———. 1982. *International Human Rights Instruments of the United Nations, 1948–1982.* New York: UNIFO.

———. 1985. *Yearbook of the United Nations.* New York: Office of Public Information.

———. 1987. *Women 2000,* no. 3. Branch for the Advancement of Women, CSDHA, Vienna.

———. 1991. *Directory of National Machinery for the Advancement of Women.* Vienna: Division for the Advancement of Women.

United Nations Industrial Development Organization (UNIDO). Unit for the Integration of Women in Industrial Development. 1989. *Women Considered: How UNIDO Is Making Women More Visible in Industry.* Vienna: UNIDO.

Vallance, Elizabeth, and Elizabeth Davies. 1986. *Women of Europe: Women MEPs and Equality Policy.* Cambridge: Cambridge University Press.

Van Holthoon, Fritz, and Marcel Van Der Linden, eds. 1988. *Internationalism in the Labour Movement, 1830–1940.* Leiden: E. J. Brill.

Ventresca, Marc. 1995. "Counting People When People Count: Global Establishment of the Modern Population Census, 1820–1980." Ph.D. diss., Department of Sociology, Stanford University.

Vogel, Ursula. 1991. "Is Citizenship Gender-Specific?" In *The Frontiers of Citizenship,* ed. Ursula Vogel and Michael Moran, 58–85. London: Macmillan.

———. 1994. "Marriage and the Boundaries of Citizenship." In *The Condition of Citizenship*, ed. B. Steenbergen, 76–89. London: Sage.

Vogel, Ursula, and Michael Moran, eds. 1991. *The Frontiers of Citizenship*. London: Macmillan.

Waggaman, Mary T. 1919. "First International Congress of Working Women, Washington, D.C." *Monthly Labor Review* 9:280–98.

Walby, Sylvia. 1994. "Is Citizenship Gendered?" *Sociology* 28:379–95.

Whitaker, Jennifer S. 1975. "Women of the World: Report from Mexico City." *Foreign Affairs* 54:173–81.

White, Lyman Cromwell. 1951. *International Non-Governmental Organizations*. New Brunswick: Rutgers University Press.

Whittick, Arnold. 1979. *Woman into Citizen*. London: Athenaeum, with Frederick Muller.

Wilson, H. T. 1992. "The Impact of Gender on Critical Theory's Critique of Advanced Industrial Societies." *Current Perspectives in Social Theory* 12:125–36.

Winick, Charles, and Paul Kinsie. 1971. *The Lively Commerce: Prostitution in the United States*. Chicago: Quadrangle Books.

Woo, Margaret. 1994. "Chinese Women Workers: The Delicate Balance between Protection and Equality." In *Engendering China: Women, Culture, and the State*, ed. C. Gilmarting, G. Hershatter, L. Rofel, and T. White, 279–95. Cambridge: Harvard University Press.

Wuthnow, Robert. 1987. *Meaning and Social Order: Explorations in Cultural Analysis*. Berkeley: University of California Press.

Zucker, Lynne. 1983. "Organizations as Institutions." In *Research in the Sociology of Organizations*, ed. S. Bacharach, 1–42. Greenwich, Conn.: JAI Press.

# INDEX

. . . . . . . . . .

Pan American Conferences: Havana (1928),
81, 82; Montevideo (1933), 81
Parental care policies, 104, 134, 138
Parents, working, 133
Paris Peace Conference (1919), 58, 86, 73
Patriarchy, 2, 13, 32, 174
Patriotism, and peace movement, 70
Peace, 63, 100, 145, 147, 159, 169
Peace congress, international (1848), 64
Peace and Disarmament Committee of
Women's International Organizations,
64
Peace movement, 57, 72; women's inter-
national, 67, 68
Peace of Westphalia, 58, 60
Peace work, and League of Nations, 80
Peckover, Priscilla, 64
Persia, ICW national council in, 26
"Person cases," 1
Personhood, 10, 172
Persons, women as, 14
Peru, 46, 50
Pethick-Lawrence, Emmeline, 66
Philanthropy, and women, 20, 42
Poisons, industrial, 56
Poland, 64, 66, 67n. 1, 131, 164; and parental
care policies, 138; and traffic in women
and children, 75n. 4
Politics, 2, 3; international, 16, 51; and labor
movement, 54; and maternalism, 70; as
part of public sphere, 13; and peace move-
ment, 72; and temperance movement, 71;
and women, 1, 4, 12, 20, 23, 32, 33, 71, 100,
145. See also Suffrage
Polynesia, women for peace in, 64
Population control, 5, 9, 140
Portugal, 50, 64, 138
Private sphere. See Domestic sphere
Professions, and women, 23
Prostitution, 158, 169; campaign against, 21,
33, 42, 43, 60, 74, 79; and diseases, 34, 35;
and League of Nations, 74; regulation of,
9, 15, 19, 34-35, 37, 40, 57, 145; and women's
economic situation, 78
Protection of women and children, 16, 100,
123, 124, 132, 170. See also Employment,
women's; Labor legislation, protective
Prussia, women for peace in, 64
Public health, 18, 34, 78, 169
Public institutions, 6, 10, 13, 139, 171
Public sphere, 13, 70, 171, 172, 173, 174, 175,

176; equality and rights in, 14; and men, 2,
23; and socialism, 32; and temperance
movement, 30; and women, 1, 2, 6, 16, 22,
25, 50, 58, 63, 83, 86, 94, 100, 104, 106, 133,
134, 139, 142, 143, 145, 166, 168, 169, 170-71.
See also Domestic sphere
Puritanism, international, 28
Purity crusade, 39

Race, 149, 158; and protective legislation, 48,
50
Rape, and domestic rights, 174
Rationalization, 140, 141, 150
Reason, and citizenship, 12
Recommendation on Women Workers with
Family Responsibilities (1965), 133
Reform associations, 65
Reform movements, transnational, 60
Refugees, 149; and League of Nations, 59, 60,
79
Religion, 5, 29, 39
Report of the Committee on the Employ-
ment of Women and Children in Mines
and Collieries (1842), 44
Research Institute for Social Development,
150
Retail, women working in, 45
Right to work, 92, 96, 97, 98, 131, 133
Rights, 10, 11, 106, 111, 173; natural, 26, 27, 100;
political, 10, 11, 15, 27, 106; public, 176, 177;
and prostitution, 42; reproductive, 159
Rights, women's, 1, 2, 9, 11, 15, 16, 17, 20, 24,
73, 100, 103, 104, 111, 114, 121, 143, 162, 168,
169, 170; and Arab organizations, 154; campaign for, 156, 160; conventions for, 130;
and economics, 166-67; and EEC, 155; and
ILO, 108; as international affair, 85-86; and
League of Nations, 60, 80; protection of,
164; and United Nations, 10
Rockefeller, John D., Jr., 76
"Role of Women in Development, The"
(report), 143
Roosevelt, Eleanor, 105
Roosevelt, Franklin D., 69
Romania, 75n. 4
Russia, 31, 41, 64, 66, 67; and labor legislation, 55; and Open Door International, 92;
and protective legislation, 50; revolution
in, 60; and suffrage, 26; and traffic in
women and children, 40; and women's
employment, 94

Library of Congress Cataloging-in-Publication Data

Berkovitch, Nitza.
   From motherhood to citizenship : women's rights and
international organizations / Nitza Berkovitch.
      p.   cm.
   Includes bibliographical references and index.
   ISBN 0-8018-6028-8 (alk. paper)
   1. Feminism—International cooperation—History.  2. Women's
rights—International cooperation—History.  3. Women—Societies
and clubs—History.  I. Title.
HQ1154.B417   1999
305.42'09—dc21                         98-45776
                                            CIP

Printed in the United States
32569LVS00003B/86

9 780801 871023